# PEOPLE
# OF THE ANDES

S M I T H S O N I A N
**EXPLORING THE ANCIENT WORLD**
JEREMY A. SABLOFF, Editor

# PEOPLE
# OF THE ANDES

By JAMES B. RICHARDSON III

St. Remy Press • Montreal

Smithsonian Books • Washington, D.C.

EXPLORING THE ANCIENT WORLD
was produced by
ST. REMY PRESS

| | |
|---|---|
| *Publisher* | Kenneth Winchester |
| *President* | Pierre Léveillé |
| *Managing Editor* | Carolyn Jackson |
| *Managing Art Director* | Diane Denoncourt |
| *Production Manager* | Michelle Turbide |
| *Administrator* | Natalie Watanabe |

Staff for *PEOPLE OF THE ANDES*

| | |
|---|---|
| *Editors* | Alfred LeMaitre |
| | Daniel McBain |
| *Art Directors* | Philippe Arnoldi |
| | Chantal Bilodeau |
| *Picture Editor* | Christopher Jackson |
| *Researcher* | Olga Dzatko |
| *Assistant Editor* | Jennifer Meltzer |
| *Photo Assistant* | Geneviève Monette |
| *Illustrator* | Maryo Proulx |
| *Systems Coordinators* | Eric Beaulieu |
| | Jean-Luc Roy |
| *Secretary* | Lorraine Doré |
| *Administrative Assistant* | Dominique Gagné |
| *Indexer* | Christine Jacobs |
| *Proofreader* | Judy Yelon |

THE SMITHSONIAN INSTITUTION

| | |
|---|---|
| *Secretary* | I. Michael Heyman |
| *Assistant Secretary for External Affairs* | Thomas E. Lovejoy |
| *Director, Smithsonian Institution Press* | Felix C. Lowe |

SMITHSONIAN BOOKS

| | |
|---|---|
| *Editor-in-Chief* | Patricia Gallagher |
| *Senior Editor* | Alexis Doster III |
| *Editors* | Amy Donovan |
| | Joe Goodwin |
| *Associate Editors* | Bryan D. Kennedy |
| | Sonia Reece |
| *Assistant Editor* | Robert Lockhart |
| *Senior Picture Editor* | Frances C. Rowsell |
| *Picture Editors* | Carrie E. Bruns |
| | R. Jenny Takacs |
| *Production Editor* | Patricia Upchurch |
| *Business Manager* | Stephen J. Bergstrom |
| *Marketing Manager* | Susan E. Romatowski |

**Library of Congress Cataloging-in-Publication Data**
Richardson, James B. (James Bushnell), 1936-.
    People of the Andes / by James B Richardson III
        p. cm. — (Exploring the ancient world)
    Includes bibliographical references and index.
    ISBN 0-89599-041-5
    1. Indians of South America—Andes Region—Antiquities. 2. Andes Region—Antiquities. I. Title. II. Series.
F2229.R53    1994
980'.01—dc20                                                    94-22754
                                                               CIP

Manufactured and printed in Canada.
First Edition

10  9  8  7  6  5  4  3  2  1

FRONT COVER PHOTO: *The majestic Kalasasaya was the ceremonial focus of Tiwanaku, the ancient world's highest capital city.*

BACK COVER PHOTO: *The ceramic artists of the Moche excelled at the depiction of individual personages. The startlingly lifelike face of a warrior adorns this stirrup-spout vessel.*

# CONTENTS

# EDITOR'S FOREWORD

The pre-Hispanic cultures of the Andean area of South America have been of great interest to archaeologists and the general public alike for many years. As a result of a recent burst of archaeological activity, scholarly knowledge of the area has grown rapidly. However, there are few up-to-date syntheses of ancient Andean cultural development and even fewer that are readily accessible to the general public. One of the reasons for this relative lack of cultural overviews is that the new archaeological research has shown that over many millennia cultural development in the Andes was tremendously complex.

There are many reasons for this complexity, but the most apparent is the great variety of environmental zones in the Central Andes. Although it is clear that the Andean environment has played a critical role in the growth of civilization, Professor and Curator James B. Richardson III skillfully shows how over time the systematic interaction of the physical environment, the environmental changes wrought by ancient peoples, and shifting climatic conditions produced the complicated cultural mosaic of Andean prehistory. Obviously, it is a Herculean task to try to bring order and clarity to this complexity, but, as readers will see in the pages that follow, Dr. Richardson is certainly up to this mission. Avoiding environmental determinism, Dr. Richardson nevertheless carefully indicates how and why such factors as the periodic El Niño events in the Pacific Ocean, recurrent droughts, and earthquakes influenced the growth of Andean civilization and differentially affected various regional zones.

Following the intellectual lead of the well-known Andean archaeologist, the late Edward P. Lanning of the State University of New York at Stony Brook, Dr. Richardson also knowledgeably develops the theme that the maritime resources available to the ancient peoples who lived on the Peruvian coast played a more crucial role in cultural growth than previously had been recognized. He clearly points out how the exploitation of such resources facilitated the construction of some of the remarkable early architectural monuments on the coast.

Dr. Richardson also pays considerable attention to the material culture of the ancient Andean peoples—their technological accomplishments, their artistic and architectural styles, their religious beliefs—and to the cultural contacts, particularly trade, that took place within the vast Andean zone and with neighboring groups. Thus, readers should obtain a well-rounded view of the cultures of the Andes, from early, mobile hunter-gatherers more than 12,000 years ago up to the renowned Inca of the 16th century A.D.

Dr. James B. Richardson III is a Professor of Anthropology at the University of Pittsburgh and Chair of the Division of Anthropology at the Carnegie Museum of Natural History. Dr. Richardson, who received his Ph.D. from the University of Illinois at Urbana-Champaign, is a well-known authority on both Andean and Northeastern North American archaeology and has published numerous scholarly articles on both subjects. He also has curated many anthropological exhibits at the Carnegie Museum and has done much to foster public interest in archaeology and ethnography.

Readers interested in finding out the latest archaeological views on such cultures as the Chavín, Moche, Nasca, Tiwanaku, Huari, Chimú, and Inca will be pleased by Dr. Richardson's well-presented discussions of these justly famous civilizations and their spectacular achievements in such realms as architecture, ceramics, metallurgy, and weaving. However, readers also will gain an appreciation of the interconnectedness of these civilizations and the key roles played by the climate and topography of the Andes in shaping their long-term development.

*Jeremy A. Sabloff*
*University of Pennsylvania Museum*
*of Archaeology and Anthropology*

A field of quinoa—known in the Quechua language as the "mother grain"—covers a hillside above the village of Yumani on the sacred Isla del body of water lies at the northern edge of the dry Altiplano, a wide, undulating plain between the two main chains of the Andes Mountains.

Sol (Island of the Sun) in Lake Titicaca. **This huge**

# 1

---

# SETTING THE STAGE

On November 15, 1533, the Spanish adventurer Francisco Pizarro and a small force of soldiers entered Cuzco, the imperial capital of the Inca Empire. How can we begin to imagine their awe as they beheld this magnificent ancient city? Only through written accounts can we catch a glimmer of the original splendor of the temples and palaces of the Inca rulers, their elegant masonry, their finely wrought gold and textiles. Only through the chronicles of the Spanish conquerors themselves can we fully understand the city's surviving archaeological treasures, for Pizarro and his band of invaders left few behind. In no time, the city—arguably the grandest center in pre-Columbian America—was stripped of its treasures.

It had taken Pizarro almost two years to reach Cuzco. During this time, Spanish expeditions had visited many of the Inca and pre-Inca cities and temple centers that archaeologists would begin to investigate only three-and-a-half centuries later. In their continued quest for the riches of the Inca Empire, the Spanish explored much of the Central Andes, learning rather quickly that gold and silver were not the only treasures that the newly conquered Inca civilization held in store. Mother Spain, in conquering what would become Colombia, Ecuador, Peru, Bolivia, and Chile, had won herself a luxurious cornucopia of new resources, ranging from llama wool to fertilizer to a variety of new foods—including the potato.

This book is about the long, slow process of fashioning that cornucopia: the migration from the Old World to the New (that is, the earliest migration to the Americas, across the Bering Strait) and the early settlement of the Andes; the building of cultures, religions, states, and empires, with their distinct traditions, ingenious solutions to problems, and art. It is also, alas, about the conflicts between the various peoples of the Andes, eventually giving rise to the Inca Empire; and, finally, about the ultimate conflict, one which was, for all intents and purposes, decided on the day Pizarro entered Cuzco.

But first, we must prepare for our journey. Like Pizarro and his occupation forces, we will encounter a myriad of environments and resources, from the Pacific Ocean, across the narrow desert coast, to the Andean peaks, and into the tropical realm of the Amazon Basin. Unlike Pizarro, we have at our disposition more than 400 years of geographical study, which others before us have taken the time to sift through and synthesize. Let us begin with a short study of the region's major environmental zones.

### OCEAN RICHES AND ARID COASTS

The prime mover in the Central Andean climate is the Peru Current (also known as the Humboldt Current). This cold, northward-flowing current washes the west coast of South America from Valparaíso, Chile, to Punta Pariña, Peru. The winds blowing across the Peru Current pick up not only its cold water, but also nutrients as rich as the ocean itself. Beginning more than 900 feet (275 meters) below sea level and rising to the surface of the ocean, the aqueous environment served by the Peru Current sustains the greatest concentration of fish, bird, and sea mammal life in the world. The most resource-rich of the Andean environmental zones, the Pacific Ocean (which fronts the Andes) until recently supplied one-fifth of the world's fish catch, used both for food and for fertilizer. These ocean riches are concentrated between 5° and 15° South latitude, an immense fishery where, as we shall see, the first Andean civilizations arose. The bounty of the current is evident—sometimes to the naked

Peru's desert coast, mountain highlands, and tropical forests provided the setting for an extraordinary cultural florescence that began some 12,000 years ago. Beginning on the coast, and then spreading into the highlands, Peru's first inhabitants slowly adapted to the challenging environments of the Central Andes, and created a way of life that survives to this day. The map on the opposite page shows the location of some of the major archaeological sites discussed in this book.

Quito●

ECUADOR

VALDIVIA ★

LAS VEGAS ★

Amazon R.

Iquitos●

*Tumbez R.*

SICHES ★
Talara

*Chira R.*

*Piura R.*

SECHURA
DESERT

*Marañón R.*

PERU

BATAN GRANDE ★
PACOPAMPA ★

*Marañón R.*

TÚCUME ★
SIPÁN ★
KUNTUR WASI ★
CUPINISQUE ★
HUACA PRIETA ★
CHAN CHAN ★
CERRO ARENA ★
Trujillo ●
CERRO BLANCO ★
SALINAS DE CHAO ★
PAÑAMARCA ★
PUNKURÍ ★
SECHIN ALTO ★
CERRO SECHIN ★
MOXEKE ★
LAS HALDAS ★
ASPERO ★

*Zaña R.*
*Lambayeque R.*
*Jequetepeque R.*
Cajamarca ●
HUACALOMA ★
*Chicama R.*
*Moche R.*
*Virú R.*
GALINDO ★
KOTOSH ★
LA GALGADA ★

HUARICOTO ★

*Nepeña R.*
*Santa R.*
*Casma R.*
CHAVIN DE
HUÁNTAR ★

HUÁNUCO
PAMPA ★

*Huallaga R.*

CORDILLERA BLANCA

BRAZIL

EL PARAISO ★
ANCÓN ★
Lima ●
GARAGAY ★
PACHACAMAC ★
MINA PERDIDA ★
CARDAL ★

*Supe R.*
*Chancay R.*
*Chillón R.*
LA FLORIDA ★
*Rímac R.*
*Lurín R.*

TELARMACHAY ★
PACHAMACHAY ★

Ayacucho ●
HUARI ★

CORDILLERA NEGRAS

*Apurímac R.*

*Urubamba R.*

*Madre de Dios R.*

MACHU PICCHU ★
● Cuzco

PIKILLACTA ★

PARACAS ★
KARWA ★

*Ica R.*
*Grande R.*

Nazca ●
CAHUACHI ★

★ PUKARÁ

BOLIVIA

*L. Titicaca*

Arequipa ●
CERRO
BAÚL ★
TIWANAKU ★
CHIRIPA ★

PACIFIC OCEAN

RING SITE ★
CHINCHORRO ★

CHILE

★ Archeological Site
● Modern City

II

Enriched by the northward-flowing waters of the Peru Current, the waters off the coast of Peru contain some of the most prolific marine resources in the world. As they have for centuries, fishermen ply the coastal waters to harvest its bounty. This photograph shows the fishing fleet at Ilo, a port in southern Peru.

eye—as one approaches the shoreline: multitudes of inshore fish and shellfish species, and, clinging to the rocky shoreline, shellfish and sea lions.

Not only does the Peru Current provide marine resources—of prime importance to Central Andean peoples past and present—but it is also the controlling factor in the creation of one of the world's driest deserts. As the warm, moisture-laden sea winds move across the cold seas of the current, they are forced to release their life-giving water before reaching land. It is not until they move upward into the Andes that they once again gather water, which falls seasonally in the mountain valleys. As a consequence, the narrow coastal strip between the Pacific Ocean and the Andes Mountains receives virtually no rainfall, thus creating the famous hyperarid coastal desert of South America. Yet while this parched landscape holds only limited and scattered resources on its own, the inhabitants have long succeeded in exploiting their environment, for crosscutting the stark deserts of Peru are 57 rivers, most of which originate in the western Andes. These ribbons of life have sustained the people of the Central Andes for more than 12,000 years. Though it must be said that before the establishment of irrigation agriculture some 3000 to 4000 years ago—which enabled the populace to spread river water onto the floodplains and onto the desert—the rivers offered little except seasonal floodwaters for limited farming along the river banks and floodplains at the coast. Without irrigation, this desert coastal zone could not support the dense populations it has known over the centuries.

It is deceptive to think of the desert as a monotonous and barren sea of sand, for the desert coast contains within it a number of individual desert environments that necessitated different adaptive responses from early Andean

12

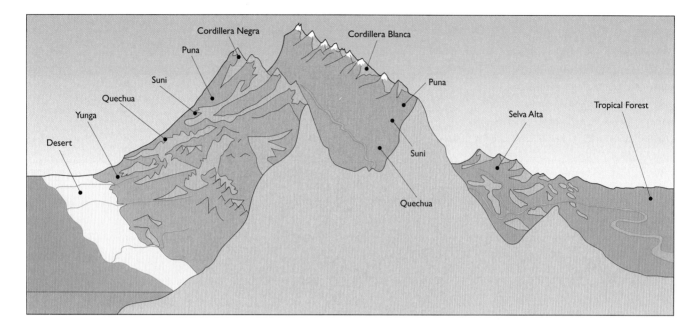

Peru's varying topography and diverse climates make it a "vertical mosaic" of environmental zones. The illustration shows the landscape rising from the arid coastal desert through the *yunga* and *quechua* zones to the high grazing lands of the *suni* and *puna*. Between the parallel ranges of the Andes Mountains—the Cordillera Negra and the Cordillera Blanca—lies an area of dry plains. East of the Cordillera Blanca, the land falls away to the tropical forest of the Amazon Basin. The diversity of Peru's natural environments plays a vital role in the lifestyle of Andean peoples.

peoples. In northern and southern Peru, for example, high plateaus that were formerly marine floors during the last Ice Age now rise precipitously at the coast to more than 900 feet (274 meters), their heights carved by deep canyons and river valleys. South of the northern plateaus, meanwhile, the 56-mile-wide (90-kilometer-wide) Sechura Desert, with its massive fields of barchan (crescent-shaped) dunes, presents a formidable barrier to population movements. Even farther south, past the Sechura, the desert narrows into a thin strip, fronting the majestic Andean mountain chain into northern Chile, where it again widens to form the Atacama Desert—one of the driest places on Earth. Still another environment, now largely destroyed by overgrazing, hardly resembles a desert at all: the elevated areas of the Peruvian coast, which support the *lomas* vegetation. There, a moist winter fog called *garúa* nurtures more than 1000 plant species that once attracted deer and the wild camelid, or camel-like animal, known as the guanaco.

### ANDEAN VALLEYS, HIGH GRASSLANDS, AND MOUNTAIN PEAKS

As one climbs the western Andean slopes, wetter conditions prevail. Between 1600 and 7500 feet (500 and 2300 meters), the *yunga* ("warm valley", in Quechua, the language of the Incas) is a warm, dry region with deep canyons and plateaus carpeted with thorn forests and such distinctive vegetation as columnar cactus and algarroba trees. From the Zaña Valley northward to Tumbez, the yunga has relict stands of a tropical forest belt. Once widespread, it was destroyed by forest clearing and the introduction of European animals. This tropical forest band was the home of animals that are common

The people of the Andes have adapted their farming techniques to the often difficult conditions of the highlands, or *quechua*. In some areas, wide valley floodplains provide extensive fertile land. Elsewhere, highland farmers have resorted to terracing in order to make efficient use of seasonal water and available land.

in the Amazon Basin: monkeys, parrots, jaguars, and, in the Tumbez River, cayman (a relative of the crocodile). Because the tributaries of the coastal rivers are numerous and are comparatively narrow, the yunga has only limited potential for irrigation. Still, it remains an important agricultural zone, for almost all indigenous Andean crops can be cultivated here as well as in the river valleys of the coast.

The land between 9200 and 11,500 feet (2800 and 3500 meters) is known as the *quechua,* named for the descendants of the Inca. The high-altitude environment encountered by early hunters and gatherers has been radically changed by thousands of years of exploitation, notably by agriculture and tree-clearing. Although there is seasonal rainfall, the region is dependent, as is the coast, on perennial river-water for irrigation and terrace farming. Here, the north-flowing rivers form long valleys that drain two-thirds of Peru eastward to the Amazon. On the slopes of these longitudinal valleys, farmers have constructed flights of terraces, expanding the agricultural potential of even the most precipitous terrain. These staircase farms and the valley floodplains produce a wide range of traditional Andean crops, including many species of potato, one of which is resistant to frost. The potato is only one of a series of tuber crops, such as *oca, ullucu,* and *mashua,* which have formed the subsistence base of Andean peoples for millennia.

Between the quechua valley system and the vast grasslands of the *puna* (in Quechua, "high plateau"), lies the narrow transitional zone called the *suni,* an environmental band ranging from 11,500 to 13,000 feet (3500 to 4000 meters) that reaches the upper limits of agriculture. Cut by deep canyons, the suni is home to the domesticated llama, alpaca, and guinea pig, all of which are important for wool and meat products. In southern Peru and Bolivia, the suni spreads into a wide, undulating plateau surrounding the famed Lake Titicaca. Lying at an altitiude of 12,500 feet (3812 meters), Lake Titicaca is 103 miles (165 kilometers) long, 40 miles (65 kilometers) wide, and 935 feet (285 meters) deep, making it the highest navigable body of water in the world. The Lake Titicaca Basin sustains the densest rural population in both Peru and Bolivia, a vibrant agropastoral society that grows many of the quechua crops and tends vast herds of llama and alpaca.

The agropastoralists of the suni utilize the puna, the highest of the Central Andean environmental zones to be occupied by humans. The puna is an open grassland above the altitude limits of agriculture. Dominated by tall bunch grasses called *ichu*, this grassland holds a mosaic of resources clustered around perennial streams and shallow glacial lakes. Among these resources are the vicuña, a wild camelid prized for its wool, as well as white-tailed and huemal deer. At between 13,000 and 16,000 feet (4000 and 4800 meters), vast herds of domesticated camelids are managed by Quechua and Aymara people. At its widest, in southern Peru and Bolivia, the puna combines with the suni zone to reach a width of about 120 miles (200 kilometers) before grading into the hyperarid Atacama Desert of Chile. At its northern extreme, this rich pasture-land constricts and disappears altogether in north-central Peru.

Towering above the puna are two parallel cordilleras, or mountain ranges, called the Cordillera Negra (black) and Cordillera Blanca (white), the latter named for its cap of snow and ice. Huascarán, the tallest mountain in Peru at 22,205 feet (6768 meters), is the centerpiece of the 75-mile (120-kilometer) Cordillera Blanca; indeed, the range boasts more than 30 mountains exceeding 20,000 feet (6000 meters). The Cordillera Negra, the westernmost of the two ranges, forms the Continental Divide and overlooks the desert coast; the Cordillera Blanca, interrupted repeatedly by major rivers heading to the Amazon and Madre de Dios river systems, is broken into a chain of short cordilleras.

East of the Cordillera Blanca, the land falls away rapidly into a series of deep river valleys that plunge toward the lowland tropical forests. Along the upper portions, at 7200 to 11,000 feet (2300 to 3300 meters), cloud forests are nourished by the persistent, damp winds from the Amazon Basin. Below these forests, the yunga environmental zone extends from 7500 to 3200 feet (2300 to 1000 meters).

Between 1300 and 3200 feet (400 and 1000 meters), the *selva alta* (high tropical forest) grades into the varied tropical forest environment, stretching thousands of miles eastward to the Atlantic Coast of Brazil. Within the tropical forest is found the greatest diversity of plant and animal life in the Western Hemisphere.

The snow- and ice-covered peaks of the majestic Andes run down almost the entire length of the South American continent, and form the world's longest mountain chain.

The people who inhabit these diverse environmental zones certainly do not depend solely upon the resources that they can produce or extract from their own land. It was the ethnohistorian John V. Murra who, during the 1970s, was the first to stress that traditional Andean peoples enjoyed direct access to land and resources in both higher and lower ecological zones. Control of resources in widely dispersed ecological zones produced a chain, or archipelago, of economic islands. This permitted the incorporation of sparse resources, first by households, then communities, then pre-Hispanic states, and, finally—under the Inca Empire—a single, unified, economic system. In the highlands, this economic integration permitted the quechua and suni agriculturalists access to the great pastures of the puna. In the Titicaca Basin, this led to the development of an elaborate agropastoral economy. In other regions, such as the coast, access to goods took place through exchange and trade, with specialized fisherfolk and agriculturalists exchanging marine products for farming staples.

**IT WASN'T ALWAYS LIKE THIS**

Although there is a paucity of geological studies on the Late Pleistocene (Late Ice Age) in the Central Andes, the little research that has been done allows us to reconstruct the changing environments of the late Ice Age and the Holocene Epoch. Even if the indigenous peoples of the Central Andes had not radically altered the landscape over millennia (a process which accelerated with the arrival of the Spanish), the modern environment would still be markedly different from that encountered by the first migrants some 12,000 years ago. In many now-arid or semiarid areas, for example, colder temperatures and greater precipitation resulted in lusher conditions.

The Talara Tar Pits, in northwestern Peru, offer archaeologists a glimpse of prehistoric climatic conditions along the Peruvian coast. The remains of several species of extinct animals have been found at the site, indicating that this arid area once received sufficient rainfall to support vegetation on which the animals could feed.

Today, 722 glaciers cover some 298 square miles (723 square kilometers) in the Cordillera Blanca in central Peru—the largest glacier-capped region in the tropics. At the height of the last glaciation, between 20,000 and 18,000 years ago, glaciers and snowfields extended downward in altitude more than 3280 feet (1000 meters) below their modern limits. Needless to say, this cold, windswept region would have been very forbidding to early migrants into the high Andes.

Much of the central Peruvian puna was covered by glaciers, and the yunga, quechua, suni, puna, and selva alta vegetation zones were forced to lower elevations or restricted to narrower zones. Even the tropical forests to the east of the Cordillera Blanca, once thought to have been unchanged for millions of years, were more restricted, and deserts prevailed in certain areas fringing the Amazon Basin. During the height of the last glacial period, the average temperature is estimated to have been 9 to 11 degrees Fahrenheit (5 to 6 degrees Celsius) colder than that of today. But by 12,000 to 10,000 years ago, the glaciers were in full retreat, ushering in the Holocene and initiating the transition to modern environments, which were in place by about 5000 years ago.

It has been said that the Peruvian coast has been a desert throughout the entire time period, but recent evidence proves otherwise. Fauna at the Talara Tar Pits provides the best evidence for the glacial Late Pleistocene climate on the northwest Peruvian coast. The now-extinct animals trapped in the tar pits include mastodons, horses, wolves, giant ground sloths, saber-toothed cats, and an extensive bird and insect fauna—all dated to 14,000 years ago. These water- and grass-dependent animals enjoyed annual monsoon rains, which supported widespread savannas, forests, lakes, and marshlands in what has since become—but was not always—a desert.

Glaciologists have learned much about the Andean region from the Quelccaya Ice Cap, located southeast of Cuzco in southern Peru. Each layer in this 164-foot-high (50-meter-high) ice cliff, near the margin of the ice cap, represents one year's worth of precipitation. Ice cores taken from the cliff have revealed information about climate changes extending as far back as 1500 years.

Further evidence of wetter conditions into the Holocene Epoch (11,000 to 5000 years ago) comes from the shell middens (mounds of discarded shells) that stretch from El Alto to the Llescus Peninsula. These shell middens are composed of mangrove shellfish species that were collected by early fisherfolk along the coast. Although mangrove swamps are now found only to the north of the Peruvian-Ecuadorian border, they had fringed the northern 233 miles (375 kilometers) of the Peruvian coast prior to 3000 B.C. Just north of the Santa River, and about 250 miles (400 kilometers) south of the mangrove shell middens, a number of 5000-year-old archaeological sites situated on a former Holocene-Epoch shoreline have yielded extensive warm-water shellfish fauna. Since at that latitude today the coast has the cold-water shellfish of the Peru Current, the presence of warm-water shellfish strongly suggests that the ocean current system was different in the past, and that a warmwater current formerly washed these shores, bringing yearly rainfall to this now-arid coast. If this was so, the central and north coasts of Peru were not the arid deserts of today, but were better watered, and probably featured grasslands and forested valleys as many as 5000 to 6000 years ago. As has been pointed out by paleontologist Harold B. Rollins, archaeologist Daniel H. Sandweiss, and myself, this would mean that El Niño, the sporadic warm-water current that brings catastrophic rainfall to the Peruvian coast, originated only in the last 5000 years.

In addition to the significant climate and environmental changes that have occurred since the end of the Pleistocene glacial period, ocean levels fell by 410 feet (125 meters) during the maximum glacial, with the water being "locked up" in the massive ice sheets of the world. Such an enormous drop in sea level exposed vast expanses of the world's continental shelves. Although not as extensive as the exposed continental landmasses along the eastern edges of the Western Hemisphere, a drop of 325 feet (100 meters) some 12,500 years ago would have exposed dry land along the central Peruvian coastline to a distance of more than 37 miles (60 kilometers) from the present coast. As the world's ice sheets retreated, they poured their meltwaters into the ocean basins. Over the next 7000 years, this land surface was submerged by the rising sea levels. Finally, by 5000 years ago, ocean levels stabilized and beach ridges formed at the mouths of the northern Peruvian river valleys. Thus the narrow desert coast of today was much wider in the past, providing early migrants with a broad landscape and coastline to exploit.

THE FOUR "NATURAL" HORSEMEN OF THE APOCALYPSE
Cultural development in the Central Andes cannot be interpreted without correlating the cultural record with geological and climatic change. This region is subject to many of the natural catastrophes that assail other areas of the world, but nowhere else do they occur in such profusion. The disasters range from

The devastating earthquake and subsequent landslide that entombed the Central Andean town of Yungay and 4000 of its inhabitants in 1970 is considered the most destructive natural catastrophe to have occurred in the New World in the last 500 years. The valley appears tranquil today, but the great expanse of boulders and debris left by the avalanche is a reminder that nature always has the upper hand.

localized avalanches, or *huaycos* (floods of liquid mud, usually transporting large boulders), to volcanic eruptions, earthquakes, and El Niño rainfall and drought events that bring severe devastation to vast areas of the Central Andes.

The huaycos can be caused by the rupture of dammed glacial lakes, or by huge rock and ice avalanches from the peaks of the towering cordilleras, some of which are the result of earthquakes. One still-remembered huayco resulted from what is known as the Huascarán avalanche. On May 31, 1970, a devastating earthquake dislodged a block of ice and rock 0.75 mile (1.2 kilometers) long and 2600 feet (800 meters) wide, which then broke away and entombed the town of Yungay and 4000 of its inhabitants. In total, the earthquake claimed more than 70,000 lives and left 500,000 people homeless; it affected 32,000 square miles (83,000 square kilometers) of territory, and destroyed 152 highland and coastal towns and cities, as well as 1500 peasant villages. It is considered the most destructive natural catastrophe to have occurred in the New World in the last 500 years.

An active volcanic chain runs from Colombia to Chile, but the chain is interrupted from southern Ecuador to southern Peru. This gap in the "ring of fire" is due to the low angle (10°) of the Nazca Oceanic Plate as it descends under the South American continent. In the active volcanic regions, the Nazca Plate slides under the Andes at steeper angles of 25° to 30°, allowing magma to rise and exit the earth's crust in the form of volcanic explosions. The largest historically known volcanic eruption in Peru was Huaynuputina, which occurred from February 9 to March 6, 1600. For seven days, the city of Arequipa was in complete darkness, and heavy ash was transported northward for 50 miles (80 kilometers); there is evidence that ash from Huaynuputina reached as far north as Nicaragua. Ash from this eruption also drifted southward, and in the Moquegua Valley, archaeologists have identified its 0.5-to-1.0-inch (1-to-3-centimeter) ash layer, which is used as a chronological marker of the early colonial period.

The passing of the Nazca Oceanic Plate under the South American continent makes the Central Andes one of the most earthquake-prone areas in the world. The subduction, or sliding, of one tectonic plate under another takes place at the junction of oceanic and continental plates. This occurs at an immense tear in the earth's crust called the Peru-Chile Trench, a chasm between 16,000 and 26,000 feet (5000 and 8000 meters) in depth. Of the thousands of earthquakes recorded between 1582 and 1974, 42 registered over 7.0 on the Richter Scale. The most active earthquake zone in Peru follows the coastline and the Andes, which is, ironically, the region where many of Peru's great pre-Hispanic civilizations developed. For centuries, inhabitants of this

The dramatic effects of the 1982-1983 El Niño show up clearly in these false-color satellite images of sea-surface temperature. In the upper image, warm water (shown as red-magenta) from the western Pacific pushes all the way to the coast of South America, preventing cool water from reaching the surface and replenishing vital nutrients. The lower image shows a return to normal circulation, with a tongue of cool water (shown as blue) stretching up the coast and out into the Pacific.

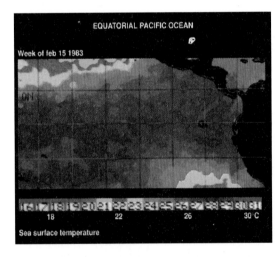

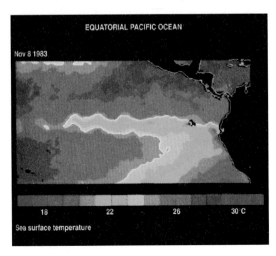

area have watched earthquakes disrupt water sources needed for irrigation, and render unusable the irrigation canal systems so crucial to these agriculturally based coastal societies.

Sometimes accompanying earthquakes are *tsunamis,* or tidal waves, which wreak havoc on coastal cities. In 1746, when an earthquake leveled Lima, a wall of water inundated the city's port, Callao, drowning more than 4000 inhabitants.

It is rare that rain falls upon the hyperarid desert coasts of the Central Andes, but when it does, in so-called El Niño years, it does so to destructive excess. El Niño, or ENSO (El Niño/Southern Oscillation), was named by fishermen for the Christ Child because of its arrival around Christmas. A warm-water current flowing southward along the northern Peruvian coast, El Niño overrides the cold Peru Current, pushing it offshore. This allows the moisture-laden clouds to unload their rain on the desert coast, producing a natural weather catastrophe for the peoples of the Central Andes.

Not only does El Niño produce torrential rainfall on the desert coasts of southern Ecuador and northern Peru, it also provokes droughts in the southern Peruvian and Bolivian Andes. In the last 450 years there have been about 70 ENSO events of varying degrees of intensity. Seven of these, including the El Niños of 1891, 1925, and 1982-1983, were among the strongest on record. (The ENSO record has been pushed back to A.D. 500 by the ice core taken from the Quelccaya Ice Cap southeast of Cuzco, which records both wet and dry periods; this work was done by Lonnie G. Thompson and Ellen Mosley-Thompson of the Byrd Institute of Polar Studies, Ohio State University.) In 1982-1983, the strongest El Niño in 100 years produced months of rainfall, shattering all established records. In southern Ecuador and northern Peru, roads and bridges were washed out, cities inundated, and irrigation systems and agricultural fields destroyed. In the southern Andes, meanwhile, the ENSO drought had a devastating impact on the llama herders, forcing them to choose between seeking pasturage at lower elevations or abandoning their herds, either by slaughtering or selling them, and forsaking the suni and puna by migrating to coastal cities and lomas pastures.

### THE SPANISH CHRONICLERS: EYEWITNESSES TO THE PAST

Not only did the Spanish take a keen interest in the mineral riches and the economic wealth of the land and sea, but they also were astonished by the sophistication and magnificence of Inca culture, and by the impressive ruins of even earlier civilizations that abounded throughout the Central Andean landscape.

Because the Inca had no written language, it became the task of the chroniclers—the Spanish soldiers, religious practitioners, and

In the early morning of March 15, 1720, heavy rains caused by El Niño unleashed floods that annihilated Zaña, once a thriving city of 80,000 people in northern Peru. The only building to remain standing was the Convent Church of San Agustín, whose eroded lower walls hint at the massive destruction caused by the floodwaters. Today, the ruined structure is undergoing repairs to ensure that its walls remain stable.

government officials—to tell the story of the history and culture of the Inca Empire and its predecessors. The writings of Captain Pedro de Cieza de León, published in 1553, provide one of the best eyewitness accounts of the early years, and are among the few to mention the brilliant civilizations that preceded the Inca. Arriving in 1547, Cieza de León traveled throughout Peru and Bolivia, and described Inca and pre-Inca cities and temples, including the ruins of the capital of the pre-Incan empire of Tiwanaku, in present-day Bolivia. Other major pre-Inca sites, such as the capitals of the Huari and Chimú empires and the ancient ceremonial center of Pachacamac, caught the attention of other Spanish chroniclers.

In 1908, the momentous discovery in the Royal Library of Copenhagen of *El Primer Nueva Corónica y Buen Gobierno*, written before 1615 by Felipe Guamán Poma de Ayala, made public 400 drawings depicting aspects of the economic, social, political, and religious systems of the Inca. This unparalleled document is the only visual history of the fateful encounter between the Spanish and Inca empires, and it is a major source for the interpretation of Inca culture by ethnohistorians and archaeologists.

Often for motives of greed rather than those involving scientific inquiry, Inca and pre-Inca ruins were mined for their golden and silver treasures, activities which continue to the present day. Yet whatever the motive, it is by this means that we have amassed much of our knowledge of Andean cultures. In addition to precious metals, the Spanish discovered elaborate ceramics, textiles, jewelry, and wood and stone carvings—treasured by-

products of looting that represented the majority of the pre-Incan civilizations that professional archaeologists would study in great depth in the 19th and 20th centuries.

## THE EARLY ARCHAEOLOGICAL DISCOVERIES

The 19th century saw the rise of the scientific approach to the explanation of both the natural and the cultural world, replacing theological interpretations of the archaeological and geological record. The earliest scientific attention to the archaeological record of the Andes came in the form of expeditions that investigated the geography, geology, flora, and fauna of South America. The pace of discovery quickened as naturalists explored throughout the Andes. Although most early investigators described the ruins that they encountered, they did not conduct organized archaeological investigations of the sites, and rarely did they speculate on the age of the archaeological record they were documenting.

One of the first archaeological reports was by Thomas Ewbanks, who in 1855 published a series of provincial Inca tomb lots from Arica (a small city which at that time belonged to Peru, and is now part of Chile), collected and shipped to the United States by a U.S. Navy astronomical expedition. In his well-illustrated report, Ewbanks remarked that:

> Whatever is to be known has to be drawn out of the ground; out of what the plough turns up; what mounds, graves, and earth-works may disclose; and what architectural ruins may afford. These are the only archives remaining of the deeds and destinies of the old inhabitants of the hemisphere; and hence everything registered in them, however trifling under other circumstances it might be considered, has a value proportioned to the insight it may give into national or social habits and conditions.

A key point in Ewbanks's profound statement is the fact that much of the cultural record of the Central Andes can be revealed only through archaeological research, for, as was previously stressed, there exists no written record of the accomplishments of Central Andean peoples before the arrival of the Spanish chroniclers.

In 1863, Ephraim George Squier arrived in Peru as the U.S. Commissioner to arbitrate between Peruvian and North American merchants of guano (bird excrement used as fertilizer). Squier was well known for the first scientific studies of the large earthworks in the Ohio and Mississippi valleys, and his friendship with the eminent historian William H. Prescott led him to spend two years of research on archaeological sites in Peru and Bolivia. His 1877 publication on his Peruvian travels included detailed descriptions of archaeological sites, and he speculated on the possibility that some of the ruins were pre-Inca in date. Rich with illustrations, his book made the public aware both of the vastness of the Central Andes and also of the magnitude of the region's numerous monuments, cities, and temples.

Among the earliest artifacts unearthed from Inca tombs were the pots shown above, which were studied and recorded by Thomas Ewbanks during an 1849-1852 expedition to South America. Ewbanks was one of the first to establish the importance of such artifacts, in the absence of any written records. These and other materials were subsequently shipped to the United States by a U.S. naval astronomical expedition.

**The 19th-century explorer Ephraim George Squier traveled extensively in Peru and Bolivia in 1863 and 1864. Squier was impressed with the massive structures and fine architecture that he encountered, and described his journey in *Peru: Travel and Exploration in the Land of the Incas*. In this engraving from the book, Squier and his party inspect the partly ruined Gateway of the Sun, at Tiwanaku.**

The modern foundations of scientific archaeology in Peru stem from the 1874-1875 excavations at Ancón, north of Lima, by the German investigators Wilhelm Reiss and Alphons Stübel. These studies stimulated Max Uhle, an assistant at the Königliches Museum für Völkerkunde in Berlin, to devote the rest of his life to Andean archaeology. Uhle published on the Stübel and Reiss collection and, with Stübel, on the ruins of Tiwanaku; thus, when he finally went to South America in 1892, he was already an eminent scholar of Andean archaeology. With financial support from his new employer, the University of Pennsylvania, he excavated briefly at Ancón before mounting a major campaign at Pachacamac, where he excavated for a full year; his 1903 report on the research at Pachacamac became a milestone in Peruvian archaeology. Uhle focused his attention on the contents of burials, and, through his analysis of cemetery data at various sites, he soon demonstrated that a whole series of art styles had a regional—specifically, pan-Andean—spread. Uhle proposed the first chronology of cultures for Peru: Early Pre-Tiahuanaco (now spelled Tiwanaku), Tiahuanaco, Pre-Inca, and Inca periods.

For more than 40 years, Uhle's ordering of major Peruvian cultures remained in vogue. Even after continued investigations to the present day, it remains the core of the modern chronological system of the Central Andes. Uhle speculated that the cultures he had discovered must be at least 2000 years old. Remarkably (considering his relatively small bank of data), he was not far wrong: the beginning of his Early Pre-Tiahuanaco Period has since been radiocarbon-dated to 2200 years ago. (All dates presented in this volume for pre-Hispanic cultures in the Central Andes are derived from the radiocarbon, or C14, technique of dating. The technique was invented by Willard F. Libby in 1949, and earned him the Nobel Prize. This method can date organic materials—such as wood, charcoal, bone, and shell—up to 50,000 years of age). Uhle was also correct in his statement that the pre-Inca societies were at least comparable to, and in many cases surpassed, the Inca in their complexity and brilliance.

Uhle left Peru in 1912, after directing the newly opened National Museum of History of Peru. He remained in South America until 1933, establishing museums in Chile and Ecuador, and amassing large collections for exhibition and for foreign museums. The year before Uhle left Peru, Hiram Bingham of Yale University was to discover the untouched Inca site of Machu Picchu in the Urubamba Valley east of Cuzco, initiating a surge of interest in Inca culture and the first major research at an Inca site.

Max Uhle was one of the founders of modern scientific archaeology in Peru. Uhle's pioneering studies of cemeteries and burials helped to establish an important chronology of Peruvian cultures.

Gordon R. Willey, shown here in 1946, implemented the settlement-pattern study of the Virú Valley Project, a chronological examination of a single valley that focused on all aspects of its cultural development.

In 1913, the first Peruvian professional archaeologist was appointed to direct the new archaeology division of the National Museum of History, Lima. Born in 1880 and educated at the University of San Marcos and at Harvard University, Julio C. Tello was a highland Indian. He was a prodigious investigator, excavating or surveying in almost every coastal valley and throughout the highlands. One of Tello's major scientific contributions was the recognition of even earlier cultures than those described by Uhle. In 1919, Tello headed an expedition to the Callejón de Huaylas in northern Peru, where he investigated the massive temple center of Chavín de Huántar. With its elaborate carved stone monuments, representing fanged jaguars, caymans, birds, and serpents, the site led Tello to conclude that Chavín de Huántar was the center of the first civilization in the Central Andes. He also proposed that Chavín culture was in part derived from cultures in the tropical forest. Tello and others subsequently encountered the Chavín art style in architecture, ceramics, and textiles along much of the coast. Thus, by the 1940s, they were able to establish that yet another period of widespread cultural interaction had preceded the Early Pre-Tiahuanaco Period.

## THE QUICKENING PACE OF RESEARCH

After World War II, the members of the Institute of Andean Research, founded in 1941, played a key role in the planning and implementation of the Virú Valley Project, the largest archaeological project yet undertaken in the Central Andes. The goal of the Virú Valley interdisciplinary research program was to conduct a holistic study of a single coastal Peruvian valley; the project included research on the early occupation of the region, the development of a precise chronology of the styles of ceramic works, and a valley-wide study of settlement patterns. This latter approach to archaeological interpretation was developed by the archaeologist Gordon R. Willey after discussions with noted anthropologist Julian H. Steward. Willey examined how settlement systems—that is, the ensemble of all the components of a settlement, including temple and public centers, dwelling sites, fortifications, and cemeteries—reflected changing political, religious, social, and economic organization of successive cultures in the Virú Valley. The monographs and numerous papers resulting from the Virú Valley Project formed the next plateau upon which the succeeding generation of Peruvian and foreign archaeologists was to build.

In concert with the Virú Valley Project, excavations by the archaeologist Junius B. Bird at the coastal fishing village of Huaca Prieta in the neighboring Chicama Valley revealed for the first time the Late Preceramic cultures (cultures not yet using pottery) that formed the foundation for later Central Andean civilizations. In 1949, just after Bird excavated at Huaca Prieta, he took advantage of W.F. Libby's newly developed radiocarbon C14 dating system and submitted botanical samples from Huaca Prieta to Libby for dating.

In 1919, Julio C. Tello's excavation of the temple center of Chavín de Huántar led the archaeologist to the belief that Chavín represented the earliest civilization in the Central Andes.

Archaeologist Michael E. Moseley was the first to present the hypothesis that Peru's earliest coastal temple centers depended upon the resources of the sea, rather than on agriculture, for subsistence.

The dates not only supported Bird's estimate of 5000 years of age for Huaca Prieta, but produced dates for 3000-year-old pottery production in Peru.

By the 1950s, the tempo of archaeology increased markedly, with numerous expeditions and excavations being initiated throughout the Andes by both foreign and Peruvian scholars. Many of the research strategies of the Virú Valley Project were applied to various Andean regions. In the 1950s and 1960s, emphasis was placed on uncovering the evidence for initial human occupation, origins of farming economies, development of coastal fishing societies, and the nature of the newly discovered, 5000-year-old Andean temple centers. Ethnohistorical sources and archaeological techniques were employed in reconstructing Inca civilization. A geological approach was introduced into the interpretation of the archaeological record, correlating climate change with cultural development. Researchers also investigated the relationships between tropical forest cultures and Central Andean societies. These new research thrusts included the continued research at many well-known sites, leading to further refinement of the cultural chronology of the Central Andes, as well as a better general understanding of the evolution of Andean civilizations.

A major issue in the late 1960s and early 1970s was which kind of resources—agricultural or maritime—had formed the subsistence pattern of cultures preceding the later Andean coastal civilizations. Archaeologist Michael E. Moseley, following up on Edward P. Lanning's work on the Late Preceramic sites in the Ancón region, developed the hypothesis that the earliest complex societies in Peru had an economic base of ocean resources, and not agriculture. For its time, this was a radical hypothesis, for all archaeologists believed that the rise of the state throughout the world was universally due to subsistence strategies based upon agriculture. Moseley supported his claim with evidence from the Ancón region shell middens and from the discovery in the 1960s of a series of 4000- to 5000-year-old coastal temple centers that offered little agricultural evidence.

It was also during this period that further large-scale, interdisciplinary research projects were initiated—the first since the Virú Valley program. In the Ayacucho region of the southern Peruvian Andes, archaeologist Richard S. MacNeish initiated a program of investigations on the early evidence for human occupation and the origins of agriculture; and in the Junín puna, archaeologists Ramiro Matos Mendieta and John W. Rick concentrated on early cave and rockshelter sites. In the Moche Valley, Moseley and his colleagues investigated the Moche capital at Cerro Blanco, the Chimú capital at Chan Chan, and the irrigation canal systems that were so essential to the agricultural economy of these state-level societies. A major program of Inca research in the Huánuco region, focusing upon local ethnic groups under Inca domination, was developed by John V. Murra and a team of archaeologists and ethnologists.

These studies have established certain norms in the field of Andean archaeology: to the present day, research continues to focus on long-term investigations of temple and urban centers, and on the examination of changing settlement patterns of river valleys and geographic regions. Not only have the sites made famous by the earliest Spanish chroniclers received renewed attention, but other little-known regions of the Central Andes have been surveyed and investigated. However, many areas still remain unknown to the archaeologist.

This volume will present our current understanding of cultural development in the Central Andes, as reconstructed from the archaeological record. As emphasized above, with the exception of the Inca Empire, all of our interpretations of the cultural evolution of the Central Andes come from archaeological research. The reason for this is that, unlike societies such as the Maya, the ancient peoples of the Andes left no written record of their accomplishments. Four unifying themes will guide our interpretation and reconstruction of the 12,000 or more years of cultural development in the Central Andes. These are continuity and change, interaction and communication, economic diversity, and the impact of natural catastrophes on the rise and fall of Central Andean civilizations.

It has been well established that there is long-term continuity between successive cultures in certain areas of the Central Andes. However, the contrary is also true, as evidenced by dramatic cultural changes in other areas. Emphasis will be placed on these continuities and discontinuities through time, as well as on their underlying causes—such as political domination, assimilation, or sweeping population changes.

The rise of complex societies 5000 years ago brought increasing trade and interaction over great distances. Not only were foreign elements present in the artifact assemblages and art styles, but much of the Central Andes region, especially after 3000 B.C., was united in a sphere of interaction through which economic resources, ideologies, and art styles flowed northward and southward, and east to west, from the tropical forest, across the Andean chain, and into the coastal valleys.

Cultural complexity led to a myriad of subsistence technologies which were developed to maximize the capture or production of resources from the ocean to the high grasslands to the tropical forests. Ingenious systems of fishing, farming, and herding emerged through time, providing the economic foundation for these states and empires.

As societies grew more complex, the impact of natural disasters became more severe. Recently, the impact of natural catastrophes has been seen as playing a key role in the rise and fall of Central Andean civilizations. The record of the natural "Four Horsemen of the Apocalypse"—avalanches, volcanic eruptions, earthquakes, and El Niño flood and drought events—will be examined to determine their role in driving cultural change.

# CENTRAL ANDEAN CHRONOLOGY

The chronological system used by archaeologists to organize the vast and complex archaeological record of the Central Andes was proposed by archaeologist John H. Rowe in 1960, and was based on the ideas of famed anthropologist Alfred L. Kroeber and archaeologist Gordon R. Willey. Later modified, it now stands as follows:

### EARLY PRECERAMIC PERIOD (10,000? TO 6000 B.C.)

This period saw the initial peopling of the Central Andes during the Late Pleistocene, when glacial conditions prevailed. Over the next 4000 years of fluctuating climate, these first inhabitants developed a series of adaptations to coastal and intermontane valleys, and to the high grasslands.

### MIDDLE PRECERAMIC PERIOD (6000 TO 3000 B.C.)

The transition to modern climates led to the first sedentary communities, the use of domesticated plants, and the growth of a llama-herding economy.

### LATE PRECERAMIC PERIOD (3000 TO 1800 B.C.)

During this period, large temple centers were built on the coast and in the Andes, supported by the exploitation of maritime and agricultural products.

### INITIAL PERIOD (1800 TO 800 B.C.)

This period saw the introduction of pottery technology, the construction of huge monuments, the spread of irrigation, and the development of new art forms and architectural styles.

### EARLY HORIZON (800 B.C. TO 200 B.C.)

The first of three periods during which the Central Andes was integrated by the spread of the Chavín religious cult, also reflected in the adoption of the Chavín art style.

### EARLY INTERMEDIATE PERIOD (200 B.C. TO A.D. 600)

The rise of the Moche, Nasca, Tiwanaku, and others produced the finest ceramics, textiles, and metalwork of any period, as well as massive irrigation and public works. This period also saw an increase in militarism.

### MIDDLE HORIZON (A.D. 600 TO 1000)

The Middle Horizon marked the zenith of the southern Andean Tiwanaku and Huari empires.

### LATE INTERMEDIATE PERIOD (A.D. 1000 TO 1470)

The renewed development of regional states—notably the Chimú Kingdom of the Peruvian north coast and the emerging Inca of the Cuzco region—led to collision and invasion.

### LATE HORIZON (A.D. 1470 TO 1532)

Having subdued their neighboring rivals, the Inca soon established the largest empire known in the Americas: Tahuantinsuyu (or "Land of the Four Quarters"), stretching 3500 miles (5500 kilometers) from Chile and Argentina to southern Colombia.

**Max Uhle's research at the Middle Horizon cemetery under the temple at Pachacamac was among the first stratigraphic excavations carried out in Peru. This illustration shows the relative positions of burials unearthed by Uhle.**

Peru's rugged northern coast is one of the world's richest sources of marine life. Enriched by the Peru Current, the coastal waters also support here. The coastal plain was inhabited as early as 10,000 years ago by people who lived almost entirely off the sea's bounty.

# THE EARLY PEOPLE

huge colonies of seabirds, such as those shown

Heated debate has raged over the date when the earliest migrants could have entered the Western Hemisphere. This debate is fueled in part by claims that some South American sites are more than 20,000 years old. Two positions have emerged from the ongoing discussion of when the first people crossed the Bering Strait into North America. Many scholars feel there is not sufficient irrefutable evidence that the crossing occurred prior to 9500 B.C.; still, other archaeologists are convinced by

Following the end of the last Ice Age, many of Peru's earliest inhabitants pursued a hunting and gathering way of life on the grasslands of the suni and puna. Cave sites in the Junín puna and the Ayacucho region have provided clues to the lifestyle of these people. Other early groups subsisted on marine foods at campsites along the coast. However, rising sea levels obliterated many of these coastal sites.

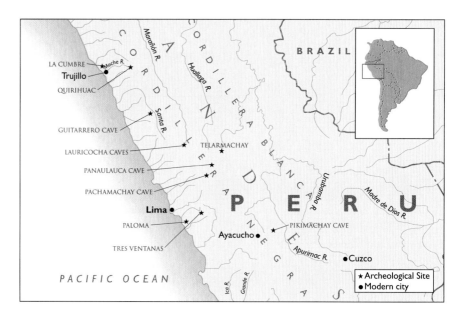

data from North and South American sites that these Old World migrants traveled into the New World long before that date. While abundant evidence demonstrates that the Americas were indeed inhabited by hunting and gathering peoples after 9500 B.C., there are a number of sites that point to an even earlier crossing.

In North America, the best current candidates for a pre-9500 B.C. occupation are the Bluefish Caves, in the Yukon, and Meadowcroft Rockshelter, in Pennsylvania. The Bluefish Caves, excavated by archaeologist Jacques Cinq-Mars, are situated north of the area covered by the massive Cordilleran and Laurentian ice sheets of the Late Pleistocene era (or last glacial age); they carbon-date to between 13,000 and 10,000 years B.C. There, the early settlers of the Arctic subsisted by hunting bison, elk, small game, and the now-extinct mammoth and horse. (The horse disappeared at the end of the Pleistocene, but was subsequently reintroduced by the Spanish.) Meanwhile, Meadowcroft Rockshelter, at the southern edge of the glacial ice sheets in southwestern Pennsylvania, holds evidence of human presence by at least 12,000 B.C.—and possibly earlier. Although the site holds no remains of extinct fauna because the earliest levels were below and beyond the roof of the shelter and subject to moisture, archaeologist James M. Adovasio has found small blades and bifacial cutting tools (flakes chipped on each side of the cutting edge) that are reminiscent of tools from the Bluefish Caves and from sites in Siberia.

The evidence from Mexico and Central America does not clarify the issue. The narrow landbridge of Central America, over which the early migrants would necessarily have funneled from North to South America, shows no convincing evidence of their having passed before 9500 B.C. The few sites that have been discovered with dates of more than 20,000 years, such as Tlapacoya and Valsequillo in Mexico, are troubled by substantial problems that leave the evidence uncertain. Still, the evidence may lie buried on the submerged continental shelf.

Meanwhile, despite the lack of Central American evidence, there remain numerous claims that South America was inhabited prior to 9500 B.C. The majority either have been dismissed as invalid or are awaiting the full publication of data. But several claims have acquired some credibility.

The telling argument centers on campsites at the Straits of Magellan in Chile, once home to hunters of the guanaco, the extinct giant ground sloth, and the Ice Age horse. At sites such as Fell's Cave, excavated by archaeologist Junius B. Bird in 1936-1937 and further studied by him and others until 1970, investigators turned up distinctive spearpoints dating to 9000 B.C. Known as fluted fishtail projectile points, they share one common feature with certain North American spearpoints, called Clovis points. Like their North American counterparts, the Chilean points have a groove—or flute—knocked out of their base. This enabled the hunter to bind the point onto a throwing shaft. This form of fluted point also is found throughout Patagonia, at El Inga in highland Ecuador, and isolated finds have been made in both Colombia and Panama. While the points themselves date only to 9000 B.C., they raise the following question: how long would it have taken early migrants to travel from North America (where they had developed the Clovis fluted spearpoint) to Fell's Cave at the tip of South America? The question has spawned controversy. In traveling south, these Arctic-adapted peoples would have traversed a myriad of environments; again and again they would have readjusted their hunting and gathering strategies and technologies to take advantage of local resources, and this process takes time. Paleoecologist Paul S. Martin holds that, after these early hunters and foragers had entered the continental United States, successive generations could have accomplished the trip of more than 10,000 miles (16,000 kilometers) in just 1000 years; yet many disagree. The constant adaptation, they feel—from temperate to tropical to arid conditions, from sea level to high altitudes—must have been a much slower process, taking the immigrants thousands of years to reach Fell's Cave.

But even if all agreed that migrants had arrived in South America as early as 9000 B.C. (as demonstrated by the fluted spearpoints), there is tempting evidence that the continent had been reached far earlier than that. Perhaps as early as 11,000 B.C., a group of settlers known as the El Jobo hunters pursued mastodons with lanceolate (or lance-shaped) projectile points at a Venezuelan site called Taima-Taima, where the butchered remains of these ancient elephants and an associated spearpoint fragment were discovered. At Tibitó, in highland Colombia, bones of mastodons, horses, and deer were found in association with flake artifacts dating to 9700 B.C. (These were produced by chipping away at a stone until its unusable core was reached; since the resulting edges were already sharp, they needed little, if any, retouching.) But the most convincing evidence that the New World was occupied before 9500 B.C. is found in the temperate forests of southern Chile, at the 11,000-B.C. site of Monte Verde. Excavated by archaeologist Thomas D. Dillehay, Monte Verde had a diversified economy of animals and plants, including mastodons and a wide variety of seeds, fruits and nuts, as well as several species of medicinal plants. The camp, which was situated along a streambed, had log foundations of semi-rectangular huts, and a structure thought to have been used for ceremonies. Tools found at the site include lanceolate projectile points, flake tools—both bifacial and unifacial—grinding stones for plant processing, as well as stone bolas, which were attached to a thong and thrown at birds or other animals. Following the seasons, the early Monte Verde hunters and gatherers moved from the interior to the coast—12 miles (20 kilometers) distant—as plant and animal resources became available. There is an even earlier cultural level at Monte Verde, with three small hearths that have been dated to an astonishing 33,000 years ago, though this data awaits verification.

Under Richard S. MacNeish, a team of archaeologists excavated several caves in the Ayacucho region of southern Peru in 1969 and 1970. Examination of Pikimachay Cave, pictured above, as well as other sites, has contributed to a long sequence of Preceramic cultures. Possible human presence is dated to before 18,000 B.C., with confirmed occupation of the caves by hunters and gatherers after 9000 B.C.

Archaeologists have yet to reach a consensus on these ancient dates: Monte Verde, Taima-Taima, and all other sites earlier than 9500 B.C. are contested by the "conservatives," who feel that the dates are incorrect or that the archaeology is not satisfactory.

In addition to the sites mentioned above, there is a cluster of sites in southeast Brazil, one of which is the Pedra Furada Rockshelter, with proposed dates of more than 30,000 years ago. (These dates also remain to be scrutinized.) Yet even if only Meadowcroft Rockshelter and Monte Verde are accepted as unequivocal evidence of human presence before 9500 B.C. (a position for which there is strong general support), a reasonable conclusion is that the earliest migrants entered the New World by at least 15,000 years ago.

There has been great controversy over the occupation date of Peru. In the Ayacucho region of the southern Peruvian Andes, two early periods of Pikimachay Cave—the Pacaicasa and Ayacucho Phases, both excavated by Richard S. MacNeish—have yielded objects at first thought to be stone tools, alongside the bones of extinct animals, all dating to between 18,000 and 11,000 B.C. with estimated dates to 23,000 B.C. The majority of the hundreds of tool-like objects are made of a porous rock called tufa, of which the cave walls are composed. But since there are no signs that these chunks of tufa were modified by humans, investigators have declared that the purported tools are merely the products of nature, and not early hunters. The succeeding Huanta Phase only has seven artifacts, which may well have fallen into the deposits from the upper levels of the rockshelter, either through human or natural disturbance of the site; thus it is only with the 9000 B.C. Puente Phase that investigators agree humans were present in the Ayacucho cultural sequence (or series of sequential cultures).

The Central Andes have no indisputable sites with pre-9500 artifacts and extinct fauna, although the La Cumbre site in the Moche Valley does offer one tenuous connection. There, investigators have found a mastodon in the vicinity of a spearpoint, dated to 10,410 B.C., that is typical of the Paiján culture. But this date is considered several thousand years too old for Paiján, since most other dates place Paiján between 8000 and 6000 B.C.

While the evidence is slim that the Central Andes were occupied prior to 9500 B.C., the situation is different in the highlands, or puna. At three highland caves—Guitarrero, Telarmachay, and Pachamachay—the earliest dates hover around 10,000 B.C. Again, these dates remain unconfirmed, for it is not until 1500 to 2000 years later, after 8000 B.C., that there is unequivocal evidence for substantial occupation. Although the early purported dates for the sites and their sparse assemblages of stone tools are discounted by some, they may indicate a brief and unsuccessful habitation of altitudes above 9000 feet (2500 meters). Though the tools are few and some believe they fell from later deposits above, early occupation seems likely because the three sites all had the same early date. One factor that would have made life difficult was the ice-age climate of the Late Pleistocene period (which ended about 10,000 years ago); other possible factors include unusually cold conditions even after the Ice Age, between 9000 and 8000 B.C., and the Younger Dryas glacial readvance. Still another consideration is the sheer physiological adaptation required to cope with the low oxygen levels of the puna. Due to low initial population levels and the birth of few viable offspring, these early hunters and foragers may have died out or retreated to lower elevations. It may have taken the next 2000 years for humans to adapt to high altitudes and the rarified oxygen content of the puna region. It has also been proposed that these early dates represent a brief summer intrusion by hunters and gatherers from lower altitudes. But if this were the case, one would expect them to have returned each summer, leaving small concentrations of artifacts throughout the intervening 1500 to 2000-year period, up until the permanent settlement of the cave sites.

On the north coast of Peru, the Paiján has two other dates earlier than 10,000 B.C., at Quirihuac Rockshelter in the Moche Valley. But the 16 other dates from various Paiján sites place this complex at between 8000 to 6000 B.C.

Although there are hints of occupation in the Central Andes at roughly the same time that settlement began in northern and southern South America, current evidence suggests that real widespread adaptation, from the coast to the puna, occurred between 9000 and 8000 B.C.

### HIGHLAND ADAPTATIONS IN THE EARLY PRECERAMIC

The highland valleys and grasslands of the quechua, suni, and puna environments have been extensively occupied since 8000 B.C. This date marks the beginning of the Holocene Epoch, during which geographic and climatic change continued until about 3000 B.C., when modern conditions stabilized. The retreat of the glacial ice, between 10,000 and 12,000 years ago, opened up the suni and puna regions to the vegetation so favored by camelids and deer, which in turn supported the hunters and gatherers. It is during this period of settlement that many common features arise in the artifacts of the region. Based on similarities between the stone tool kits (spear points and cutting and scraping tools) of the valley and puna sites, archaeologist Thomas F. Lynch has proposed a Central Andean Preceramic Tradition that encompasses Chobshi, Guitarrero and Lauricocha caves, and the Junín sites. The hunters and foragers of these sites, in the Andean mountain valleys and the puna grasslands, utilized a variety of lanceolate and triangular spearpoints to hunt game, and an assemblage of scraping and cutting implements to process the animal and vegetable products at the heart of their subsistence. Stone tools also were used to manufacture bone and wooden artifacts, which were employed in a wide range of activities, including the manufacture of clothing and woven or skin containers.

Guitarrero Cave, overlooking the Santa River at 8500 feet (2580 meters) in the Callejón de Huaylas, is dated securely to 8000 B.C., and is one of the few highland valley sites to have received attention. The faunal and floral remains from Guitarrero reflect a broad spectrum of resources, including wild and domesticated plants. The flora, surprisingly, consists not only of berries and other collected wild plants, but also domesticated peppers, *oca* (a tuber), *lucuma* (a fruit), beans, and *quinoa* (a grain). The diverse fauna includes deer, camelids, rabbits, *viscacha* (a rodent), tinamou (a bird), and pigeons. Although the Guitarrero hunters and foragers were normally valley dwellers, they may also have included the puna in their seasonal exploitation of resources.

In the puna of north-central Peru, at altitudes of between 13,000 and 14,000 feet (3950 and 4250 meters), there are a series of caves and rockshelter sites whose inhabitants lived mainly by hunting camelids and deer, and by gathering plants

**Overlooking the Santa River in the Callejón de Huaylas, Guitarrero Cave is one of the most important early highland sites to have been explored. The site is dated securely to 8000 B.C. Resources found in the area include a variety of wild plants and berries, but also domesticated peppers, tubers, and grain—the oldest cultivated plants found in the New World. The hunters and foragers who lived here might have moved seasonally to the puna in search of more resources.**

Guitarrero Cave was excavated in the late 1960s by a team led by archaeologist Thomas F. Lynch. This photograph shows members of the excavation team screening deposits found within the cave. In the distance rears snowcapped Huascarán, Peru's highest mountain.

along the streams and glacial lake edges. Due to the abundance of camelid herds in the puna, Stanford archaeologist John W. Rick has proposed that the hunters and gatherers at Pachamachay, Panaulauca, Telarmachay, and other Junín sites were year-round occupants of the puna; unlike the Guitarrero people farther north, Rick believes, these high-altitude dwellers did not move seasonally through different environmental zones to take advantage of seasonal resources. Evidence that the people of the puna were sedentary camelid hunters comes from traces of both wet- and dry-season fauna and flora at the sites, and also the fact that all tools were made from strictly puna quarry sources.

There is little evidence of any interaction between the Andes and the coast, for highland sites have yielded only a few marine shell ornaments (a favored trade item in later periods). The only evidence of any trade whatsoever is at the valley site of Chobshi Cave in southern Ecuador. This cave, at 7900 feet (2400 meters), holds evidence of long-distance access to obsidian, the volcanic glass used for sharp-edged tools. Chobshi is at the northern edge of the Central Andean Preceramic Tradition, 186 miles (300 kilometers) to the south of obsidian quarry sites; the volcanic glass was either quarried by the cave-dwellers themselves or obtained through trade with neighboring groups to the north. Here, also, there is little evidence of interaction with the coast, for obsidian, so prized for its sharp cutting edges, is not found in early Ecuadorian Preceramic coastal sites. Neither is there much evidence of contact between coastal peoples and the dwellers of either the Toquepala Cave or the open-air site of Asana (11,600 feet or 3540 meters) on the western side of the Cordillera Negra in southern Peru, in spite of the fact that, on the rare clear days, the inhabitants could have seen the coast.

Farther south, Andean hunters in northern Chile seasonally exploited the puna and the lower valleys. But, as the Chilean glacial lakes of this hyperarid region dried up at the end of the Pleistocene (about 6000 B.C., coinciding with the end of the Early Preceramic), the region was depopulated until the Late Preceramic (about 3000 B.C.).

## COASTAL ADAPTATIONS IN THE EARLY PRECERAMIC

It has only been in the last decade that researchers have established solid evidence of the Early Maritime Tradition, when fish and shellfish foods took on great importance. The main reason for the delay is that most of the evidence (all prior to 3000 B.C.) lies submerged on the continental shelf. But, of course, it was not always under water. The wide coastal plain of the last glacial and

early Holocene periods was between 12 and 37 miles (20 and 60 kilometers) wider on the central coast of Peru until 3000 B.C., by which time modern sea level was reached and the shelf was finally submerged. In other areas of the coast the former shoreline was within only .5 to 1.5 miles (1 to 2 kilometers) of the modern coast, thus preserving evidence of the use of ocean resources by early peoples. Only a few early maritime sites are preserved—most others lie drowned on the continental shelf—but the surviving sites, located high on terraces or at inland sites, hold evidence of the seasonal exploitation of the former coast. These surviving sites either formed part of a hunting and gathering subsistence pattern, including exploitation of the now-drowned Holocene coasts, or else were situated on elevated terraces to take advantage of the lomas.

On the east coasts of the New World the continental shelves are broad plains (now submerged), but the western continental shelf is narrow. However, the narrowness of the shelf did not drastically inhibit settlement. On the east coasts there are only a few maritime sites that predate 3000 B.C. (since the pre-3000 B.C. sites are underwater), yet recent evidence from southern California, southern Ecuador, northern and southern Peru, and northern Chile confirm that the earliest West Coast peoples took great advantage of the bounty of the sea. It has been stressed by a few investigators that the earliest coastal migrants, who would instantly recognize the tremendous resources offered by the ocean and its coast, may in fact have used watercraft to move southward from the Bering Strait.

Two groups known for their versatility in adapting to a coastal lifestyle are the Las Vegas and Amotape-Siches people. Inhabitants of the Santa Elena region of southern Ecuador and of the Peruvian north coast both exploited a variety of resources, including those of mangrove swamps, ocean, and inland areas. The Las Vegas peoples (8000 to 4600 B.C.) of Ecuador subsisted on shellfish, marine fish, deer, and small game. Although no plant remains have been recovered, gourds and either wild or domesticated squash were identified from phytoliths, the silica crystals contained in plants. On the northern Peru *tablazos*, or raised Pleistocene marine floors, the Amotape (9000 to 6000 B.C.) and the Siches (6000 to 3000 B.C.) adapted to the mangrove resources in the river estuaries along the coast. The disappearance of the mangroves from northern Peru reflects the final transition, after 3000 B.C., from a wetter environment to the arid conditions of today. The Las Vegas and Amotape-Siches are known for a unifacial stone tool industry, but instead of stone projectile points, they used projectile points made of bone.

A distinctive feature of the Las Vegas was their burial tradition, one that was shared by the maritime-adapted Cerro Mangote people of Panama: the long bones of the deceased were bundled together and covered by their ribs, and their skulls were placed at the top. This similar approach to burial has led archaeologist Karen E. Stothert, the excavator at Las Vegas, to conclude that there was a cultural interaction between Ecuador and Panama before 5000 B.C.

Much evidence of maritime habitation has been lost to changing sea levels. One gets a hint of this loss from studying areas where the former Peruvian coast was comparatively wide. South of the Sechura Desert, for example, between Lambayeque and Lima, are to be found significant Paiján artifacts. Characteristic Paiján projectile points, along with bifacial and unifacial stone tools, have turned up on the Peruvian north coast from Chiclayo to the Casma Valley, with a scattering of Paiján points as far south as Ica on the south coast.

North of the Chicama Valley, in the Pampa de Los Fósiles, archaeologist Claude Chauchat excavated a series of Paiján sites that had an abundance of marine fish and lizards. Remains of viscacha, fox, deer, pigeons, iguana, and geckos were recovered, all of which occur in the lomas environment

From approximately 9000 B.C. to 6000 B.C., the Amotape people successfully adapted to the environment of the river estuaries of the Peruvian north coast. These shells, found at an Amotape campsite overlooking the Talara Tar Pits, point to the exploitation of the mangroves that once flourished in the river estuaries.

today. The Paiján were far inland from the early Holocene coast, which they visited during the summer months to take advantage of the lizards appearing after their winter hibernation. The marine catfish, mullet, drumfish, and several other fish species vary in size, leading faunal specialist Elizabeth S. Wing to conclude that such a range of species must have been caught using nets. Today, these Paiján sites are located 9 to 22 miles (14 to 35 kilometers) from the shoreline, which at 8000 B.C. would have been 12 miles (20 kilometers) farther out from its present position. Not surprisingly, only a few fragments of marine shell have been found at the sites, as shellfish would not be an economical resource to transport such a distance. However, dried fish would have been easy to take along, explaining the variety of fish skeletons on-site. It is believed that these inland Paiján sites represent part of the seasonal round of Paiján hunters and gatherers, which, as the evidence shows, included the use of marine resources on the coast of the now submerged continental shelf.

This interpretation is supported by a series of sites in northern Chile: the Tiliviche I Complex (8000 to 5500 B.C.). Samples from the Tiliviche sites, located 25 miles (40 kilometers) from the coast and at an elevation of some 3100 feet (950 meters), contain more than 50 percent marine products—fish, shorebirds, shellfish, and sea mammals—indicating regular travel to the coast; the remaining 50 percent indicates exploitation of riverine oases rich in terrestrial game and plants. A number of other sites in northern Chile provide similar evidence of coastal adaptations, including the 8000 B.C. site of Las Conchas with a midden (a heap of decayed refuse) containing 24 species of marine fish, sea mammals, mollusks, birds, and terrestrial animals.

In southern Peru, near Ilo, the Ring Site, excavated by archaeologist Daniel H. Sandweiss and myself, shows almost exclusive use of marine resources by 8500 B.C. Now partially destroyed, the Ring Site was formerly a large shell ring 85 feet (26 meters) in diameter and between 8 and 26 feet (2.5 and 8 meters) in height. Radiocarbon dates from the lowest levels of the ring's base show occupation from 8500 to 5700 B.C. Unifacial stone tools comprise the vast majority of intentionally modifed objects excavated from the Ring Site; the only other artifacts are seven bone-and-shell fishhooks and one bone harpoon. No projectile points were recovered in the excavations, although some were present on the site surface.

Faunal specialist Elizabeth J. Reitz's analysis of Ring Site fauna has shown that the inhabitants relied heavily upon marine fish, shellfish, and shorebirds. All the birds except one were coastal or oceanic species, with pelicans and cormorants a major food source. The fish indicate that the Ring Site people extensively fished the near-shore waters using fishhooks. Twenty species of fish were identified, with two species of drumfish being the most abundant. The shellfish that make up this midden are from rocky headland and sandy shore environments. Interestingly, while sea mammals were represented by a few sea otters and seal, there is a total lack of land mammals. This is puzzling because the nearby lomas must have supported both guanaco and deer.

As we can see, there is ample evidence that the earliest Central Andean inhabitants made good use of the ocean's horn of plenty. With such evidence, it is not startling to consider that a maritime economic system was completely in place before 8000 B.C.

The picture that is emerging for the Early Preceramic is of two distinct and exclusive traditions. The first, as we have seen, is the Central Andean Preceramic Tradition in the highlands. Enjoying a mixed economy of animal and plant exploitation, the highlanders relied on deer, camelids, and small game supplemented by both wild and rare domesticated plants. Among these

The Ring Site, near Ilo in southern Peru, takes its name from a circle of discarded shellfish and refuse dated to more than 10,000 years ago. The inhabitants of this settlement stayed close to the shore, and subsisted almost exclusively on fish, shellfish, and shorebirds. Fishhooks made of bone and shell have been found at the site, as well as a bone harpoon. The upper portion of the shell ring has been destroyed. In this photograph, archaeologists examine the massive accumulation of shells and other foodstuffs discarded by its early inhabitants.

highland people, two patterns of exploitation were practiced: the seasonal movement of hunters and gatherers upward from quechua to puna; and the sedentary hunting and gathering of those encamped in the Junín puna. The second is the Maritime Tradition of the coasts, whose inhabitants depended on the resources of the ocean, lomas, and valley environments. As in the highlands, there are also two subsistence strategies on the coast: sedentary communities relying almost solely on marine foods; and nomadic groups that moved from coast to interior, taking advantage of seasonal resources.

### SETTLING DOWN: THE MIDDLE PRECERAMIC

The Middle Preceramic period (6000 to 3000 B.C.) was a time of significant developments—changes that would lead ultimately to the rise of the great civilizations of the Central Andes. There is increased diversity within both the Central Andean Preceramic and the Maritime traditions as these populations continue to adapt to the transition from glacial to modern conditions.

In the Middle Preceramic there is an intensification of plant use, leading to the domestication of many of the crops central to later agricultural economies on the coast and in the Andes. The advent of farming also introduces water management, which was of key importance not only on the arid coast but in the highlands as well. In the high Andes, camelid management leads to the domestication of the llama and the alpaca, and also to a herding economy in the suni and puna regions. On the coast, the maritime economy becomes firmly established not only along the shore, but also in the lomas environment. The Middle Preceramic holds the key not only to the development of agricultural, herding, and maritime economies, but also the seeds of the sociopolitical and religious systems expressed in the large temple centers of the Late

Preceramic. It was in the Middle Preceramic that sedentary communities developed residential architecture, and there is evidence of ceremonial structures. Significantly, the few sites that have received intensive investigation point to larger populations. Alas, the Middle Preceramic is the least researched of all the Andean time periods. Thus, we have only glimpses of the threads that would soon form the cultural fabric of the Late Preceramic.

The evidence of the Middle Preceramic comes mainly from the same Andean rockshelters and cave base camps mentioned in our discussion of the Early Preceramic, from open-air sites in the Zaña Valley of northern Peru, from the Osmore drainage region of southern Peru, and from the central Peruvian and northern Chilean coasts.

In the puna, the Early Preceramic way of life continued largely unchanged in the Middle Preceramic, with hunters and gatherers relying on the predictable camelid and wild plant resources. One key theme here—and a source of much debate—is the domestication of the llama and the alpaca from the guanaco, their wild camelid ancestor. The transition from hunting to herding took place largely in the suni and the puna, extending across a period of semi-domestication when wild camelids may have been controlled through corralling. Telarmachay Rockshelter in the Junín puna, containing a ton of camelid bones, is a good place to start. Until 5000 B.C., the bones are of wild camelids, but after 5000 B.C. there is a dramatic shift that indicates domestication. Whereas among the early bones there are numerous fetal remains of hunted pregnant females, these are abruptly replaced by the skeletal remains of newborn animals. This is interpreted by archaeologist Jane C. Wheeler as reflecting the beginnings of the coralling of wild camelids. The semi-domestication of llamas and alpacas occurred by 4000 B.C., and full domestication by 2500 B.C.

Evidence varies, of course. In Panaulauca Cave, also in the Junín puna, archaeobotanist Deborah M. Pearsall's analysis of plant remains shows that the herding of semi-domesticated camleids may not have begun until some time after 2000 B.C., with full domestication 400 years later. Pearsall bases her conclusions on the weedy plants, such as quinoa, that would have thrived on the floors of the manure-rich corrals. These plants were valued for their seeds, and grown in abandoned corrals—but not at Panaulauca Cave—until about 2000 B.C.

In either case, llama and alpaca herding—the hallmark of the early agropastoral economy in the Central Andes—was in place sometime around 2000 B.C. In the Moche Valley of the coast, llamas had become an important food source somewhere between 1500 and 1100 B.C. In other parts of the high Andes too, llama and alpaca may have been independently domesticated at various times.

The *cuy* (guinea pig) is the other important comestible animal—in fact, in many regions it is the only animal protein available. This small rodent, prized as a pet in many other countries, is consumed by Andean peoples even today. Due to their short gestation period—only three months—a female will bear

Llamas once roamed wild throughout the upper elevations of the Andes, but were domesticated by about 2000 B.C. They later became valuable for their meat and wool. The versatile animal also served as a beast of burden. On the puna, llama herding was a source of great wealth for highland peoples. Today, llamas like this one are still an essential part of the Andean economy.

One of the most important staple foods of the world today, potatoes have been cultivated in the Andes for nearly 10,000 years. More than 2500 varieties have been recorded. The potato is well adapted to high altitudes, and Peruvian farmers sometimes plant up to 200 different kinds in a single field. Some species have even been developed to withstand the sub-zero temperatures of the puna.

Another tuber that is grown successfully at various altitudes in the Andes is the *ulluco*, also known in both English and Spanish as the *melloco*. Its many forms vary in size and shape from that of a pea to a potato. With its attractive outward appearance, the ulluco has been likened to a botanical jewel.

four litters in a year, usually of three or four young. Anywhere from 8 to 15 cuys are kept in the home, eventually to be boiled, roasted, or cooked in a stew. The cuy also figures prominently in festivals, and is valued in folk medicine for both diagnosis and therapy. The earliest records of the cuy come from the Ayacucho Caves dating to 5000 B.C., from the 2000 B.C. temple site of Kotosh (in the Huallaga River basin, east of the Cordillera Blanca), and from Late Preceramic sites on the coast.

Camelid herding and the breeding of cuys are joined by the domestication of grains and tuber crops, an elemental ingredient of the agropastoral economic systems of later Andean empires. It is probable that these high-altitude crops were first domesticated in the quechua and suni zones above 7500 feet (2300 meters). With the exception of the potato, the grain and tuber crops of the Inca and their predecessors are still relatively unknown outside the Andes; yet in that region, they remain important staples. They are also convenient: when dried or processed into flour, they can be stored for years. Highly nutritious, they serve as a major source of protein, starch, and oil for Andean peoples, as well as for livestock, which in turn provide meat, wool, and manure for fertilizer and fuel.

Quinoa, *kiwicha*, and *tarwi* are the vital grain crops, providing seeds for producing flour that is used in baked goods and stews. Tarwi has the added gift of containing useful vegetable oil. Quinoa was considered by the Inca as the *chisiya mama*, or mother grain, and was noted by the early chroniclers as second only to potatoes in importance. It is found in the Ayacucho Caves by 5800 B.C., at Panaulauca Cave circa 2000 B.C., and at Chiripa in the Lake Titicaca Basin at 1350 B.C.

There are more species of starchy tuber crops in the Central Andes than anywhere else on Earth. The domesticated potato alone has more than 2500 distinct varieties, as recorded at the International Potato Center in Lima. First domesticated in the Central Andes, the potato was later introduced to the Old World by the Spaniards. Today, the potato ranks as one of the 20 staple foods that feed the world's population. In a single field, Andean farmers can grow more than 200 different potato varieties, which have a wide assortment of shapes and colors. A number of species have been perfected to withstand the killing frosts at 13,800 feet (4200 meters) in the puna, and these are processed into a freeze-dried food called *chuño*. Preparation begins with stomping the water from the tubers, which then can be stored indefinitely. Although wild potatoes were used for food at the 11,000-B.C. Monte Verde site in Chile, the earliest cultivated potatoes date to 8000 B.C. These were found at Tres Ventanas Cave in the upper Chilca Valley of Peru. Other important Andean tuber crops include *oca, ulluco,* and *mashua*, all ideal for soups and stews. Once again, 8000 B.C. figures as the date when oca and ulluco are first domesticated, at Guitarrero Cave and at Tres Ventanas Cave, respectively.

The common bean did not grow well at high altitudes, so the Andean people developed their own large-seeded bean known today as the lima, examples of which are shown above. A major source of protein, this bean has become one of the most widely cultivated legumes in the world today.

In the upper yunga and the lower reaches of the quechua zones, peanuts, common beans, lima beans, and a number of tree fruits, including guava and lucuma, were probably developed as domesticated plants; all are present in coastal sites by 2500 B.C., in the Late Preceramic period. Earlier dates may be possible, but studies of floral remains can be tricky, and sometimes results are hard to interpret, as the following case illustrates. Fireplace charcoal in the Nanchoc Complex sites, in the yunga of the upper Zaña Valley, dated the plants, which included quinoa-like grain, squash, peanuts, and manioc (a tropical root crop), to between 6400 and 5600 B.C. Yet recently a new radiocarbon technique was used to date directly these domesticated plants, proving them to be only a few hundred years in age. Nonetheless, archaeologist Jack Rossen, the excavator, feels the archaeological context (a location that he believes has been undisturbed for millennia) still supports the earlier dates, and calls into question the radiocarbon dates on the plants.

Except for a few plants, the earliest cultigens (crops or domesticated plants) come from two sites: Guitarrero and Tres Ventanas caves. The next archaeological occurrence is either from the Middle Preceramic sites of Ayacucho or in the Late Preceramic period on the coast. Guitarrero Cave, excavated by Thomas F. Lynch, has received rigorous examination, and 8000 B.C., at the beginning of the Holocene Epoch, is firmly established as a key date for the growing of domesticated plants. The Tres Ventanas material awaits further study.

Other uncertainties are apt to arise in the study of flora. An example occurs on the arid coast of Peru, where dry conditions have preserved evidence of domesticated plants in a later period, the Late Preceramic. Yet this very

With its origins in tropical forest regions of South America, manioc (or *yuca*) is today one of the world's most important tubers. Meal processed from the root is widely used as a cereal substitute. Radiocarbon dating of plant remains from Tres Ventanas Cave and the Nanchoc sites date as early as 8000 B.C. and 6400 B.C., respectively. However, these early dates for the plant's domestication remain to be verified.

preservation gives us an exaggerated picture of their importance in the coastal diet. In fact, agriculture, while playing a role in the coastal subsistence pattern, did not play a critical role (as will be evident in the next chapter). Most plants consumed or otherwise used on the coast were not domesticated there. Instead, such plants as manioc, cotton, avocado, sweet potato, and maize were introduced from Mesoamerica, northwestern South America, the Amazon Basin, or the high Andes. This argues for a long period of human manipulation of plants elsewhere during the Early and Middle Preceramic prior to their introduction to the coast after 3000 B.C.

The domestication of maize was an astounding human achievement. Early agricultural engineers took *teosinte*, a wild Mexican grass, and developed one of the world's most important foods. Teosinte, the wild ancestor of maize, is known only from Mesoamerica, which is considered the womb of this golden crop. The center of domestication of the plant is believed to lie in the Río Balsas region of southwest Mexico; some distance away, in Tehuacan, Mexico, small maize cobs have been found in dry caves, and date to 5000 B.C. Through the use of improved radiocarbon dating techniques, these are now thought to date to a few thousand years later. There is also evidence of maize pollen dated to 5000 B.C. in Panama, in Colombia, and in the Amazon of Ecuador. On the Ecuadorian coast, there is evidence of maize phytoliths in Las Vegas between 5000 and 6000 B.C. In Peru, maize is documented by 4000 B.C. in the Casma Valley on the coast, and in the Ayacucho Caves. Farther south, in northwest Argentina and in northern Chile, there are a number of similar sites with dates of between 4000 and 6000 B.C.

It has been thought that maize was introduced into the Central Andes by land, but the similarities in burial ceremonies between the maritime Las Vegas peoples of Ecuador and the inhabitants of Cerro Mangote in Panama suggest it may have arrived through seaborne trade. Although maize was present in Peru after 4000 B.C., it does not appear to have been an important crop in the Central Andes until the period of the Early Horizon.

In addition to being eaten, maize also was transformed into beer, or *chicha*. Unique to the Andes, this fermented drink is important in the ritual and social settings not only of the Inca and their predecessors, but also of Andean peoples today. The earliest evidence comes from the Callejón de Huaylas, where ceramic vessels used for processing and storing chicha are known by 200 B.C.

Another important Andean crop is the mildly narcotic coca plant, whose leaves even today are chewed by millions of people in the Andes. Once thought to be used only to deaden hunger pangs, coca has recently proven itself a nutritional complement to food consumption; 3.53 ounces (100 grams) of coca leaves provides the recommended daily allowance of calcium, iron, phosphorus, Vitamin A, and riboflavin. Coca was destined to become an important state product of the Inca, but during the Middle Preceramic period it remained known only locally; not until the Late Preceramic was it introduced to the coast from the eastern valleys of the Cordillera Blanca. (In this century, of course, coca's prime importance is in the production of cocaine; it is also used as a flavoring agent in commercial cola drinks, although the coca used for this purpose nowadays is treated to remove its narcotic properties.)

It is during the Middle Preceramic that sedentary communities were established, especially on the coast; it is there that we find ample evidence of small villages. Between the Chilca Valley and Paracas are a number of Middle Preceramic villages, of which the best known is Paloma. Dating from 5700 to 3000 B.C., Paloma is located in the lomas north of the Chilca Valley, 2.5 miles (4 kilometers) inland from the modern coast. This site, excavated at various times by archaeologists Frédéric-André Engel, Jeffrey Quilter, and Robert Benfer, produced a sample of 251 burials and 42 houses from its 37-acre (15-hectare) area.

More than 90 percent of the subsistence at Paloma came from the ocean, mainly from fish and shellfish, which were caught along the rocky and sandy shoreline. Since many of the fish are small schooling species—the anchovy and the herring, for example—Elizabeth J. Reitz feels the inhabitants must have had nets or scoops to catch them. In some areas, 50 percent of the midden was composed of salt, leading to the conclusion that fish were salted for storage. The few bones of land animals include those of guanaco, deer, and, surprisingly, puma, along with one spider monkey femur. Monkeys are found today in the extreme northwest of Peru and the Amazon Basin, while the puma inhabits the higher reaches of the Andes. In the past, they were also found occasionally in the coastal lomas zone.

The shellfish at the Paloma site include mussels commonly known as *choros*, found at depths of 13 to 98 feet (4 to 30 meters). Analysis of the human burials reveals that eight of the males had auditory exostoses, an inner ear bone growth attributed to diving in cold water—in this case, presumably, diving for shellfish. (As we shall see in Chapter 5, this abnormality is also present, in both male and female burials, at the 3000-B.C. village of Huaca Prieta in the Chicama Valley.) And the pursuit of marine resources was not without more sudden dangers as well, for the burial of one 17-year-old Paloma male indicates he lost his left leg to a shark.

The plant remains at Paloma consist of lomas species—including a tuber that may have been semi-domesticated—and a few beans, squash, and gourds. As mentioned earlier, the preponderance of fish and shellfish remains indicates that plants and land animals probably did not contribute more than 10 percent of the local diet.

The trade sphere of the Paloma people brought them raw obsidian for the manufacture of projectile points; the source of this valuable volcanic glass was 250 miles (400 kilometers) away, at Huancavelica in the southern Andes. Together with the spider monkey and puma bones mentioned above, these all reflect contact with far-flung regions.

At the coastal site of Paloma, located north of the Chilca Valley, the burial of the dead was a simple procedure: the body of the deceased was placed in the ground beneath the floor of the reed-covered house. Here an archaeologist excavates a burial by removing the house poles and grass insulation.

It is estimated that more than 400 houses existed at Paloma, but that only 2 to 10 of them were occupied at any one time over the 3000-year history of the site. If the average family size was five people, the population at the village would have fluctuated between 10 and 50.

Indeed, life must have been hard at Paloma during the Middle Preceramic, for the analysis of the burials has shown that 45 percent of the population did not live past childhood, and that the average age of buried adults was between 20 and 35 years of age. The burials exhibit a simple mortuary cult: many bodies were placed under the floors of the inhabitants' small, circular, reed-covered houses; others were buried outside the house, but still nearby. A number of the graves contained textiles, ornaments of bone or shell, and items of everyday use.

The careful burial of the dead is also a feature of many other coastal and highland sites of the Middle Preceramic, and even of a few Early Preceramic sites. The most complex mortuary pattern of the Middle Preceramic is at Chinchorro (5800 to 1800 B.C.), in northern coastal Chile. The Chinchorro people mummified their dead, sometimes by simply drying them, but often through an elaborate mummification process in which they removed the organs, stripped the flesh, and rebuilt the bodies using sticks to stiffen the limbs, then finally wrapped the limbs and body with rope. The skin was sewn back together where it had been cut, and a face mask was modeled in clay and adorned with the body's hair, completing the individual's preparation for the afterlife. The body then was displayed and subsequently buried alongside what appear to be family members.

As well as single and multiple burials, the Las Vegas people of Ecuador also practiced secondary burials in ossuaries. The bodies were defleshed; then their bones were gathered into bundles and buried in groups of up to 38 individuals, accompanied by only a few goods.

Such evident concern with the deceased shows that the Early and Middle Preceramic peoples had a religious ideology, one that helped them cope with the transition from life to death. Thus are sown the seeds of the elaborate postmortem rites found in all later Central Andean societies.

As we have seen, the Early to Middle Preceramic witnessed an increase in population, development of sedentary communities specializing in specific sets of resources, and access to exotic goods originating hundreds of kilometers from their settlements. Agriculture became a minor part of the subsistence pattern, and burial ceremonialism was well established. The development from the small-village way of life of the Middle Preceramic to a temple-centered society is the major achievement of the Late Preceramic, which we shall explore in the next chapter.

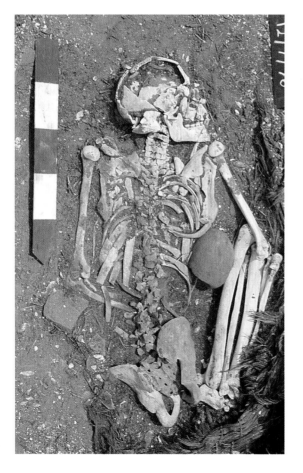

The skeleton of a 17-year-old male from Paloma was found without its left leg. This is thought to be the result of a shark attack while the youth was diving for shellfish. His elaborate burial points to the importance attached to fishing by coastal peoples.

**The Late Preceramic site of El Paraíso, in the Chillón Valley, is one of the earliest structures to have been constructed according to a U-shaped complexes are separated by a wide plaza, with a multiroomed temple, shown in its reconstructed state, forming the base of the U.**

# 3

# FOUNDATIONS OF CIVILIZATION

At the same time that Pharaoh Khufu was being laid to rest in the Great Pyramid at Giza, civilization was emerging in the Central Andes. Large temple centers arose along the Pacific Coast and in the highlands during the Late Preceramic, presaging the even greater public works of the Initial Period and the Early Horizon. These ceremonial centers, with their multiroomed temples, circular sunken plazas, and U-shaped layouts, represent the earliest appearance of complex society in the Americas. Even the Olmec, the first Mesoamerican civilization, did not arise until 1000 years after civilization was well established in the Central Andes.

Only recently did we find evidence that the genesis of the later Andean states and empires occurred in the Central Andes—and in the Late Preceramic (3000 to 1800 B.C.). Indeed, the seeds of civilization appear slow to germinate in other areas. For example, in the 1940s, the work of Junius B. Bird in northern Chile and at Huaca Prieta in the Chicama Valley portrayed the Late Preceramic peoples as living in small coastal fishing villages with limited farming. It would be another 10 years before investigators revealed evidence of the highland hunting and gathering groups of the Early and Middle Preceramic. The accepted view of the Huaca Prieta lifestyles in the Late Preceramic preconditioned archaeologists to assume, as did Julio C. Tello, that the first civilization in the Central Andes was the Chavín of the first millennium B.C. (The Chavín civilization had long drawn the attention of archaeologists because of its imposing architecture and complex art style—both in sculpture and ceramics.) The first evidence that there were large temple centers that preceded Chavín came with the 1957 discovery of Las Haldas by archaeologists Edward P. Lanning and Frédéric-André Engel. Las Haldas, south of the Casma Valley, is an enormous terraced hillside with a series of rectangular courtyards and circular sunken plazas stretching out parallel to the coast. The architecture at Las Haldas has proven to be Initial Period in date (circa 1600 B.C.), a discovery that startled the archaeological community, for nothing this grand was suspected to have existed so early in Central Andean cultural development. The discovery of Las Haldas was soon followed by another startling find, when, in the early 1960s, archaeologists Edward P. Lanning and Thomas C. Patterson came across El Paraíso in the Chillón Valley. An enormous discovery both figuratively and literally, El Paraíso is the largest temple center known for the Late Preceramic. And at the same time, archaeologists Seiichi Izumi and Kazuo Terada excavated the Kotosh site in the eastern Andes, on the Higueras River of the Huallaga Basin. The 11 single-roomed temples of the Kotosh site dated to 2000 B.C. and are the first Late Preceramic structures to turn up on the eastern side of the Andes. With this new knowledge expanding their visions, archaeologists soon found dozens of pre-Chavín temple centers throughout the coast and highlands of Peru.

The origins of these early ceremonial structures can be traced back to the Middle Preceramic, where small earthen mounds have been interpreted as functioning for religious purposes. At Nanchoc, in the upper Zaña Valley, several small, three-tiered platform mounds, reinforced with stones, have been dated to 5000 B.C. The Nanchoc mounds were accompanied by residential dwellings of nearby hunters, gatherers, and possibly farmers who used elementary irrigation techniques. A few other Middle Preceramic sites on the Peruvian central coast also have what appears to be non-domestic architecture.

At Aspero, one of the larger Late Preceramic coastal temple centers, 17 large and small mounds cover a total area of 32 acres (13 hectares). Among the discoveries made during the excavation of Huaca de los Idolos (Mound of the Idols), one of the largest of Aspero's mounds, were small clay figurines of the type shown here.

As was stressed in the previous chapter, the Middle Preceramic is not well known, so it seemed to archaeologists that the Late Preceramic centers appeared on the landscape without any precursors. It must also be kept in mind that the archaeologist is faced with the end-product of hundreds of years of building, expansion, and remodeling at such temple centers. Even now, not one of these Late Preceramic sites, with their monumental architecture, has been extensively excavated. Thus, we do not know, as we do for some Maya temples, the building sequences through time. Do they begin as modest installations and later increase in size? It is intriguing that the distribution of these Late Preceramic temple centers also lies along the portion of the coastline where the continental shelf is at its widest—and ocean riches at their greatest—in the whole Central Andes region. Therefore, it is possible that the evidence of even earlier temple centers—also from the Middle Preceramic—may be submerged on the continental shelf, for modern sea level was reached about 5000 years ago, at the same time that the temple centers appeared on the coast. This possibility remains to be investigated by archaeologists, as do questions of their origin in the Middle Preceramic.

Before describing these earliest monumental structures in the New World, it will help the reader to know that there are four major religious traditions reflected in temple architecture during the Late Preceramic: the Aspero, the Kotosh, the Salinas, and the Paraíso religious traditions.

### THE ASPERO TRADITION

Between the Chancay and Supe valleys is a cluster of sites having stone and earth mounds with stone-walled rooms on their summits. While our knowledge of the sites remains limited, we do know that they were under construction by

2800 B.C. Of the three best-known sites—Río Seco, Bandurria, and Aspero—the last has received the most attention. Although Aspero was discovered by Max Uhle in 1905 and excavated by Gordon R. Willey in 1941, it was not until 1971 that Michael E. Moseley, accompanied by Willey, demonstrated that Aspero was one of the larger Late Preceramic temple centers on the coast. Then, in 1973, archaeologist Robert A. Feldman, a student of Moseley and Willey, revealed for the first time the magnitude of the achievements of the Aspero people.

Aspero has 17 large and small mounds and refuse middens covering 32 acres (13 hectares). Feldman directed his excavations at two large mounds: Huaca de los Idolos (Mound of the Idols) and Huaca de los Sacrificios (Mound of Sacrifices). These two temple structures were composed of layers of rooms, separated by walls of rough-cut basaltic rocks set in a mud mortar. Used to carry out religious rituals, the rooms were intentionally filled in periodically in order to erect a new room complex. The final cluster, then, represents the last stages of temple construction.

Only the top third of Huaca de los Idolos has been excavated, and this room level is dated to 2600 B.C. Entrance to the summit rooms is through an entry court that allowed restricted access to interior rooms. The small central room has three small niches and a bench that may have served as an altar. In this central shrine, there was a cache of 13 small, unbaked clay male and female figurines. All the figures were depicted sitting cross-legged, except for one standing male. The clay figurines provide a glimpse of the dress styles of Aspero society, and feature turban-like hats, thigh-length skirts, and necklaces and bracelets. A few other examples of clay figurines are known from Río Seco and Bandurria.

In the Huaca de Los Sacrificios temple, dated to 2800 B.C., the elaborate burial of a two-month-old infant was found wrapped in a mat beneath an inverted four-legged, basin-shaped grindstone. On the infant's head was a cap of shell and bone beads. Whether the infant and a poorly preserved adult nearby were sacrificed in a religious ritual is unknown, but their burial in the sacred precincts of the temple indicates they were accorded special status in Aspero society.

Interspersed throughout the Aspero site are the dwellings of the inhabitants, which await future excavation. It is clear from both the midden deposits and the unexcavated houses, however, that there was a large resident population at Aspero, estimated at between 1500 and 3000.

## THE KOTOSH TRADITION

Archaeologists Richard L. Burger and Lucy Salazar-Burger first defined the Kotosh Religious Tradition based on single-roomed temples found at six sites in the Andes of central Peru. In addition to a group of sites in the Huallaga River Basin on the eastern slopes of the Andes—Kotosh, Waira-jirca, and Shillacoto—there are three other Kotosh temple centers. One is at Huaricoto,

In keeping with Kotosh custom, the Templo de las Manos Cruzadas (Temple of the Crossed Hands) at Kotosh was ceremonially buried beneath succeeding temples. The temple was excavated by a University of Tokyo expedition in the 1960s. The well-preserved square structure has several niches along each of its four walls. Beneath two of them are pairs of crossed hands modeled in clay, one of which is shown here.

The Kotosh Tradition site of La Galgada is situated on the Tablachaca River in the arid yunga region, on the western slopes of the Cordillera Negra. La Galgada boasts a number of temples, each set on a terraced mound. Pictured here is the North Mound during excavations carried out in the late 1970s. Dating to the Late Preceramic and Initial periods, the North Mound has a circular sunken plaza in front of its main staircase.

in the Callejón de Huaylas; another at Piruru, at 12,467 feet (3800 meters) in the Tantamayo drainage; and another at La Galgada, on a tributary of the Santa River on the western slope of the Cordillera Negra.

There is a remarkable similarity in the architecture of the Kotosh Tradition sites, which are found in all the highland zones, up to the edge of the puna. The round-cornered, single-roomed buildings are about 30 feet (9 meters) square, with plastered floors and wide benches containing a central fireplace with flues and niched walls. As with the Aspero Tradition, the mounds that contain these small-roomed buildings are themselves comprised of filled-in rooms with subsequent rooms constructed on top.

This distinctive religious architecture was first discovered by the University of Tokyo expedition at the site of Kotosh on the Higueras River, a waterway that flows into the Huallaga and from there into the Amazon Basin. Eleven temples of the earliest Preceramic period, called Mito, were excavated in a 46-foot-high (14-meter-high) mound at the site. The most spectacular was the Templo de las Manos Cruzadas, or Temple of the Crossed Hands. This square building, constructed of mortared rough stone and plastered walls, is entered through a stairway painted red—remarkably, the red paint survives. In each of the walls are several niches, and the participants in the religious ritual sat on a rectangular bench around the central hearth. Across from the doorway, two of the niches display crossed hands modeled in clay. In these and the other niches were found the burned bones of camelids and guinea pigs—probably sacrificial offerings. The entire room was roofed over with logs. Great care was taken with the filling of this temple, including the protection of the niches displaying the crossed hands with a layer of sand.

51

The buried temples of the Aspero and Kotosh religious traditions indicate a shared belief in the renewal of religious structures, possibly correlating with agricultural or fishing rituals or some other form of cyclical ceremony. The architecture of these two traditions is, however, significantly different, for Aspero has interconnecting room units, while Kotosh centered its religious activities in single-roomed temples.

La Galgada is situated in the arid yunga zone, on the Tablachaca River, a tributary of the Santa that empties into the Pacific. Excavated by art historian Terence Grieder and archaeologist Alberto Bueno Mendoza in 1976, La Galgada has—as well as numerous circular residences—a series of temple structures set on a terraced mound. With their plastered walls of river cobbles and trimmed stone, their niches, benches, and central fireplaces with flues, these temples mirror the architectural canon of the Kotosh site on the other side of the Andes. The arid conditions of the yunga preserved materials apt to decompose, leaving us textiles, baskets, and other perishable objects placed in the burials within the temple rooms. The deceased were laid on mats and wrapped in cotton, accompanied by baskets, gourd containers, cotton bags, and the shell and bone ornaments that the La Galgada people would have enjoyed in everyday life. The cotton bags are emblazoned with intricate designs of front-facing human figures, birds, and serpents woven with black, yellow, blue, orange, red, and green thread. This textile iconography is well known at Huaca Prieta and Asia on the coast, and will be discussed later.

Although the nature of the rituals in the dark temple rooms is unknown, the main activity appears to have been to feed the fire and make offerings to the gods. In the analysis of the ash of the central fireplaces, Grieder found chile pepper seeds; these he believes were thrown into the fire, stinging the eyes to create tears. Why? Perhaps it was a symbolic renewal of water sources. Water was crucial for La Galgada agriculture, an important element of which was cotton. Irrigation canals and fields for cotton production are located near the site, and cotton is found throughout the middens.

In addition to the single-roomed temples, there is a circular sunken plaza in front of the main mound, linking La Galgada conceptually to coastal sites of the Salinas Religious Tradition. The Kotosh Religious Tradition dates to between 2400–2000 B.C., and probably even earlier. Slightly later in time, at the end of the Late Preceramic, there emerge two new traditions: the Salinas and the Paraíso.

### THE SALINAS TRADITION
The Salinas and Paraíso religious traditions mark a radical departure from the Aspero and Kotosh. No longer are temples intentionally buried to create single large mounds filled with architectural levels. In the Salinas Tradition, rather, hillsides are cut into stepped platforms, which are then fronted with rectangular courtyards and circular sunken plazas.

As a result of earthquakes, sand dunes now separate the Late Preceramic site of Salinas de Chao from the coast. The temples of this Salinas Tradition center, located in the Chao Valley, were not buried, as in previous traditions. Instead, they were cut into the hillside in stepped platforms. The addition of both rectangular and circular sunken plazas, such as those visible in this photograph, is characteristic of the Salinas Tradition.

Salinas de Chao, in the Chao Valley, is one of a number of Late Preceramic sites at the edge of the former coastline of what was once a bay; since raised by the force of an earthquake, the area is now filled with sand dunes. Platforms cut into a hillside are fronted by rectangular enclosures, walled with rough-cut stone set in mud mortar, and two circular sunken plazas. Stairways lead from the enclosures up the elevated platforms, while two opposite stairways provide access to the circular sunken plazas. There, an encircling bench allowed spectators to view or participate in ceremonial activities. Evidence suggests a resident population in the rectangular room clusters, not only at the main temple center, but also at a village strung along the edge of the former bay. In the limited excavations at Salinas de Chao, a few cotton textiles and fishhooks were found.

A number of other Late Preceramic sites with circular sunken plazas are known in the Supe, Casma, and Moche valleys. At Alto Salaverry in the Moche Valley, the small, circular sunken plaza is set apart from the domestic residences and two above-ground structures. Numerous later sites, also with circular sunken plazas, are known from coastal valleys dating to the following Initial Period. Although there are no ceramics at Alto Salaverry, Salinas de Chao, or Huaynuná (to be discussed later), the few dates—1800 to circa 1400 B.C.—place the occupation at the very terminus of the Late Preceramic. As archaeologists Shelia Pozorski and Thomas Pozorski point out, these sites without pottery might have been inhabited concurrently with the pottery-producing sites of the Initial Period. Archaeologist Jeffrey Quilter, however, feels that there are too few dates from these only partially excavated Salinas and

El Paraíso is the largest temple center known from the Late Preceramic period. It is thought that a religious leader directed and organized the populace in hauling *shicra* (bagged stones) from a nearby quarry prior to construction. The walls of its multiroomed buildings were built of roughly trimmed stone blocks joined with clay mortar, filled with shicra, and faced with red and yellow plaster.

Shicra were made from reeds twisted together to form bags, which could then be filled with stones and rubble. These remarkable building blocks were used for wall construction and room filling. The shicra remnants shown above are from Mina Perdida, an Initial Period site located in the Lurín Valley.

Paraíso sites to conclude that they are Initial Period in date. Whatever the case, the circular sunken plazas become a distinguishing architectural feature of not only Initial Period sites, but of Early Horizon temple centers more than 1000 years later.

Awaiting future investigation is a gigantic mound from 2500 B.C., an earlier date than the rest of the Salinas structures. Known as Los Morteros for its abundance of mortars (grinding stones), it is walled with a row of upright stone blocks that restrict access to the summit, where once there were a number of rectangular houses. Los Morteros is so large that it is impossible to see or to get at the lowest levels without coring the structure with a drilling rig or similar instrument to bring up material for analysis. If, indeed, it is an artificial mound—and not merely a natural landform—coring should unearth cultural debris, which would in turn prove it to be one of the largest Late Preceramic structures in the Central Andes.

At the same time that the Salinas Religious Tradition makes its appearance on the coast, another distinctive architectural style is present in the Chillón Valley.

## THE PARAÍSO TRADITION

At least pending investigation of Los Morteros, the largest temple of the Late Preceramic is El Paraíso, 1.2 miles (2 kilometers) from the coast in the Chillón Valley. Covering 13 acres (58 hectares), El Paraíso is an enormous U-shaped temple complex. The U-shape designation for this architectural ground plan comes from two parallel, 1300-foot-long (400-meter-long) wings with three-story room complexes, separated by a 590-foot-wide (180-meter-wide) plaza covering 17.5 acres (7.2 hectares). A multiroomed temple building forms the

One of the most thoroughly explored Late Preceramic sites in the Central Andes is the fishing village of Huaca Prieta (Black Mound). This site had no temple, and its houses were built below ground, probably to escape the strong coastal winds. The population, which settled here some 5000 years ago, was dependent on the ocean for food, as evidenced by the fishing nets of various mesh sizes that have been unearthed at the site.

back of the U-shaped layout. Although excavated by Frédéric-André Engel in 1965, and later by archaeologist Jeffrey Quilter in 1983, the surface of El Paraíso has only been scratched.

The building at the end of the U, reconstructed by Engel and called Unit 1, is a four-tiered temple with 16 rooms and two stairways, all of which were constructed in four phases. The temple is built of roughly trimmed stone blocks laid in two rows with clay mortar and finished with red and yellow plaster. In the oldest section of the temple is a red-painted room. Its rectangular sunken area and circular charcoal pits at each corner suggest that the room was the focus of ceremonial activities, but beyond that, little can be deduced about the site. Few artifacts were recovered in the excavations, and the burials do not provide significant information about mortuary patterning.

The construction at El Paraíso and the earlier Aspero site included the use of *shicra*, or bagged fill. The shicra are simple net bags, made of reeds and filled with between 37 and 79 pounds (17 and 36 kilograms) of rocks or cobbles. The bags are believed to have been filled and carried one by one from the nearby quarries for room filling and wall construction in the temples, but were never used for building houses. As well as expanding our knowledge of local building materials, the shicra provide us with a rare glimpse of the human contribution to these large public buildings. It is thought that a religious leader must have organized and directed the populace in the laborious task of hauling and placing shicra at the building site, a method of construction that continued into the Initial Period.

El Paraíso was not just a religious center, for the density of the midden deposits has led Quilter to conclude that a large resident population (probably numbering in the thousands) occupied the site.

We have discussed the temple centers that dominate the Central Andean landscape, but little has been said about how the members of the general populace were making their livelihood. Huaca Prieta, excavated by Junius B. Bird in 1946 and 1947 as part of the Virú Valley program, remains the best explored Late Preceramic fishing village. It is entirely residential, and has no temple.

Huaca Prieta (Black Mound) is an oval, 39-foot-high (12-meter-high) accumulation of dwellings and refuse located on a coastal shelf at the northern edge of the Chicama Valley. The fishermen who settled at Huaca Prieta with their fishhooks and cotton nets arrived around 3000 B.C.—the very beginning of the Late Preceramic.

As the midden grew in size, a monument to hundreds of years of discarded food refuse, retaining walls were built to stabilize the slopes of the mound. The most spectacular artifact find of the Late Preceramic was uncovered in the burial of an elderly woman. Wrapped in a mat made of *junco* (a wild plant fiber material) and cotton, she was accompanied by certain possessions, including a cotton pouch. It is easy to imagine Junius B. Bird's surprise when he opened the seemingly insignificant bag and inside found two small gourds, each decorated with human faces. The designs were executed by a technique called pyroengraving, similar to present-day woodburning, but employing a simple burning stick.

Bird writes that "the gourds were powdery and extremely delicate...," and to preserve them he painstakingly injected a preservative into the fragments with a hypodermic needle, thus saving these treasures of the Late Preceramic. Out of 10,770 gourd pieces subsequently found at Huaca Prieta, a total of 13 are decorated, and only these two bear elaborate designs. The rare human-face motifs on these gourds link Huaca Prieta with the Valdivia culture in coastal Ecuador 388 miles (625 kilometers) to the north. Valdivia pottery bears similar motifs, which establishes another rare example of long-distance cultural contact. The gourds must have been highly prized by their owner.

In the upper levels of the mound, excavators found subterranean houses of one or two rooms; the walls of the rooms were constructed of cobbles, while the roof beams were of wood and whalebone. That the houses were built underground is probably due to the strong coastal winds that would have made above-ground living very unpleasant.

It is textiles that give expression to the art and iconography of the Late Preceramic. Art in other forms is rare at temple sites. Although the red- or yellow-plastered walls would have provided an excellent medium for displaying religious motifs, they were left plain.

At Huaca Prieta, religious iconography was portrayed in cotton textiles woven with dyed threads; Junius B. Bird painstakingly reconstructed the designs (the colors had been lost with time), revealing, in addition to geometric designs, front-facing human figures with flowing snakes at their waists,

The excavations at Huaca Prieta, carried out by archaeologist Junius B. Bird in 1946 and 1947, threw new light on the lifestyle of a people whose existence depended almost entirely on the resources of the Pacific Ocean. In this photograph, Bird examines specimens of textiles, plants, and cordage unearthed from the coastal site.

double-headed serpents, crab monsters, and condors and other birds—all of which represented the mythology of the Huaca Prieta fisherfolk. The double-headed serpent is also found at Asia, on the south-central coast, and at the Kotosh Religious Tradition site of La Galgada. (Interestingly, the double-headed serpent has recently been identified as the common bristle worm, which at first glance appears to have two heads; the 39-inch (100-centimeter) worm resides in U-shaped burrows accompanied by crabs.) While red and blue prevail at Huaca Prieta, orange, tan, and green are also found at La Galgada, where bags made of looped and twined fibers are decorated with human figures, birds, and snakes. A number of the motifs found at Huaca Prieta and La Galgada continued into the Early Horizon, suggesting some continuity in mythologies for the next 1000 years.

The importance of fishing at Huaca Prieta is evident in the quantity of cotton fishnets and gourd net-floats found throughout the midden. An astounding find was the discovery of a fragment of fishnet with eight attached gourd floats and a stone weight. The net is assumed to have been 100 feet (30.5 meters) long, and has a 1-inch (2.54-centimeter) mesh. Two mesh sizes were used by the Huaca Prieta fishermen: the 108 small-mesh nets, with squares between 0.15 and 0.35 inches (0.4 and 0.9 centimeters); and the 234 large-mesh nets, whose squares were from 1.5 to 2.2 inches (1 to 5.5 centimeters). The choice of mesh depended on the size of the fish sought. The large-mesh nets were probably used for seining the fish, a technique in which the net is drawn through the surf by fishermen and then hauled back to the shore with the catch. While there is no evidence for watercraft, it is nonetheless difficult to imagine that these coastal-adapted maritime people had no form of seaworthy boats. Finds of *Spondylus* at Aspero and the human-face gourd containers at Huaca Prieta attest to long-distance contact with Ecuador.

Again, as at La Paloma, the hazards of diving for fish are evident in auditory exostoses of the external ear canal. Although this abnormality was present only in males at La Paloma, it occurs in three females and six males (out of a total 27 individuals examined) at Huaca Prieta. Constant contact with the cold Peru Current in the pursuit of fish and shellfish created this bony growth in the outer ear canal.

### THE MARITIME ORIGIN OF CENTRAL ANDEAN CIVILIZATION

The discovery of temple centers 1000 years older than anyone would have expected was not the only revelation that the Late Preceramic held in store. Once the antiquity of the temple centers was established, archaeologists became curious about the economic and social-political-religious systems behind these public monuments.

The excavations at Huaca Prieta led to the recognition that the economy of this burgeoning civilization was heavily dependent upon marine resources.

Bird's research at Huaca Prieta was followed some 15 years later by the work of Edward P. Lanning, Thomas C. Patterson, and Michael E. Moseley on Preceramic sites in the Ancón-Chillón region. The results of the excavations at the Ancón-area shell middens prompted Moseley to publish his startling hypothesis that the temple centers were based not on agriculture as previously assumed, but instead on a subsistence pattern featuring seafoods. Moseley's hypothesis, published in *The Maritime Foundations of Andean Civilization*, was immediately countered by a number of archaeologists who argued, without much evidence, that agriculture—rather than fishing and shellfish gathering—was the major component of the diet of these Late Preceramic temple-oriented societies. Prior to Moseley's hypothesis, the evidence from all other early civilizations—such as Egyptian, Near Eastern, Chinese, and Mesoamerican—clearly placed agriculture at the base of their economic system; thus the proposal by Moseley, that Peruvian civilization owed its origins to ocean foods, met with considerable skepticism.

Since Moseley's pronouncement, 20 years of archaeological research has provided substantial proof that maritime resources were indeed a major part of the Late Preceramic coastal diet. In order to test Moseley's hypothesis further, Jeffrey Quilter focused his attention on the refuse middens at El Paraíso. Moseley was vindicated. Fish turned out to be the overwhelming animal protein source at El Paraíso, with the anchovy being the most common. But there was more: the analysis of plant and animal remains in middens revealed that plants—both wild and cultivated—were clearly more than just an incidental part of the diet. The plants included the everpresent Late Preceramic squash, beans, tree crops, gourds, and cotton.

What remains uncertain is what percentage of the diet was derived from farming. Without irrigation, less than five percent of the river valleys would have been arable. Since cotton and gourds are found in such great profusion in Late Preceramic sites on the coast, it is clear that the cultivation of these industrial plants was of paramount importance for fishing technology.

Cotton was not domesticated first on the Peruvian coast; it is more likely that this domestication took place in coastal Ecuador and in the Amazon, where the wild ancestors of cotton are found, with the plant subsequently being brought to the Peruvian coast and highlands. The use of cotton for clothing, mats, bags, fishnets, and fishline made it a crucial part of the material culture of the Late Preceramic. As previously mentioned, cotton is found throughout the deposits at La Galgada, and it is assumed to have been grown in the irrigated fields nearby. Quilter also proposes that the cotton at El Paraíso may have been produced in irrigated fields near the site. Since

One of the most exciting moments in the excavations at Huaca Prieta came with the discovery of two small gourds, buried in a bag with the body of a woman. This one is decorated with four human faces. The preservation of these delicate objects required painstaking treatment.

fishing was so critical to the economic system, cotton became the premier crop. Some have suggested that cotton—or finished cotton products—may have been an important exchange commodity.

## TRADE AND COMMUNICATION

During the Middle Preceramic there was little contact between the coast and highlands, let alone with Ecuador. Yet in the Late Preceramic, interaction between the coast and highlands is found both in trade goods and in architectural elements. Beads of redstone, from an unknown source, are found both in the coastal sites and at La Galgada in the highlands. Marine shells are present at many Kotosh Religious Tradition sites. It was also at this time that highland-domesticated root and tree crops were introduced to the coast. Even doorway thresholds, made of the *fourcroya* tree at the coastal site of Río Seco, must have been traded or otherwise procured from 4800 feet (1450 meters) on the western cordilleran slopes.

Looking northward, the Huaca Prieta human-face gourd containers are similar to those on Valdivia pottery vessels from Ecuador. *Spondylus* shell artifacts and fragments occur at coastal centers and at La Galgada, yet the thorny, red-shelled oyster grew only in Ecuador; it was to become an important item of exchange for the next 5000 years. Along with *Spondylus* and the iconography of the Huaca Prieta gourds, cotton may have been introduced from Ecuador at about the same time.

At the Salinas Religious Tradition site of Huaynuná, north of the Casma Valley, archaeologists Shelia Pozorski and Thomas Pozorski uncovered a hillside temple with four terraces linked by a central stairway to a circular sunken plaza. In their exploration of a small mound, they discovered a tiny, rectangular, stone-walled room boasting a central fireplace with a flue that is reminiscent of the temples of the Kotosh Religious Tradition. This may reflect an introduction of the Kotosh religion to the coast by means of trade interaction with the highlands.

## LATE PRECERAMIC SOCIETY

The social-political-religious organization of Late Preceramic societies remains poorly understood. Although there are claims that these huge coastal temple centers are products of a type of social structure known as a chiefdom, there is little evidence to support this interpretation. A chiefdom is a stratified society in which status is measured by genealogical closeness to the chief, who also may be the religious leader. The chiefdom thus usually has two classes: a small chiefly elite and the general population. If the political organization was based on a chiefdom, there should be ample evidence in the burial patterns of the Late Preceramic. One would expect that the chiefly class would have been buried with sumptuous grave offerings, yet Late Preceramic graves show little status differentiation; in most cases, the occupants are accompanied by artifacts for everyday

The spiny, red-shelled *Spondylus* oyster is a native of Ecuadorian waters. Its presence among the artifacts of many Peruvian sites indicates that long-distance trading took place by land or sea routes, even though no evidence of boats has been found from the period.

use—articles that they themselves probably made. Even the elaborate grave of the infant at Aspero (the one containing the four-legged, basin-shaped grindstone) was probably intended to consecrate the new temple on the top of Huaca de los Sacrificios. Also, burial sites aside, the prestige goods that one would expect to form the wealth of chiefs or rulers are rare during the Late Preceramic. It is not until the Initial Period that there is reliable evidence for chiefdoms.

More convincing than the chiefdom hypothesis are theories on family and community structures. In a recent study of house shapes of the Middle and Late Preceramic, archaeologists Michael A. Malpass and Karen E. Stothert have shown that prior to 2500 B.C., dwellings were circular in shape, while after 2500 B.C. they were rectangular structures. The shift from circular to rectangular houses, as archaeologist Kent V. Flannery first recognized in the Near East, reflects a fundamental change in social organization. Whereas the Middle Preceramic circular houses were only large enough for a few people or a small family to occupy, the multiroomed Late Preceramic dwellings could accommodate large family kin groups.

The coastal peoples of the Middle Preceramic not only hunted and gathered as a community, they also participated in the sharing of the accumulated food (all the while living in immediate-family units). This communal society was replaced during the Late Preceramic by one that emphasized the household or extended family as the basic unit of economic production and consumption. Sedentary communities, at coastal temple centers and fishing villages, constructed rectangular houses. The rectangular design facilitated the growth of the family, for it is much easier to add rooms to a rectangular dwelling than to a circular one.

Just as the change from circular to rectangular houses reflected a shift in social organization, the planning and construction of the large Late Preceramic temple centers saw the emergence of leaders; someone had to direct these community building projects. Whether these leaders were part-time or full-time, secular or religious, is not known. What is certain is that religion played a key role in holding the community together, and some form of leadership was required to organize these large labor projects.

The large buildings and plazas of the coastal temple centers reinforced the communal religion by uniting large groups of people in public festivities and rituals. In the highland Kotosh Religious Tradition, however, things were different. There, small groups, probably individual families, practiced their religion in the privacy of their single-roomed temples. The construction of monumental public works on the coast would have necessitated large numbers of laborers; the Kotosh temples, on the other hand, according to Richard L. Burger, could have been built by a dozen people in just a month or so.

Although temple centers appear confined to the central coast and north-central highlands of Peru, recent discoveries by archaeologist Mark S. Aldenderfer, at a mountain site called Asana, demonstrate that even Andean hunters and gatherers incorporated religious structures into their temporary campsites. At Asana, located 11,270 feet (3435 meters) up in the Osmore drainage basin of southern Peru, Aldenderfer uncovered a ceremonial structure with a prepared clay floor, altars, and hearths surrounded by five rectangular shelters. This small settlement is interpreted as having been used by hunters and foragers who moved seasonally from Asana into the puna as plant and animal resources became available. Future research in the Central Andes will undoubtedly turn up further evidence of religious architecture outside the present core area.

The southern Peruvian mountain site of Asana, shown prior to excavation, offers clear evidence of the stratification resulting from a succession of cultural layers. This site seems to have been a temporary campsite for hunters and foragers, who moved seasonally up to the puna in search of plant and animal resources.

In the next chapter, we shall see that the highland Kotosh Religious Tradition continues relatively unchanged into the following Initial Period, while the Salinas and Paraíso religious traditions of the coast reach a new plateau of social-political-religious complexity. Not only is there an increase in the number and size of temple centers, but these complexes also begin to appear in the valleys away from the coast, where the agricultural economy is intensified. We shall come to understand the ways in which the transition from Middle Preceramic hunting and gathering to Late Preceramic temple-oriented societies established the basis for the rise of later Central Andean civilization.

The main pyramid of Moxeke, an Initial Period site in the Casma Valley, stands more than 100 feet (30 meters) in height. The pyramid is famous the clay sculptures excavated at the site. At its zenith, the Moxeke pyramid center probably sustained a population of about 2500 people.

not only for its robust architecture, but also for

# 4

# THE RISE OF CIVILIZATION

The Initial Period (1800 to 800 B.C.) ushers in a number of remarkable developments, setting the stage for all subsequent Andean civilizations. One notable change is a dramatic intensification of farming, which comes to overshadow the Late Preceramic dependence upon ocean resources. The limited floodwater farming on the coast during the Late Preceramic was reserved for producing cotton and gourds, which, as we have seen, were critical to the fishing economy; but the wide range of food plants in the middens clearly indicates that these part-time farmers were well aware of the dietary value of domesticated plants. In the highlands, the mixed economy of farming, plant collecting, herding, and hunting soon gave way to a greater reliance upon farming. The key to this transformation was the control of water to nourish crops. This prompted an irrigation revolution that brought with it a greatly expanded agricultural landscape, including the ability to produce two crops annually, as well as a dramatic population increase.

Irrigation agriculture pulled the populace away from the coastal temples to the interior of the valleys, where an amazing number of pyramid centers were soon erected. Independent irrigation-based societies, clustered around pyramids and plazas, dotted the valley floors of the coast and the highlands in the Initial Period.

Another innovation that sets the Initial Period apart from the Late Preceramic is the use of pottery containers. With its diverse regional shapes and styles, pottery becomes the artistic medium that enables the archaeologist to define not only cultural boundaries, but also trade and interaction between neighboring and far-flung cultural groups. The ubiquitous potsherd—simply a broken piece of earthenware—becomes an important chronological marker, as the forms and design motifs of ceramic vessels come and go with the rise and collapse of Andean states and empires.

Pottery is a late development in the Central Andes, for the use of clay containers had been known elsewhere in South America for at least 2000 years before its use here in the early Initial Period. One of the earliest centers of pottery production in South America lies in the Lower Magdalena drainage of Colombia. Here, archaeologist Augusto Oyuela-Cayceda recently discovered, at a site called San Jacinto, small bowls and neckless jars dating to 4000 B.C. Another pottery center is in the lower Amazon River, where ceramics are dated to 3000 B.C. The third major center is on the coast of Ecuador, where pottery of the Valdivia culture, excavated by archaeologists Betty J. Meggers, Clifford Evans, Jr., and Emilio Estrada in the late 1950s and early 1960s, has been dated as far back as 3200 B.C.

In Peru are found two major traditions of early pottery manufacture that are unrelated to other South American ceramics. The first tradition exists on the coast, where all of the earliest pottery has two vessel shapes: a bowl, and a neckless *olla*, or globular water vessel. What is distinctive is that the designs on them differ from region to region—and in some cases from valley to valley. Even in the Callejón de Huaylas, in the northern highlands at Huaricoto, the bowl and olla shapes prevail.

The second tradition has its origins in the tropical forest of the upper Amazon. At Lake Yarinacocha, an old oxbow of the Ucayali River in Peru, archaeologist Donald W. Lathrap revealed an elaborate ceramic sequence that he dated to 2000 B.C. On the early period bowls, designated Early Tutishcainyo (after a local Indian name), there is a representation of a cat that

Lathrap connects to the feline religious iconography of the later Early Horizon in the Andes. Meanwhile, in the Huallaga Valley in the eastern Andes, the sites of Kotosh and Shillacoto also have sophisticated pottery, which shows relationships with Early Tutishcainyo ceramics. Both of these eastern Andean ceramic styles were well developed, and it is assumed that they probably originated in some unexplored region of the upper Amazon Basin.

The question that is often posed is this: Why did it take more than 1000 years before Peru received the knowledge that clay could be formed and fired to construct a pottery container? Pottery is dated to between 1700 and 2000 B.C. for northern and central Peru, but ceramics were not accepted by southern Peruvian and Bolivian societies until about 1000 years later. Certainly there is evidence of contact with coastal Ecuador, where the Valdivia ceramic tradition flourished, and with Late Preceramic Peruvian societies. At Preceramic Huaca Prieta the gourd faces are similar to Valdivia ceramic motifs, and the Ecuadorian *Spondylus* shell is found at Aspero and La Galgada. What is more, the people of Valdivia are known to have had seafaring abilities, for Valdivians settled La Plata Island in the Guayas Basin 14 miles (23 kilometers) off the Ecuadorian coast.

The explanation may be in the fact that the Late Preceramic gourd bowls and bottles, baskets, and textile bags initially were more than sufficient for food and liquid storage. In addition, the predominantly marine diet on the coast, where fish and shellfish could be dried or cooked over a fire, did not require pottery containers until the Initial Period, when diet shifted to more extensive use of crops or domesticated plants that required boiling. Similarly, in the highlands during the Late Preceramic, tubers could be roasted and meat dried or cooked over the fire. Whatever the reason pottery was not accepted before 2000 B.C., it soon became the most widespread artifact at all Andean sites.

Two other technological achievements also emerge in the Initial Period: gold and copper metallurgy and loom weaving. Sheets of beaten gold and a metalworker's tool kit, dating between 1900 and 1400 B.C., have been found in the southern highlands of Peru at Waywaka. Copper smelting is present at Wankarani sites in Bolivia by 1200 B.C. At Mina Perdida, in the Lurín Valley, investigators have discovered hammered copper sheets and evidence of copper smelting dating to 1000 B.C. These metals provided the material for the rich artifacts that were to be produced for the ruling classes of later states and empires. In textile manufacturing, the Late Preceramic techniques of netting, looping, and twining continued to be used in the production of cloth and bags; but it is the new loom textile technology, first introduced during the Initial Period, that will prove instrumental in the production of the magnificent textiles of later time periods.

The changes brought by the new irrigation farming economy, and by the incorporation of pottery and metal-producing technologies, had a profound impact upon Central Andean cultures. The Salinas and Paraíso religious

The main pyramid at Sechín Alto was
long considered to be the largest of its
kind in the New World for this period.
In this aerial view, the pyramid mound
appears as a large, light-colored square
area near the top of the photograph.
A series of plazas, some with circular
sunken courts, stretches away from the
pyramid. Although largely unexplored,
the site has received greater attention
in recent years.

The circular sunken plaza is a common feature of many Initial Period sites. Here, at **Las Haldas**, a coastal site located south of the **Casma River**, the sunken plaza is clearly visible in the foreground, with a large rectangular court in the background. Las Haldas is significant not only for the layout of its temple complex, but also for a Late Preceramic village located beneath the surface construction.

traditions continued to dominate the central coast of Peru in the Initial Period, while a new religious tradition, the Cupisnique, arose on the Peruvian north coast. Temple centers of these and other little-known traditions are found from the Mala Valley on the south coast northward 578 miles (930 kilometers) to the Piura Valley. Three areas that have received long-term archaeological attention will form the basis for our interpretations of cultural developments on the coast during the Initial Period: the Rimac and Lurín valleys (which lie next to each other and constitute one area), the Casma Valley, and the Moche Valley.

### THE SALINAS RELIGIOUS TRADITION

Architect Carlos Williams was the first to recognize the geographic core of the Salinas Religious Tradition. Williams noted more than 50 major temple centers, with their distinctive circular sunken plazas, at some 36 sites in the Supe Valley alone. The circular sunken plazas and attendant pyramids, rectangular court-yards, and room clusters are distributed between the Chancay and Chao valleys.

Las Haldas, 12 miles (20 kilometers) south of the Casma, seemed to be just another coastal hill to Edward P. Lanning and Frédéric-André Engel in 1957. They soon realized, however, that the 164-foot-high (50-meter-high) natural hill was modified into a series of terraced platforms with entry stairways. But that was not all. Stretching 984 feet (300 meters) along the coast were four rectangular courts, the second holding one of the site's two circular sunken plazas. It was a major find, for Las Haldas is the only Initial Period center adjacent to the Pacific Ocean. Beneath the temple complex is a Late Preceramic village, which may have had religious significance to the Initial Period people who erected the temple.

The most outstanding feature of the temple at Cerro Sechín, in the Casma Valley, is its spectacular stone carvings depicting a military victory. The standing warrior shown below is adorned with the severed heads of enemies slain in battle. Although scholars disagree on whether the Cerro Sechín carvings represent historical or mythological events, all acknowledge the visual power of the work.

The most thoroughly studied and impressive number of Initial Period monuments of the Salinas Religious Tradition are found in the Casma Valley. So enormous are these monuments that they have caused speculation ever since Ephraim George Squier discussed them in 1877. In 1937, Julio C. Tello excavated at Cerro Sechín and Moxeke, and was convinced that the two sites were related to the Chavín civilization that he had investigated at Chavín de Huántar in 1919. Near the juncture of the Sechín and Casma branches, which join to form the Casma River 7 miles (12 kilometers) from the coast, lies Sechín Alto. This massive site has the same basic ground plan as Las Haldas, with a main pyramid, flanking temples, rectangular courtyards, and three circular sunken plazas. The enormity of Sechín Alto dwarfs Las Haldas, however, for its massive presence—nearly 1 mile (1.5 kilometers) in length—dominates the Lower Casma Valley. Sechín Alto dates to the early Initial Period, but it is the later Initial Period construction phases that are most visible. The main pyramid is faced with stone blocks weighing two tons, each set in mud mortar. Sechín Alto was the largest pyramid complex in the New World in the second millennium B.C., and exceeded in volume the mammoth Pyramid of the Sun at Teotihuacán in Mexico, which was erected some 2000 years later. Unfortunately, little archaeological research has been conducted at the site.

Comparable in area to Sechín Alto is the Moxeke pyramid center, located 11 miles (18 kilometers) from the Pacific Ocean in the Moxeke Valley. Moxeke covers an area of more than 544 acres (220 hectares), and consists of the pyramid of Moxeke and the storage center known as Huaca A, the two structures being separated by more than 1 mile (1.5 kilometers) of rectangular plazas, 70 small temple mounds, and hundreds of single- and multiroomed houses. The 100-foot-high (30-meter-high) Moxeke pyramid was excavated by Julio C. Tello, and on the third terrace he found a series of niches containing two types of clay sculpture: standing figures, dressed in mantles, tunics, or shirts, and holding snakes; and large, painted clay heads.

The low, 30-foot-high (9-meter-high), platform of Huaca A has been investigated by Shelia Pozorski and Thomas Pozorski, and has proved to be a warehouse for food storage. Huaca A was built in two stages

The temple center of Cerro Sechín is one of the most important sites of the Initial Period. Viewed here from the air, the temple reveals its unusual rounded corners, as well as the trenches made by archaeologists during excavation of the site. The architects of Cerro Sechín made creative use of the natural setting, extending the temple platform into the surrounding hillside.

between 1800 and 1400 B.C., and the second phase consists of 77 rooms superimposed over a similar, earlier stage of construction. The rooms have rows of niches that are believed to have been used for food storage. This conclusion is supported by the analysis of pollen that shows the niches held cotton, peanuts, beans, potatoes, sweet potatoes, and avocados. Thousands of rodent bones indicate an infestation problem. Huaca A also has large courtyards in the front and in the back. In the rear courtyard is a circular sunken plaza. On the exterior of the entry room are friezes of two opposing feline creatures. While the pyramid of Moxeke hosted religious activities at this enormous site, Huaca A was used to store agricultural products produced by the resident population, which was controlled by some form of religious authority.

Another important Casma Valley site is Cerro Sechín, also excavated by Julio C. Tello, and most recently by the archaeologists Henning Bischof and Lorenzo Samaniego. Cerro Sechín has long been recognized for its exceptional stone sculptures, and it is undoubtedly the most famous Initial Period temple.

The three-tiered platform temple of Cerro Sechín hugs the side of a hill, and probably once had a circular sunken plaza in front. This elaborate small temple is only 171 feet square (53 meters square), with rounded corners. In the earliest of three construction stages, the entrance to the central chamber of the room complex was built. There, the visitor was greeted by two opposing painted feline figures, much like those at Huaca A. Beautiful as they are, those figures are not the most spectacular artwork at the site.

Carved on stone blocks and upright slabs set into the temple walls is a spectacular military scene. Two lines of armed warriors march along the sides of Cerro Sechín, interspersed with the ghastly severed human heads, arms, legs, and gouged-out eyes of the vanquished. The victims are depicted with bashed-in heads, flowing blood, and slashed stomachs, some attempting to push their intestines back into place. The two marching columns emanate from the back of the temple and converge on the central entrance stairway, where we meet the battle standards of these two military troops. This horrific display was put in place during the last building stage.

The military formation has been interpreted by Shelia Pozorski and Thomas Pozorski as a war memorial to commemorate the invasion of the Casma Valley by foreign troops from the highlands. Such a view is not universally held, for as Richard L. Burger points out, the earliest temple had similar representations 500 years earlier, demonstrating the continuity of this tableau. These warriors and their victims may represent a mythological battle central to the religious ideology at Cerro Sechín or an actual historical event, which was incorporated into the temple architecture. Cerro Sechín is the only site with this type of theme, although a few similar scenes appear on isolated stone sculptures at other Initial Period sites.

In the neighboring Nepeña Valley, Julio C. Tello excavated at Punkurí, 17 miles (27 kilometers) from the coast. In the center of the main stairway, Tello found a large painted clay sculpture of a feline figure, its claws raised menacingly to intimidate the visitor, who is forced to walk around this fearsome creature in order to proceed into the upper sanctuary of the temple.

### THE PARAÍSO RELIGIOUS TRADITION

The U-shaped architectural plan of Late Preceramic El Paraíso—with the temple at the junction of two flanking wings enclosing a large plaza—is the basic layout for more than 20 U-shaped pyramid centers constructed during the Initial Period. As Carlos Williams has noted, the U-shaped pyramid centers are concentrated in the Lurín, Rimac, Chillón, and Chancay valleys of the

Brightly painted clay friezes, like the example pictured here, decorate the atrium of the Middle Temple at Garagay. This detail shows the head of a supernatural being, resembling a spider. The band around the head suggests a spiderweb.

central Peruvian coast, but only a few have been excavated. The two Rimac Valley centers that have received attention are La Florida, investigated by archaeologist Thomas C. Patterson, and Garagay, which was excavated by archaeologists Rogger Ravines and William Isbell. Of the five U-shaped monuments in the Lurín Valley, only Cardal and Mina Perdida—the latter excavated by Richard L. Burger and Lucy Salazar-Burger—have been investigated.

The U-shaped pyramid centers have a set of common architectural features, including a massive pyramid with entry stairways leading up to a room complex on the summit, and two long, flanking wings enclosing a large plaza. The materials of the facing include rough-cut and uncut stone blocks, set in mud mortar. In the late Initial Period, circular sunken plazas were added to many sites, reflecting the incorporation of Salinas religious elements into the Paraíso religious system.

La Florida, 7 miles (11 kilometers) from the coast, is the earliest Initial Period U-shaped pyramid complex. After the abandonment of La Florida, it was replaced by Garagay, 1 mile (2 kilometers) farther down the valley. The 75-foot-high (23-meter-high) pyramid has the typical stairway leading up to summit rooms. The Garagay atrium contains brightly painted clay sculptures representing supernatural spider motifs and the lower half of standing warriors bearing shields. A circular sunken plaza is also located in the central plaza of Garagay.

In the neighboring Lurín Valley, Cardal is the most extensively excavated of any U-shaped pyramid complex. It is 9 miles (15 kilometers) from the coast,

Cardal, in the Lurín Valley, is one of many U-shaped pyramid centers dated to the Initial Period. The architectural format of these sites had a pyramid at the base of the U with stairways leading to the summit. Two long walls extending from the pyramid enclose a large plaza. This photograph shows the right-hand wing of the Cardal complex with the temple remains in the foreground.

and covers 50 acres (20 hectares). The summit of the 56-foot-high (17-meter-high), flat-topped pyramid is reached by 34 steep steps. There, prior to entering the sacred precinct of the temple, religious practitioners were greeted by a clay mouth painted red and yellow, with interlocking teeth. The main public activity took place within the plaza, and even though the plaza could have held 65,000 people, population size was less than the 18,300 residing in the lower Lurín Valley at the time of Spanish contact. Late in the use of the complex, a circular sunken plaza was dug into the central plaza, and two more into one of the flanking wings. In addition, there are seven more circular sunken plazas elsewhere within the site boundaries, reflecting a melding of the northerly Salinas Religious Tradition with that of Paraíso.

### THE CUPISNIQUE RELIGIOUS TRADITION

On the far northern coast of Peru, there arose a new religious tradition called Cupisnique. Cupisnique was first defined by archaeologist Rafael Larco Hoyle in 1929, from his discovery of elaborate stirrup-spout vessels (so named for their hollow, stirrup-shaped handles, which end in a spout at the top) bearing human and feline designs. Although Cupisnique is centered in the Chicama Valley, its ceramic style is found throughout the north coast from Virú to the Lambayeque Valley. Little is known of the temple architecture of the Cupisnique Religious Tradition, but in general, the temples consist of step platforms with staircases to the upper courtyards and rooms, and two short wings that flank a rectangular court.

Huaca de los Reyes (Mound of the Kings), in the Moche Valley, is one of the best-explored examples of a Cupisnique temple. Although Michael E. Moseley associates this temple center with the Paraíso Religious Tradition, certain distinctive elements set it apart from the U-shaped temples of the central coast: notably, its short wings, lack of a major pyramid, and absence of a circular sunken plaza. Richard L. Burger includes Huaca de los Reyes in what he terms the Cupisnique culture of the Peruvian north coast. Discovered by Michael E. Moseley and excavated by Thomas Pozorski, Huaca de los Reyes, 10.5 miles (17 kilometers) inland, is part of the Caballo Muerto (Dead Horse) mound complex. Huaca de los Reyes was constructed in eight phases, according to architect William T. Conklin, beginning with a small platform and two courtyards, and concluding with a 656-foot-square (200-meter-square) building. It was in phase five that six massive heads, with interlocking canine teeth, were set into niches along a façade facing the courtyard between the temple wings. The heads, with dimensions of 67 by 51 by 24 inches (170 by 130 by 60 centimeters), were made of a core of stone and cobbles, which was then plastered over with yellow clay. In phase seven, the colonnaded temple wings were ornamented with a series of friezes depicting standing human figures, wearing snakes as belts and flanked by fanged creatures. One of these human figures is standing upon two severed heads. The iconography of this Late Initial Period temple, along with the architectural art and designs on ceramics, includes a number of elements that are at the heart of the later religious art of the Chavín during the Early Horizon.

Six massive adobe heads, including the fierce, feline-like figures shown in this photograph, adorn the Cupisnique temple complex of Huaca de los Reyes, in the Moche Valley. The heads are composed of stones and cobbles plastered over with yellow clay. Although Huaca de los Reyes dates from the Initial Period, investigators consider the grimacing heads to be a precursor to what would become the style of the Chavín tradition.

## THE NORTHERN HIGHLAND QUECHUA TEMPLE CENTERS

It may be premature to speak of a Northern Highland Quechua Religious Tradition, but there are enough striking similarities in temple architecture, art, and ceramic styles to conclude that these temple centers were part of a widespread shared religious ideology that included interaction with the coast and tropical forest zones. Between the Cajamarca and Chotano river valleys are prominent hills that have been modified into pyramids. The hills were terraced into platforms, with wide stone entry staircases and courtyards, and, on the summit, standing buildings. Many have ingenious systems of subterranean stone-lined canals that drain the room complexes and terraces. The systems have been related to the ritual use of water, so important in the agricultural economy. The sculptural and ceramic art at these sites portray felines, snakes, and birds, which continue as important religious symbols into the Early Horizon.

Just 93 miles (150 kilometers) south of the Ecuadorian border is the temple complex of Pacopampa. This site, excavated by archaeologists Ruth Shady, Hermilio Rosas, and Rosa Fung Pineda, consists of three rectangular plat-

Two pairs of stone sculptures, similar in style to Chavín sculptures, decorate the staircase leading to the sunken plaza at the hilltop site of Kuntur Wasi in the upper Jequetepeque Valley. The frontal fanged face is clearly visible on this example, with the central image framed by serpents in profile.

forms cut into the sides of a hill. On the summit of the rectangular temple are sunken rectangular courtyards and buildings, with an elaborate drainage system. The stone sculpture of a snake-bird hybrid, similar to one found at Huaca A at Moxeke, as well as ceramics bearing felines, birds, and snakes, all show strong connections with the Salinas, Paraíso, and Cupisnique religious traditions of the coast.

At the site of Huacaloma, in the Cajamarca Valley, University of Tokyo archaeologists Kazuo Terada and Yoshio Onuki encountered a small, rectangular structure dating to the early Initial Period. This building is reminiscent of the single-roomed temples of the Kotosh tradition In the late Initial Period, Huacaloma was transformed from single-roomed temples into a stepped platform, faced with painted clay murals of felines and snakes. A main stairway led to the summit rooms, which were drained by subterranean stone-lined canals. The larger nearby site of Layzón, also excavated by the same expedition, is a six-tiered pyramid cut out of a hill, again with the ever-present drainage system.

In the upper reaches of the coastal Jequetepeque, Zaña, and Lambayeque river valleys are a number of Initial Period temple centers that are closely affiliated with the northern highland Quechua sites. At Kuntur Wasi, at 7216 feet (2200 meters) in the Jequetepeque Valley, a natural hill was shaped into a 32-acre (13-hectare) stepped pyramid with sunken plazas, wide staircases, and a subterranean canal system. At Poro Poro, in the Lambayeque drainage, archaeologist Walter Alva excavated a terraced platform with the distinctive canal feature, and the finest cut-and-polished stonework of the Initial

Pacopampa, one of the largest Initial Period temple complexes, is built on a hilltop in the northern Peruvian highlands. Its builders terraced and leveled a natural hill, providing platforms on which to place temples, sunken courtyards, and other public buildings, as well as an elaborate drainage system.

Period. The ceramics found at these sites link them to Pacopampa and the Cajamarca temples, as well as with the Cupisnique Tradition on the coast below. The northernmost coastal temple center that is known lies on Cerro Ñañañique at Chulucanas in the upper Piura Valley. The hill is cut into platforms, and the ceramics have affinities with the northern styles of the Highland Quechua temple centers.

Most of these pyramid centers are located in the frost-free quechua production zone, where tuber crops, as well as maize, beans, and fruits are grown today. In 1553, the chronicler Cieza de León stated that this region was one of the most fertile in the Central Andes and was noted for its high agricultural yields. Due to the lack of preserved cultigens, it is assumed that the plant foods found at the earlier Preceramic sites in the region continued to be the mainstays of the agricultural diet. The analysis of animal bones from Pacopampa and Huacaloma showed that over 85 percent of the meat consumed was from wild valley deer, with the remainder made up of guinea pig and camelids.

It is in this northern region that the Andes are at their lowest. This allows for convenient access to the coastal valleys that originate in the Cordillera Negra, as well as to the Amazon Basin by way of the 12 mid-cordilleran river valleys that flow to the Marañón River. South of the Cajamarca Valley, the Kotosh Religious Tradition continues to hold sway in the Huallaga Valley of the eastern Andes, in the Callejón de Huaylas in the northern highlands, and in the upper Santa River drainage of the Pacific slopes of the Cordillera Negra.

The Cumbemayo canal, high above the Cajamarca Basin, is an extraordinary example of Initial Period hydraulic engineering. The 5.5-mile (9-kilometer) canal, cut into bedrock, takes water from the Pacific drainage across the Continental Divide to the Atlantic drainage. The photograph shows an open section of the canal; for part of its length, the Cumbemayo also runs underground.

## THE KOTOSH RELIGIOUS TRADITION

A number of sites reflect the continuation of the Kotosh religion into the Initial Period, but, with the exception of Huaricoto in the Callejón de Huaylas, the single-room temples of the Kotosh Religious Tradition are replaced at the end of the Initial Period by much larger and more public religious constructions. At three coastal sites in the Casma Valley, however, there are seven ventilated-hearth structures that relate to the Kotosh Tradition.

At La Galgada, for example, one of the mounds of single-roomed temples was remodeled, and on the summit a walled platform was erected, permitting increased public interaction with the ritual activity being performed at the central hearth. A number of specially constructed tombs contained grave offerings of elaborately decorated bone pins, shell and stone beads, textiles, as well as a few ceramic vessels, one of which had a lid and, on its side, facing snake motifs. The most elaborate artifacts, in the corner of the main staircase, were four disks of Ecuadorian *Spondylus* and orange shell that formed part of a dedicatory offering. Carved or mosaic designs on the disks bore motifs of birds and monsters—some with fangs—both of which are also associated with the Paraíso, Salinas, and Cupisnique religious tradition sites, and which also appear in later Chavín art.

Long-distance trade in finished artifacts, raw materials, and foreign ceramics is evident at Kotosh Religious Tradition sites. At Kotosh and Shillacoto in the eastern Andes, marine shell artifacts are present, as are ceramics portraying tropical forest animals such as monkeys, owls, and snakes—creatures that are not native to the Huallaga Basin, but rather to the Amazon Basin. The ceramics reflect influence from the Yarinacocha region of the Peruvian Amazon, the highlands, and the coast. Clearly, Kotosh and the Huallaga Valley sites were part of a line of communication linking the highland Kotosh religious centers in the Callejón de Huaylas and La Galgada with the tropical forest, and also with the coastal societies of the Salinas and Cupisnique religious traditions.

South of the Callejón de Huaylas, there is little evidence for Initial Period temple centers until the Early Horizon. The Initial Period communities in southern Peru and Bolivia continue their emphasis upon puna herding, highland and coastal farming, and coastal fishing and shellfish gathering.

## THE IRRIGATION REVOLUTION

As noted above, the movement from the coast to the valley floors in the Initial Period has been correlated with the intensification of irrigation agriculture. Water-management technology is well documented in the northern highlands, where, at Late Preceramic La Galgada, a small-scale irrigation and field system (with planting rows linked by small channels) was in place by 1500 B.C. Although interpreted as having been constructed for religious and drainage purposes, canals such as those at the Northern Highland Quechua temple sites demonstrate that the planning and engineering skills for moving water over great distances was well established in the Initial Period. The construction of a 5.5-mile (9-kilometer) canal in the Cajamarca Basin during the Late Initial Period was a magnificent feat of engineering (though it is not believed to have been constructed solely for irrigation, but also for religious purposes). Partially cut into bedrock and branching in subterranean segments, this narrow canal brought water from the Pacific to the Atlantic watershed.

Quite possibly, irrigation technology was introduced to the coast from the northern highland region. On the coast, the evidence for Initial Period irrigation is circumstantial, as it is based on the relocation of coastal sites to the interior of the valleys, where temple administrators could control the water intake canals. Since irrigation systems require a natural gradient to move and disperse water to farming fields, it is assumed that the pyramid centers were placed up-valley to coordinate the maintenance and management of small-scale irrigation works so crucial to agricultural production in the arid coastal valleys. Not only does the relocation of the pyramid centers from the shoreline up to the higher valley locations signify a dramatic change in the economic systems from the Late Preceramic into the Initial Period, but the abundance of cultigens in Initial Period sites also indicates a tremendous increase in agricultural production. As we have seen, the maritime and limited floodwater farming of the Late Preceramic was replaced by an irrigation-based agrarian economy on the coast during the Initial Period, one which was to become the mainstay of the coastal economy until the Spanish invasion.

The settlement and subsistence pattern that developed from this new agrarian orientation on the coast was an exchange system that incorporated the valley pyramid centers and coastal fishing villages. Comparing four sites in the Moche Valley, Shelia Pozorski has demonstrated that in the Late Preceramic the desert coastal settlements of Padre Aban and Alto Salaverry had a preponderance of marine foods, industrial plants, and limited farming crops. Yet by the Initial Period, there is a dramatic rise in agricultural products at the coastal site of Gramalote—a settlement otherwise similar to Padre Aban and Alto Salaverry. At the same time, the Caballo Muerto mound center, 10.5 miles (17 kilometers) from the coast, was receiving more than 50 percent of its meat volume from marine foods and the other 50 percent from hunted deer

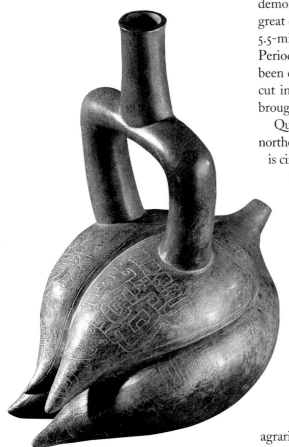

The Cupisnique manioc-tuber vessel shown above is typical of a style that influenced the later Chavín potters, as well as those of the Moche Period. Cupisnique ceramics are marked generally by dark colors, stirrup spouts, and depictions of humans, birds, vegetables, fruit, and architectural forms.

and camelids. Although no cultigens have been found at Caballo Muerto, the location of the mound complex—which includes Huaca de los Reyes—is interpreted as controlling an irrigation-based agricultural system. It is believed that the settlement's marine foods were received from coastal dwellers in exchange for agricultural products.

This network of agricultural-marine exchange has also been documented in the Casma, Rimac, and Lurín valleys. In the Lurín Valley, Richard L. Burger also includes the farming villages in the yunga zone—where coca was grown—as part of this new coastal agrarian economy. In the Northern Highland Quechua and Kotosh religious traditions, deer, camelids, and guinea pigs comprised the meat diet, and although poor preservation has left us little evidence of cultigens, it is agreed that the Andean crops found in the earlier Preceramic sites continued into the Initial Period as the basis for the agricultural economy.

The sheer size of the coastal-valley pyramid centers has led archaeologists Jonathan Haas, Shelia Pozorski, and Thomas Pozorski to propose that only a social-political organization at the level of the state could have marshaled the labor and resources necessary to construct such grandiose monuments. The planning and construction of these huge centers, they argue, must have been administered by a strong, centralized authority. They go on to nominate Sechín Alto, in the Casma Valley, as the capital of an Initial Period state that controlled or influenced six neighboring valleys. Other multi-valley states are also proposed for the Moche, Supe, and Chillón-Rimac valleys.

**The Cupisnique ceramic tradition also gave rise to this enigmatic vessel: the jaguar peering out from a clump of San Pedro cactus may represent a shaman, a view that holds with the identification of the cactus as a hallucinogenic variety.**

However, there is a problem with this theory. If there was a state-level society present in the Initial Period, archaeologists should have encountered the sumptuous tombs of the rulers, evidence of an upper class, full-time craftsmen, and more homogeneity in architecture, ceramics, and art. Although the burials of the Initial Period exhibit some status differentiation, the wealth that would have been expected to accompany the burial of a state ruler has not been found. It is interesting that only in the Kotosh Religious Tradition are there tombs for higher-status individuals accompanied by a small quantity of elaborate grave offerings. This is ironic because Kotosh society is thought to represent small-scale local farming communities centered around the temples—communities that would not have known high-status rulers.

Richard L. Burger has stressed that big monuments do not automatically translate into a state level of social-political organization. "Big" starts out as "small", and what seems an incredible feat of human energy is in reality the efforts of many small groups over a long period. Nonetheless, the end product—these magnificent edifices that figured so prominently in early Andean civilization—remains an impressive human achievment, the result of long-term planning and the organization of limited manpower. Only 7000 people live in the Casma Valley today, and archaeologist David J. Wilson estimates a population of only about 11,000 people during the Initial Period, certainly too small for a large labor force. The excavators of the following sites estimate 350,000 person-days for the construction of Huaca de los Reyes, 6.7 million for La Florida, and 2 million for Cardal. Yet these figures are misleading; for as I have emphasized previously, these pyramid centers underwent hundreds of years of construction, expansion, and renovation before they reached the final configuration viewed by archaeologists today. This is very evident at Huaca de los Reyes, which was created in eight sequential stages of construction. It started out as a small temple structure before reaching 10 times its original size in the last building stage—some 200 years later! Similarly, at La Florida, Thomas C. Patterson estimates that 500 to 1000 people laboring for two months between the agricultural cycle could have constructed this massive pyramid in under 200 years. At Cardal, Richard L. Burger and Lucy Salazar-Burger suggest that 100 persons working for two months per year over a 400-year period could have built this temple complex.

Neither does ceramic and architectural evidence bear out the state hypothesis, for pottery styles vary between centers and between valleys, and the individual orientations and layouts of the pyramid centers strongly suggest independent, self-sustaining agrarian chiefdoms. These valley communities were focused upon a single pyramid center, linked by subsistence exchange with coastal fishing villages and other farming hamlets in the yunga; at most, 1000 to 2000 people were associated with each pyramid center.

Many local community pyramids are embellished with monumental architectural art, depicting the sacred themes underlying the Initial Period religions. This external display of religious art brings the theology of the Late Preceramic out into the plazas in front of the pyramids, where large numbers of the public could now participate in ritual activities formerly observed by a small elite. The pyramid centers were controlled by either part-time or full-time priests, and the similarity in religious art reflects a shared ideology throughout the coast and highlands. Yet among the shared elements in the art is evidence of friction between communities, shown at Cerro Sechín by mutilated bodies and elsewhere by severed heads carved into stone vessels and painted onto ceramic vessels—and even, at a number of Initial Period sites, actual human trophy heads. There is, however, no indication of fortifications that would suggest large-scale warfare in the Initial Period.

It is not known what ritual ceremonies were carried out in the circular sunken plazas, the rectangular courtyards, or the room complexes of the pyramids. But the ideology underlying the fearsome feline, snake, spider, and bird motifs—all present in Initial Period architectural and ceramic art in the Salinas, Paraíso, Cupisnique, and Northern Highland Quechua religious traditions—forms the iconography of the Chavín religion, which was to dominate and spread throughout central and northern Peru during the Early Horizon.

The remains of the circular sunken plaza of the Old Temple at Chavín de Huántar perfectly evoke the mystery and grandeur of Chavín culture.
slopes of the Cordillera Blanca at the confluence of the Huachecsa and Mosna rivers, and was the center of the first widespread religious cult in

The temple site is located below the eastern
the Central Andes.

# 5

# THE AGE OF THE JAGUAR CULT

No other site in the Central Andes evokes such a sense of aura and mystery as Chavín de Huántar. The multistoried temple, with its labyrinth of galleries, drainage and air-flow systems, courtyards, and stone sculptures of demonized jaguars, caymans, birds, and snakes, still exudes the power of the Chavín cult. It was here, at Chavín de Huántar, that the momentous ceremonial and economic developments of the Initial Period culminated in the Early Horizon (800 to 200 B.C.).

Chavín de Huántar was visited by Pedro de Cieza de León in A.D. 1548, and he was told by the villagers that the impressive temple was built by giants whose likenesses still graced its walls. Even though it had been abandoned for more than 1500 years, it remained a revered site in the colonial period, where local religious practitioners continued to carry out their rituals. While a number of archaeologists visited the site in the late 1800s and early 1900s, it was not until Julio C. Tello excavated in 1919 that it unveiled its critical secrets of the rise of civilization in the Central Andes.

Nor were its riches exhausted by that initial study. Although Chavín de Huántar suffered a landslide in 1945, subsequent excavations by Peruvian archaeologist Luis G. Lumbreras and Yale University archaeologist Richard L. Burger—as well as studies of the Chavín art style by archaeologists John H. Rowe, Donald W. Lathrap, Peter Roe, and others—confirmed the vibrance of the terror-inspiring Chavín cult.

Chavín de Huántar is dramatically situated at the junction of the Mosna and Huachecsa rivers, at 10,335 feet (3150 meters) above sea level. It is hard to imagine a more strategic location. The Mosna eventually flows into the Marañón River, allowing for communication with the tropical forest in Amazonia. In addition, a series of trails leads westward from Chavín de Huántar over the mountains into the Callejón de Huaylas, allowing access to the coastal valleys. In the shadow of the 20,608-foot (6395-meter) snow-capped mountain of Huantsán, the temple sits stolidly with its back to the Huachecsa River, which emanates from the Cordillera Blanca. At the same time, the site is only a few hours walk from the puna grasslands favored by llama herders. Surrounding the site today, Andean tuber and grain crops support the modern villagers.

As with all other temples, Chavín de Huántar was erected in stages. Richard L. Burger has defined three phases of the temple's development: Urabarriu (1000 to 500 B.C.), Chakinani (500 to 400 B.C.), and Janabarriu (400 to 200 B.C.). The oldest part of the unique monument, called the Old Temple, was built in the Late Initial Period, circa 1000 B.C. The Old Temple is U-shaped, enclosing a circular sunken plaza within its short flanking wings; these are architectural features of the Initial Period Cupisnique and Salinas religious traditions. The temple is masterfully constructed of alternating rows of narrow and thick cut stone blocks, some transported from quarries more than 12.4 miles (20 kilometers) away. The four-story walls vary between 36 and 53 feet (11 to 16 meters) high. Protruding from the exterior walls, 33 feet (10 meters) above the ground and 9.8 feet (3 meters) apart, is a series of huge feline heads, sculptured in stone, representing the progressive transformation of a priest into a jaguar. These fearsome heads, each one weighing more than half a ton, appear suspended in the air before the temple face; in fact, they are well supported by a stone column (or tenon) projecting out of the back of the sculpture.

In the U-shaped courtyard is a circular sunken plaza, 68.9 feet (21 meters) in diameter, that is estimated to have held 550 worshippers. Along a portion of the circular walls are elaborate friezes of jaguars and part-human, part-animal figures bearing shields and San Pedro cactus—a plant whose hallucinogenic flowers are used today by shamans, who consult the supernatural world on matters of health and fortune.

In the U-shaped temple and under its courtyard are long galleries and rooms at different levels, connected by staircases. The main chamber, shaped in the form of a cross, holds a 14.8-foot-high (4.53-meter-high) granite sculpture weighing two tons. Named the Lanzón by Julio C. Tello because of its lance-like form, scholars now believe that the sculpture represents the Great Image, the central god in the Chavín pantheon. With its fanged, snarling mouth, clawed hands and feet, long circular ear pendants, bracelets, and snakes writhing out of its head, the Great Image is a ferocious human-feline monster. Above the Great Image is a room where a floor slab could be removed, creating an opening through which the priests—inspired with divine words—could speak for the deity.

Some of the galleries still retain traces of yellow-, white-, and red-painted plaster, and in one gallery, carvings of *Spondylus* and fanged fish in the stone roof beams are painted red, green, and blue. It is not hard to imagine the terror of acolytes ushered by priests down narrow corridors, their painted walls alive with dancing torchlight, into the dread presence of the Lanzón. And if the Lanzón was painted, the experience probably would have been doubly terrifying.

In the Galería de las Ofrendas (Gallery of the Offerings) a massive food offering was made to the temple gods. The evidence comes from more than 800 fragmented ceramic bowls and bottles, interspersed with bones of camelids, guinea pigs, deer, marine fish, and shellfish—and humans (suggesting ritual cannibalism). This elaborate ritual offering represents a single event in this darkened and eerie gallery, after which the gallery was sealed. The pottery is exceptional, not to be found in any other deposits at that site, and it is assumed to have been introduced from the coast and northern highlands, at a distance of 124 to 186 miles (200 to 300 kilometers). Other galleries are thought to be for the storage of ritual paraphernalia and accumulation of tribute. The Galería de los Caracoles (Gallery of the Snails) contained cut *Strombus* shells imported from Ecuador.

The four-story Old Temple is a tremendous feat of Chavín engineering, for precise planning was required to incorporate its galleries, air ducts, and drainage system. The network of inaccessible air ducts, opening onto the roof and through the sides of the temple, brought air to the windowless galleries. The ingenious drainage system prevented damage from the region's five to eight months of rainfall by funneling rainwater to the Mosna River. As Lumbreras has demonstrated, the rushing water would have created such a roar as to turn the temple into a huge auditory chamber.

The New Temple at Chavín de Huántar was constructed during the Chakinani and Janabarriu phases (500 to 200 B.C.). The increasing size and popularity of the town had by that time made it an important center of pilgrimage. A large, rectangular plaza built in front of the New Temple was intended to accommodate an increasing number of devotees.

In addition to the tenoned heads and the Great Image, there is yet another impressive granite sculpture that dates to the Old Temple: the Tello Obelisk. Discovered in the corner of a courtyard of the New Temple, the Tello Obelisk is the most complex of the Chavín sculptures. (A replica of the sculpture graces the tomb of Julio C. Tello at the Museo Nacional de Antropología y Arqueología in Lima) The obelisk is a granite column 8.2 feet (2.5 meters) high, around whose four flat sides are wrapped the profiles of two facing monsters with cayman characteristics—the first time that a crocodilian creature appears in the iconography of the Central Andes. The analysis of the creatures on the Tello Obelisk by Donald W. Lathrap is one of the great tour de force interpretations of Central Andean art. Lathrap, who was referred to as the Gran Cayman by his students, showed that the reptiles—who are depicted as mating—were supernatural beings representing the forces of the underworld and sky world. The underworld cayman is festooned with plants that grow

Located in a subterranean chamber at the center of the Old Temple of Chavín de Huántar is a 14.8-foot-tall (4.53-meter-tall) granite sculpture known, because of its lance-like form, as the Lanzón. Its carved surface depicts a human-feline monster, and is believed to represent the Great Image, the central deity in the Chavín culture. Its great height and upward thrust seem to symbolize the deity's role as a conduit between the underworld, the earth, and the heavens.

below the surface of the earth, and at its head there is the deep-ocean *Spondylus* shell. The sky-world cayman, on the other hand, is decorated with above-ground plants, and at its head flies a bird. Although the ideology and origin myths associated with the mating caymans is not known, the Tello Obelisk presents a detailed model of the Chavín cosmos.

For 500 years, the Old Temple was a pilgrimage center for distant converts. Only about 500 people lived around the temple, supporting themselves by growing tuber and grain crops, by hunting camelids, deer, and small game, and by herding llamas. This small, self-sufficient community also drew upon the dispersed villages in the region for the labor necessary to construct and maintain the Old Temple.

The next 100 years signaled major changes to come at Chavín de Huántar as the Chavín cult grew in importance. In the Chakinani phase (500 to 400 B.C.), population increased to more than 1000 inhabitants, and large-scale irrigation systems were constructed in the Mosna Valley. The mixed hunting and agropastoral economy of the Urabarriu phase shifts to a strictly herding and agricultural subsistence pattern. Richard L. Burger suggests that this change reflects the beginning of long-distance transport of goods by llama caravans. The marked increase in exotic goods—including ocean fish and shellfish, raw obsidian (for tools) from 292 miles (470 kilometers) to the south, and pottery from far-flung regions in the northern highlands and along the coast—attests to greatly increased contact over long distances.

In the Janabarriu phase (400 to 200 B.C.), the population reached 2000 to 3000, transforming Chavín de Huántar into a small urban center. The settlement now occupied the valley floor, and housing terraces were established on the steep mountain slopes to accommodate the burgeoning population. The economic system continued, with a marked increase in the long-distance trade of raw obsidian (replacing local stone for toolmaking), unmodified *Spondylus* shells, marine foods, and pottery both from the coast and the highlands. The Old Temple was expanded, with the new structure and its forecourts becoming the focus of religious activities at the site.

The New Temple was enlarged in two stages, using the same architectural design of cut-and-polished stone set in rows as in the Old Temple. At the front of the New Temple, a monumental branching staircase permits entrance into the inner sanctuaries. At the entrance there are two round columns supporting a massive stone lintel.

The flanking columns are adorned with a sculptured hawk and an eagle, and on the 33-foot-long (10-meter-long) lintel is a row of stone-carved eagles and hawks that served as guardians and sky messengers for the cult deities.

Facing the New Temple is a rectangular plaza that measures 279 by 344 feet (85 by 105 meters), with a sunken courtyard 164 feet square (50 meters square), large enough to accommodate not only the increased population, but also the pilgrims who flocked in ever-growing numbers to Chavín de Huántar. The New Temple also had the same system of galleries, air ducts, and drainage conduits.

The Lanzón continues as the supreme deity in the New Temple, where a small sculpture of a front-facing Lanzón figure wears the distinctive earrings, bracelets, and intertwined snakes for hair. Only 20.9 inches (53.3 centimeters) high and 22.8 inches (57.8 centimeters) wide, this diminutive version of the fanged and clawed being bears the sacred *Strombus* and *Spondylus* shells associated in Central Andean mythology with male and female power.

The latest of the sculptures at Chavín de Huántar goes by two names: the Raimondi Stone, named for its discoverer, the Italian geographer Antonio Raimondi; and the Staff God, as it was later renamed by John H. Rowe. Although it is not known from which part of the New Temple it was taken, it is possible the sculpture may have been set in the temple's outer wall. A slab of granite 6.5 feet (2 meters) tall, 29 inches (74 centimeters) wide, and 6.7 inches (17 centimeters) thick, the Staff God depicts a front-facing figure holding two staffs and wearing a tall headdress of upside-down feline faces.

The Raimondi Stone, originally named for Italian geographer Antonio Raimondi, has come to be known as the Staff God, and is another representation of the supreme Chavín deity. The 6.5-foot-tall (2-meter-tall) slab of granite depicts a front-facing figure holding two staffs and wearing a headdress designed with upside-down feline faces.

This god is a continuation of the Lanzón deity, with the addition of staffs. As we will see in the next chapter, a god bearing staffs becomes the main deity of the Tiwanaku and Huari religions.

## THE SPREAD OF THE CHAVÍN CULT

Chavín de Huántar was the most important pilgrimage center in the Central Andes by 400 B.C. It is thus surprising that its stunning temple architecture and sculptural art was not transplanted to other regions under Chavín influence. In the northern highlands, the Initial Period temple centers of the Northern Highland Quechua Tradition did incorporate the Chavín cult into their religious system. At Pacopampa, Kuntur Wasi, and other sites,

The Chavín religion probably involved the ingestion of hallucinogens. This small stone mortar and pestle, carved in the form of a feline, is thought to be part of the ritual paraphernalia used in the preparation of hallucinogenic substances.

rectangular sunken plazas and new temples were constructed with Chavín sculptural art adorning columns, stairways, and granite stelae (stone columns).

On the coast it was a different matter, for most of the Paraíso, Salinas, and Cupisnique pyramid centers were abandoned. The pyramid-laden Casma Valley, meanwhile, saw construction during the Initial Period of only a few large residential complexes with plazas and small platform mounds. In his survey of the Casma Valley, archaeologist David J. Wilson noted that population slid from a high of 11,000 in the early Initial Period (1800 to 800 B.C.) to less than 5000 between 1000 and 350 B.C. The situation in the Rimac and Lurín valleys is also similar, for no pyramid centers were erected after the abandonment of Garagay, Cardal, and Mina Perdida in 900 B.C. Although the best agricultural land in the valleys was now only sparsely inhabited, the coastal fishing villages continued to receive agricultural products from valley farming hamlets.

The abrupt abandonment of the coastal pyramid centers—a demographic change that straddled the end of the Initial Period and the beginning of the Early Horizon—could quite possibly be due to the natural destruction of the irrigation systems, so critical to the societies that worshipped at the enormous temples. On the northwest coast of Peru are three sets of eight to nine Holocene beach ridges, one of which was formed at roughly 1000 to 700 B.C. These ridges are thought to have been formed by enormous El Niño rainfall events or a closely spaced series of El Niños—the same disasters that periodically disrupt Peru's economy today. Months of rainfall would have washed out irrigation systems and placed severe stress on the economic system of these

temple-oriented societies. The collapse of the irrigation agricultural economy could easily have prompted the coastal societies to forsake the religion that did not protect them from this disaster.

If the central coast temple societies were indeed destroyed by a natural disaster, the best evidence at hand points to a major El Niño flood catastrophe. In the circular sunken plaza at Las Haldas, the University of Tokyo expedition found that the site was abandoned after torrential rains around 900 B.C. A glacial re-advance in the highlands confirms that this was a period of severe environmental stress. Still, another theory has been proposed, and has received some attention.

Junius B. Bird discovered evidence of a tidal wave at Huaca Prieta, which his son, ethnobotanist Robert McK. Bird, has dated to 850 B.C. Bird postulates that alluvial deposits at temple sites from Chicama to the Lurín valleys are the result of an enormous *tsunami*, or tidal wave. It is thought that the tsunami was 230 feet (70 meters) high, a wall of water that raced 3.7 miles (6 kilometers) up the Rimac Valley before destroying the temple of Garagay. Although there exist a few records of huge tsunamis elsewhere, a tidal wave of this magnitude and geographic coverage is hard to imagine and few archaeologists subscribe to this theory.

In the Casma Valley there is a dramatic population increase to more than 40,000 after 350 B.C. This population explosion is accompanied by the first fortifications in the Central Andes, a potent sign of unsettled times and the need for protection against foreign invaders. The largest fortress on the Peruvian coast, at 656 by 1312 feet (200 by 400 meters), sits high on a hill overlooking the abandoned Moxeke pyramid center. Chanquillo, first mapped by Ephraim George Squier in the 1860s, is a superb example of military engineering, consisting of three encircling walls enclosing one rectangular and two circular structures. The 20-foot-high (6-meter-high) walls of rough-cut stone (quarried nearby) were covered with yellow plaster. The entrance to the citadel was through baffled doorways that would have slowed any attack. If attackers successfully breached the first doorway, they would run straight into a wall forcing them left and right through a narrow, right-angled corridor, allowing the defenders to dispatch their enemies with ease. If, however, the enemies were not defeated at that stage, they would have to breach two more similar walls before encountering the two circular "castle keeps" where the defenders could hold out. Chanquillo may have had a small garrison, but it probably functioned as a defensive position where the valley populace could have found refuge should their towns and villages be attacked.

In the Santa Valley, also surveyed by David J. Wilson, 21 forts of the late Early Horizon were located on the valley hillsides; 13 of the sites were towns with an attached fortress. Many of these majestic forts had elaborate bastions that protruded from the walls, allowing the defenders to throw spears at the backs of the attackers as they tried to breach the defenses. The temple

Weapons such as this stone mace head have been found at some Chavín sites, and are suggestive of the increasing turmoil along the northern coast during the third century B.C. This period saw the construction of great fortresses, as population grew and competition for agricultural land increased.

PREVIOUS PAGE: The circular sunken plaza, enclosed by the wings of the U-shaped Old Temple at Chavín de Huántar, is estimated to have held up to 550 people. Although the exact nature of Chavín ritual is not known, archaeologists believe that the plaza was probably designed as a setting for ceremonies to honor the Staff God, as portrayed in this illustration.

architecture in the valley had platform mounds, circular sunken plazas, and elite residences with ceramics displaying, once again, Chavín feline motifs. In the nearby Nepeña Valley at Cerro Blanco, a small temple with feline friezes of mud plaster clearly indicates that the Chavín cult had arrived on the north-central Peruvian coast by 350 B.C.

The source of the disruptions in the Santa, Nepeña, and Casma valleys is not known, but the construction of the area's majestic forts was prompted by one of two causes: increasing population pressure and competition for agricultural lands by independent valley societies; or foreign raids and invasion. It has been suggested that invasion from the highlands may have been a factor, but in addition to a lack of fortifications in the highlands, there is no evidence of a replacement of coastal valley cultural traditions by a highland one.

The spread of the Chavín cult in the Janabarriu phase brought no great temples comparable to Chavín de Huántar. As Michael E. Moseley has stressed, the well-established local cultures were free to accept, reject, or modify the ideology and iconography of the Chavín cult when it was introduced into the north, central, and south coasts of Peru. The spread of the cult, then, is reflected mainly in the magnificent stirrup-spout ceramic vessels, painted and woven textiles, gold metalwork, and carved stone vessels. At the looted cemetery of Karwa, south of the Paracas Peninsula on the Peruvian south coast, a high-status personage was wrapped in red-orange, brown, green, and blue painted textiles depicting the iconography of Chavín de Huántar; the designs included the Staff God, birds, feline-headed serpents, and numerous representations of the Great Cayman. It has been suggested that these large textiles—13.8 feet (4.2 meters) long and 8.9 feet (2.7 meters) wide—had originally hung on the adobe walls of a temple, replacing with textiles the stone sculptures of the deities at Chavín de Huántar.

## HOW THE CHAVÍN CULT WAS SPREAD

The Chavín cult has been thought to have been spread by missionaries carrying the "true" religion to the heathens, similar to the spread of Christianity. The missionization theory also includes the dissemination of the Chavín cult through the use of military force. Recently, however, Thomas C. Patterson has proposed that the Chavín cult spread through the establishment of branch centers of the main oracle—the Lanzón. The Patterson oracle model of Chavín religious spread comes from the historically known oracle at Pachacamac, near Lima.

On January 30, 1533, when Hernando Pizarro entered the sanctuary of the great temple at Pachacamac, he was aghast at the pagan rituals being practiced, and he cast out the wooden idol into the plaza and destroyed the shrine where it was housed. (This same idol was found in 1938 and is on display at the

The hilltop fortress of Chanquillo, in the southern Casma Valley, is surrounded by thick walls up to 20 feet (6 meters) in height. Clearly visible in this aerial view are the offset or baffled entrances that pierce the two outer walls.

museum at Pachacamac.) At the time of the Spanish invasion, the temple center of Pachacamac housed the most powerful oracle in the Central Andes. The main idol was accessible only to the high priests, who consulted with the oracle about the most auspicious times to make war, to plant, and to harvest crops, and also to plead with the oracle to protect them from diseases, earthquakes, and other disasters. So revered was the oracle of Pachacamac that even the Inca ruler Topa Inca, whose armies had recently conquered the coast, was obliged to fast for 40 days before he could gain an audience with the priests who acted as the oracle's spokesmen.

Distant communities pleaded to have branches of the Pachacamac oracles established in their towns. The sons and daughters of the high priest were thus sent to set up satellite shrines in return for land, offerings, and tribute, and from these far-flung shrines, annual pilgrimages were made to Pachacamac.

The Pachacamac shrine network was independent of local state religions, and the branch oracles were incorporated into the local religions of a diversity of coastal and highland cultures.

The Inca-period Pachacamac model has been applied to the spread of the Chavín cult. The Old Temple's Lanzón was the oracle, which both forecast the outcome of future events and warded off evil. This talking deity was managed by the high priest, who spoke through a hole above the Lanzón to the priesthood cowering below, waiting to relay the pronouncements of the Great Image to the multitudes of pilgrims in the plazas of Chavín de Huántar. The establishment of the Chavín branch oracles at regional temple centers throughout the central and north coasts and highlands of Peru would not have necessitated transplanting Chavín de Huántar temple architecture, only the iconography of the Chavín pantheon.

## CHAVÍN SOCIETY

What kind of a society produced this elaborate cult of demonized creatures so charged with supernatural power? Among other things, it was a society with an economic hierarchy: for the first time there is ample evidence of social stratification, measured in the accumulation of wealth by the elite rulers and priests. There are rumors of a gold treasure snatched from a tomb at Chavín de Huántar, but to date no high-status burial has been found by professional excavators. At many of the northern highland Chavín-influenced temple sites, there are large resident populations, and the few known tombs show varying access to exotic wealth. At Kuntur Wasi, the 1989 University of Tokyo expedition found shaft tombs in the temple's sunken rectangular plaza. Some of the tombs of the kneeling males and females included gold crowns, gold pectorals, plaques, and ear ornaments—all decorated with Chavín motifs—as well as ceramics, Ecuadorian *Strombus* shells, and thousands of beads.

Similar tombs, with Chavín designs on gold crowns and earspools (spool-like ornaments inserted into a pierced ear), are reported to have been looted in the upper Lambayeque Valley. These finds, as well as the previously mentioned looted tomb of the painted textiles at Karwa, are all dated to the Janabarriu, the period when long-distance llama caravans brought great loads of exotic goods from the central and northern highlands and the coast to Chavín de Huántar.

Llama caravans were, and are, a very cost-effective means of transport. Each llama can carry a load of up to 132 pounds (60 kilograms), and 20 llamas, feeding on local grasses as they move through the highlands, can be controlled by a single herder. On the coast, archaeologist Colleen M. Beck has identified roads, dating to the Initial and Early Horizon periods, in the Chicama, Moche, and Virú valleys; these roads argue for llama caravans being part of a highland-coastal economic exchange system. The stone walls that flanked the roads were up to 2.5 feet (.8 meter) high, and would have prevented llamas

A system of roads dating to the Initial and Early Horizon periods has been identified in several valleys along the northern coast, implying the existence of extensive regional trading networks. The Chavín cult itself was probably spread by the movement of llama caravans along these routes. The remnants of retaining walls flank this road.

from straying into the adjacent cultivated fields. Llama commerce is also documented for Bolivia and the northern Chilean coast at the same time.

It is suspected that the acceleration in commerce brought about by the llama caravans ranging from Ayacucho to the Piura Valley—a distance of 715 miles (1150 kilometers)—may have been responsible for increased communication with far-flung regions. This contact would have resulted in the dissemination of the Chavín cult, which was embraced by local societies of the coast.

Population growth in the Early Horizon resulted in the establishment of villages clustered around temple centers. The temple arts and offerings—magnificent stone sculptures, beautiful ceramics and textiles, and spectacular goldwork—argue for a class of full-time artisans. Employed in the production of religious trappings for the temples, they also created treasures for the ruling elite. The leadership and organization of the public works and ritual offerings was accomplished by priest-rulers, whose rare tombs provide us with a glimpse of their earthly power. The increasing cultural complexity of the Early Horizon in the northern Peruvian highlands and coast has led archaeologists to conclude that the chiefdoms in the Central Andes were on the verge of developing a state level of social-political-religious complexity by 200 B.C.

### THE ORIGINS OF CHAVÍN

Ever since Julio C. Tello declared that the Chavín cultures derived from the eastern tropical forest, Chavín specialists have followed his lead, stressing that the animals portrayed in Chavín art clearly show links with the

The production of gold artifacts, such as this hammered gold plaque depicting a fanged feline, reached new heights during the Early Horizon. A new class of full-time craftspeople emerged to supply the many new temple centers. The holes in this 4.1-inch-long (10.4-centimeter-long) piece would have enabled it to be attached or sewn to a costume.

Amazon Basin. However, as Richard L. Burger has clearly stated in his magnificent book—*Chavín and the Origins of Andean Civilization*—the architecture of Chavín de Huántar, with its U-shaped plan and its circular and rectangular sunken plazas, originates not in Amazonia but on the desert coast. He also points out that if the Chavín cult had originated in the highlands, the deities would have taken the form of llamas, deer, condors, guinea pigs, foxes, and the tuber and grain crops central to the economy of the Chavín de Huántar residents (as they would remain in the later Inca economy and religion). The ceramics are coastal and highland by shape and design styles. Thus, if the Chavín cult was introduced to the highlands by tropical forest peoples, those missionaries transmitted virtually none of their architectural styles and material culture.

It is evident from the coastal pyramid centers of the Initial Period that much of the iconography of the later Chavín appeared first in coastal temple art and on ceramics. The list is long: the fanged mouth frieze at Cardal, the fanged deities at Garagay, the facing jaguars at Cerro Sechín and at Huaca A,

**Early Chavín textiles were decorated with felines, birds, serpents, and deities. This Chavín cotton panel, from a south coast tomb, bears a fanged deity motif. This piece is an early example of a design woven by loom into the fabric rather than applied afterwards.**

94

The Paracas Necropolis, a burial
ground on the Paracas Peninsula, yielded funerary bundles that amazed the
site's excavator, Julio C. Tello. Among
the 429 bundles that he examined, 40
belonged to high-ranking individuals
who had been buried in elaborately
woven and embroidered garments.
The design of the colorful burial fabrics
represented the religious and social
beliefs of Paracas society.

Chavin ceramics strongly influenced the
art styles of other cultures. However,
the design of this Paracas resin-painted
ceremonial jar seems to bear no relation
to the fearsome, fanged Chavin deities.
The round-eyed anthropomorphic figure,
formed by incising the design while the
clay was still soft, may represent the
Oculate Being, a deity that appears on
later Paracas ceramics.

the monumental fanged heads at Huaca de los Reyes, and the staircase jaguar at Punkuri—to mention only a few examples. The ceramics from
sites such as Ancón and Cupisnique all depict much of the iconography that
makes up the Chavín cult, and Cupisnique vessels even depict priests being
transformed into jaguar beings—the same theme that is on the great tenoned
heads at Chavín de Huántar. Thus, much of the iconography and architectural
elements of Chavín de Huántar were present on the coast more than 500 years
prior to the rise of the great religious cult.

The conclusion that Chavín architecture and material culture first developed on the coast forces us to consider another possibility as well: that the
tropical forest animal-deities in Chavín art also originated on the coast. The
relict tropical zone in the upper Zaña Valley, which Antonio Raimondi
described as being situated between 1181 and 4480 feet (360 and 1366 meters),
had tropical forest fauna, including monkeys and jaguars. In later Moche art
there are monkeys and occasional scenes of jaguars being hunted, reflecting
their presence on the western side of the Andes.

Little is known of the tropical forest environment on the western
cordilleran slopes, an environment that probably stretched northward to
Tumbez at the Peruvian-Ecuadorian border. It is known that the cayman
was found in the Tumbez River, where whalers from New England ports
recorded in their logbooks during the 1800s that the river was teeming with
alligators. During the 1925 El Niño, ornithologist Robert Cushman Murphy
reported caymans as far south as Paita.

The most stunning legacy from the Paracas cultural tradition is its wealth of woven textiles. Spanning nine hundred years and covering a wide geographical area the Paracas culture displayed different styles of image construction. This Ocucaje tunic from the Ica Valley shows an anthropomorphic figure woven into the cloth but one which stands out clearly from the background.

But what about the harpy eagle, the major guardian or messenger deity of the Chavín cult? This Chavín bird has been reinterpreted as a parrot, rather than as a tropical forest eagle. Parrots certainly make up part of the bird life along the coast, and both parrots and toucans are also portrayed in Moche art. The plants depicted on the Tello Obelisk—such as manioc, peanuts, bottle gourds, and peppers—are certainly known from the coast in the Initial Period or even earlier. The sacred *Spondylus* and *Strombus* shells from coastal Ecuador that appear in Chavín art are also present at Late Preceramic and Initial Period sites on the coast, and in great abundance at Chavín de Huántar. Thus, it appears that all the elements of the Chavín cult originated neither in the highlands nor in Amazonia, but on the coast or on the western slopes of the Cordillera Negra.

The Chavín cult is not just a reordering or makeover of Initial Period and Early Horizon religious beliefs. On the contrary, it boasts a new and powerful pantheon of deities that sweeps through the Central Andes for the first time during the late Early Horizon. This first great pan-Andean cult reached its peak between 400 and 200 B.C., when oracle branches were established in the highlands and on the coast. The long-distance trade pattern of the Late Preceramic and Initial Period was intensified in the late Early Horizon, and great quantities of economic goods were being exchanged with far distant cultures all the way from Ecuador to the southern Peruvian highlands.

But at the end of the Janabarriu, according to Luis G. Lumbreras, Chavín de Huántar suffered a severe earthquake that collapsed the black-and-white portal of the New Temple and seriously damaged the subterranean galleries. This catastrophic event may have shaken the confidence of the worshippers in the power held by their priests over the deities, for soon thereafter the Chavín cult disappears as a practicing religion in the Central Andes.

Though the Chavín cult has captured our imagination, there were also other momentous developments occurring in the same time period along the Peruvian central coast and in the Lake Titicaca Basin of Peru and Bolivia.

**THE PARACAS CULTURAL TRADITION**

One of the most spectacular discoveries in the Central Andes was made—again by Julio C. Tello—on the Paracas Peninsula in 1925. There, Tello and his assistant, Toribio Mejía Xesspe, excavated 429 funerary bundles. Forty of the bundles held high-ranking individuals cloaked in dazzling mantles and dressed in richly embroidered tunics, ponchos, shirts, turbans, and headbands. The other bundles held the remains of men, women, or children wrapped in nondescript textiles. Paracas textiles are considered by art historian Anne Paul to be the most sophisticated ever to have been made; the elaborate, brilliantly colored designs embody the social, religious, and environmental themes of Paracas society.

By 600 B.C., the Paracas Cultural Tradition has begun, but the spectacular achievements of ceramic and textile art occurred only between 450 and 175 B.C. The textile embroideries of human figures dressed as birds, felines, fish, foxes, and priests were worn by the society's high-status leaders. The incredible textile wealth is glimpsed in just two of the funerary bundles, which have been estimated to have taken a total of 47,000 hours to make.

The Paracas Tradition embraced a six-valley area from Cañete to the Nazca, a distance of more than 124.3 miles (200 kilometers). A recent survey of the desolate Paracas Peninsula region by archaeologist Helaine Silverman has shown that there were extensive fishing settlements for miles along the bay; the population of just the peninsula itself is estimated at between 2500 and 5000 inhabitants. Not surprisingly, the economic mainstay of Paracas society was ocean resources. An elite class emerged, managing the rich ocean resources and exchanging them for the agricultural products of the farming societies in nearby valleys.

**THE ORIGIN OF LAKE TITICACA CIVILIZATION**

In addition to the achievements at Chavín de Huántar and Paracas, developments in the Lake Titicaca Basin would also contribute to the reshaping of the cultural landscape of the Central Andes over the next 2000 years. The intervening region beyond the reach of the Chavín cult, yet not within that of the Lake Titicaca Basin culture, was dominated by prosperous village farmers and camelid herders. But south of these village societies a wholly different religious tradition arose in the Lake Titicaca Basin, a tradition which culminated in one of the greatest civilizations of the Central Andes—the Tiwanaku.

The Lake Titicaca Basin is dominated by Lake Titicaca—103 miles (165 kilometers) in length, and the world's highest navigable body of water—which really consists of two lakes joined by a natural channel. The larger of the two lakes (Chucuito) is distanced from the small southern lake (Huiñamarca) by the Copacabana Peninsula, around which runs the linking channel. It is beside this inland "sea" that the foundations of the Tiwanaku Empire were laid by a number of originally independent societies.

**The Paracas Tradition evolved among a people who lived close to the ocean. Not surprisingly therefore, many of its artifacts had marine origins, such as this *Spondylus* shell intricately inlaid with a feline mosaic of gold, turquoise and shell.**

In the second millennium B.C., a camelid-herding and agricultural society called the Wankarani arose 12.4 miles (20 kilometers) south of Huiñamarca. The Wankarani villages had circular houses grouped within a circular adobe wall, each settlement ranging from 15 to 780 houses, with populations of between 75 and 3900. As well as herding camelids, the residents smelted copper and participated in the caravan trade to the south in northern Chile. Their artwork is distinguished by stone effigies of llama heads; the deities represented by these effigies must have been worshipped in family shrines, for no temple architecture has yet been discovered.

By 1300 B.C. the first settlements of an important branch of the Titicaca tradition, the Chiripa culture, appear along the lakeshore of Huiñamarca and the northern margins of Chucuito. The main site of Chiripa is on the Taraco Peninsula, jutting out into Huiñamarca; it has been investigated by archaeologists Alfred Kidder II, David L. Browman and Karen Mohr-Chávez, who divided the development of Chiripa culture into three phases. In the Early Phase (1300 to 900 B.C.), the shoreline was occupied by peoples whose pottery is related to that of the earlier Wankarani culture. These early lake-dwellers exploited the rich fish, waterfowl, and aquatic resources of the lake, and continued the agropastoral economy of their Wankarani predecessors. By between 900 and 600 B.C., the site consisted of a mound with retaining walls, and the Late Phase (600 to 100 B.C.) saw construction of a temple with a rectangular sunken plaza and 16 elite residences. Rectangular structures on the summit of the mound had inner walls that were segmented into storage bins, accessible only by small openings; investigation shows that these bins held potatoes and quinoa and other commodities.

The shift from the circular houses of the earlier Wankarani to the rectangular structures of the Chiripa is a sign—as it was for the Late Preceramic of the Peruvian coast—of a shift from a communal economy to one controlled by extended family units.

The religion at Chiripa has been defined by Karen Mohr-Chávez and Sergio J. Chávez as the Yaya-Mama Religious Tradition, whose principal cult deities are two figures—one male and one female, each accompanied by snakes—carved on stone stelae. These Yaya-Mama cult figures, along with the architectural elements of Chiripa, continue into the powerful Tiwanaku Empire that soon dominated the Lake Titicaca Basin.

Another lake-adapted society, the Qaluyu, emerged along the northern shores of Chucuito, and was distributed as far north as Marcavalle, near Cuzco. Little is known of Qaluyu ceremonial developments, but its economic pattern clearly paralleled that of the Chiripa further south, with an emphasis upon lake resources and agropastoralism.

As well as the Chiripa and the Qaluyu, there are other complex societies along the lakeshore and its hinterlands, but little is known about these. Sillimocco, for example, on the west side of Chucuito, was only recently discovered by archaeologist Charles Stanish. According to Stanish, future investigations may demonstrate that a mosaic of chiefdoms struggled for control of the region.

Archaeologist Alan Kolata has attributed the rise of Chiripa—which had the first known temple architecture for the Titicaca Basin—to the combination of Lake Titicaca resources and the agropastoral economy inherited from their Wankarani predecessors. The question that then arises is this: if the lake resources were so critical to the economy of the Chiripa (and also to the Qaluyu), why was the lake not used before these people established their settlements on the lakeshore by 1300 B.C.? The answer is quite simple—Lake Huiñamarca did *not* exist before 2000 B.C., and Chucuito was much smaller than it is today.

Chucuito, the larger of the two lakes, averages 443 feet (135 meters) deep, with its greatest depth at 932 feet (284 meters). Huiñamarca, the small lake, is on average 30 feet (9 meters) deep, reaching only 138 feet (42 meters) at its deepest point. Coring of Huiñamarca has demonstrated that there were two lower levels of Lake Titicaca (the combined area of the lakes and their linking channel): one between 5700 and 5250 B.C., and another between 5250 and 2000 B.C. During the first period, the lake dropped 164 feet (50 meters)—so at this time Huiñamarca would have been dry. Between 4000 and 2500 B.C., levels were still 82 to 98 feet (25 to 30 meters) lower than today, and Huiñamarca remained mostly dry. During both these lower stages, Chucuito also shrank markedly. However, between 2000 B.C. and A.D. 0, the water level rose to within 33 feet (10 meters) of today's level, but Huiñamarca was so shallow that only the northern half of the lake would finally have contained water, and parts of Chucuito still would have been exposed. Exploitation may well have occurred earlier than these dates, but, as with early evidence of ocean foods, evidence for early use of lake resources may lie underwater.

These changing levels of Lake Titicaca profoundly affected the economic base of its dependent human populations. Even in drought periods today, the lake is lower, farming becomes precarious, and cattle, sheep, and goats are herded to lower elevations in search of pasturage and water. Yet at its zenith, Lake Titicaca provided a rich economic foundation for the subsequent rise of civilization in the southern Andes.

The end of the Early Horizon (200 B.C.) in the Central Andes saw the first well-recognized states with their magnificent capitals. In the next chapter, we will explore the origins of the dominant states and follow their spread through the Early Intermediate Period.

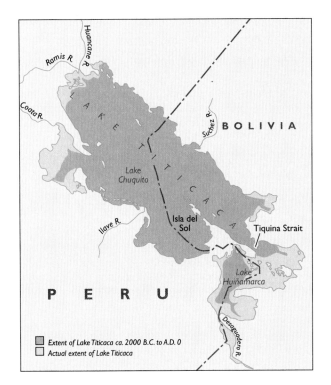

Straddling the border between Peru and Bolivia, in southeastern Peru, Lake Titicaca is one of the world's highest bodies of water. Its larger half, Chucuito, is linked to the smaller (and shallower) Huiñamarca by a narrow channel. Investigators have shown that the lake's water level has changed dramatically over the centuries, with decisive impact for the peoples living around its shores.

Shimmering testimony to the creative imagination and technical skill of Moche (or Recuay) metalworkers, this gold ornament is only one of many lurgy paid homage to the gods and to the deceased. The status of the bearer or the recipient was emblazoned in ritual objects and adornments

# 6

# THE GREAT ARTISANS

A time of great artistry, unequaled in Central Andean prehistory, unfolded during the Early Intermediate Period (200 B.C. to A.D. 600). The masterful pictorial ceramics, the elaborate textile art, and the shimmering gold, silver, and copper creations attest to the elegance of the earliest Central Andean states. In addition to the great artistic merit of these artifacts, their technological sophistication reflects the unparalleled cultural achievements of Early Intermediate societies.

unearthed from this rich period. Moche metal-
such as this.

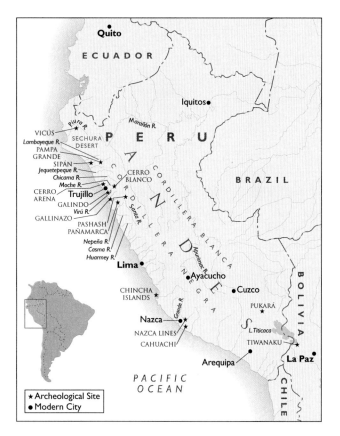

By a process of expansion and military conquest, the Moche State at its peak covered an area that stretched from the Huarmey Valley in the south to the Piura Valley in the north. Much of our knowledge of Moche expansion has been gleaned from scenes of combat, sacrifice, and burial painted on ceramics.

The question most frequently asked is this: when did the first recognizable states emerge? Some scholars believe that a state level of social-political-religious organization was attained in the Initial Period or at least by the Early Horizon; however, there is not sufficient evidence of the hallmarks of the state until the Early Intermediate Period. Only then do we find cultures that, through military expansion, incorporated large territories into their realms. For the first time there is abundant evidence for a strong ruling class, state capitals, and distant administrative centers with sufficient bureaucracy to manage the production, storage, and distribution of commodities produced by full-time craft specialists.

The Early Intermediate is a period of significant population increase and the clustering of people into ever-larger urban centers. Along with this increase in human numbers came technological, industrial, and cultural growth. To support the burgeoning populations, entire coastal valleys were overlain by sophisticated irrigation systems. In the highlands, the step-terracing of hillsides and the development of the ingenious raised-field agricultural system in the Lake Titicaca Basin brought additional lands into farming production.

Communication followed a network of roads over which llama caravans moved large quantities of goods to and from the far-flung reaches of these expansionist states. Transport by sea was also an important part of the communication system on the Peruvian coast, where seafarers plied the shoreline from Piura to the Chincha Islands. The public architecture and art styles, although not completely homogeneous within each state, adhered to the individual canons of well-developed states; especially in ceramics and textiles, the architecture and art styles of these early states are recognizable throughout their individual domains. Many Early Intermediate Period states have received only limited investigation, and are known primarily by their ceramic art styles. We will devote our attention to those areas where archaeological research allows us to reconstruct a state's origin, development, and spread.

### ORIGINS OF THE MOCHE STATE

The beginnings of the Moche State can be traced to the Salinar and Gallinazo cultures that arose between the Chicama and Casma valleys. During the Salinar Period, defensive fortifications continued to be built in the Casma, the more southerly of these two valleys, while throughout the north coast of Peru there appeared sites with elite residences, irrigation networks, road systems, and llama corrals. In the unfortified Moche Valley, the largest site in the valley at this time was Cerro Arena, situated near the later Moche capital at Cerro Blanco (White Hill). Cerro Arena had 2000 single-room stone structures and a number of 20-room dwellings, interpreted as elite residences.

In the Gallinazo Period that followed, the dominant center was the Gallinazo Group in the Virú Valley, an urban center of 30,000 rooms that some scholars believe to have been the capital of the first multi-valley state. Other smaller Gallinazo sites in neighboring valleys are thought to be administrative centers that exerted valley-wide political control over the populace. It is also during the Gallinazo Period that rectangular adobe bricks, mass-produced in molds, became the major construction material on the coast—and thus they would continue until colonial times. In the upper valleys of the north coast, extensive irrigation works were implemented to bring river waters farther out on the desert plain of the middle and lower valleys. Although still shrouded in mystery, the Salinar and Gallinazo accomplishments of the early part of the Early Intermediate soon led to the first recognizable state on the Peruvian north coast: the Moche.

At its height, the Moche State controlled the coast from the Huarmey Valley northward for 373 miles (600 kilometers) to the Piura Valley. Cerro

**The massive Huaca del Sol, located at the site of the Moche capital of Cerro Blanco, is the largest adobe pyramid in the Americas. Astonishingly, the structure is but a third of its original size. In 1602, gold-hungry Spaniards diverted the nearby Moche River—on the opposite side of the huaca in this photograph—to erode the pyramid's sun-dried mud bricks more quickly.**

One hundred and forty-three million adobe bricks were cast, transported, and assembled to create Huaca del Sol, a detail of which is shown at right. The project was carried out in eight phases, employing many generations of engineers, masons, and laborers. The brick at far right shows the maker's identity mark. The system of marking bricks helped the authorities ensure that each community had supplied the requisite number of bricks for the project.

Blanco, the Moche capital, was 3.5 miles (6 kilometers) from the sea. There, Huaca del Sol (Temple of the Sun)—the largest adobe pyramid in the New World—dominates the site. At a distance of 1640 feet (500 meters) to the south of Huaca del Sol is Huaca de la Luna (Temple of the Moon), a huge multiroomed adobe platform temple that hugs the base of Cerro Blanco. (It should be stated that these structures were named by the Spaniards, and their designation as temples of worship to the sun or moon is only speculative.)

Today, Huaca del Sol remains one of the most impressive construction achievements on the coast. It is even more astounding when one realizes that the present pyramid—at 525 by 1116 feet (160 by 340 meters) wide and 131 feet (40 meters) high—is only a third of its original size, for when the Spanish arrived, they undertook to pillage the treasures that they felt a monument of this size must contain; in 1602, they went so far as to divert the Moche River against the pyramid's northern flanks to facilitate mining of the site! These two platform pyramids must have been awe-inspiring at their pinnacle of development, for Huaca del Sol was plastered and painted red, and Huaca de la Luna was multicolored, with brightly painted interior rooms. Buried 20 feet (6 meters) between both pyramids are cemeteries and the residences of the elite, indicating that the capital had a considerable urban population.

The construction techniques of these centerpieces of the Moche capital provide a glimpse into the organization of labor. Huaca del Sol was built in eight phases, using 143 million adobe bricks; Huaca de la Luna in four phases, using 50 million bricks, many of which bear more than 100 distinguishing marks (such as dots, lines, and curvilinear motifs). Archaeologists Michael E.

Diminutive when compared to its nearby sibling pyramid, the Huaca de la Luna is nonetheless a robust architectural construction in its own right. Yet size is not the only difference between the two structures: rich polychrome murals adorn the interior walls of the Huaca de la Luna, as shown below. The large openings that are visible in the side wall of the huaca, at right, are the entrances to tunnels excavated by looters.

Moseley and Charles M. Hastings have noted that these two temples were built in vertical segments and that bricks with the same makers' marks were stacked together. These construction details, they feel, represent a labor tax system where more than 100 communities were mandated by the ruling elite to provide adobe bricks for the building of the two public monuments over time. Each community used its own mark to prove to the authorities that they had indeed supplied the proper number of bricks to the project. Since there is no evidence that there was a monetary tax system until the colonial period, it thus appears that taxes were paid in labor. Throughout the Moche realm, many public works were built using marked adobes, and this labor system was to continue as a method to organize and tax the populace through Inca times.

### THE SPREAD OF THE MOCHE STATE

After consolidating control over the Moche and Chicama valleys, the Moche began to conquer their neighbors; the success of their militaristic expansion can be traced in the Moche ceramic record. In 1948, Peruvian archaeologist Rafael Larco Hoyle noted that the stirrup-spouted vessels from Moche cemeteries had five distinctive spout forms, indicating five different phases: Phase I had short spouts with thick spout lips; in Phase II the tips are reduced; Phase III spouts flare and have no lip rim; in Phase IV the spout is taller with straight sides; and in Phase V the spout tapers to the lip. Since such vessels were used in conquered areas, these and other changes in form allow the archaeologist to trace the conquest to the southern boundaries of the multi-valley Moche State.

During Moche III and IV, the capital at Cerro Blanco reached a peak of development. During these periods, the ceramics show an increase in battle scenes; depictions of captured prisoners being sacrificed provide us with insights into Moche battle strategy. Warriors are portrayed in individual combat, and not in battle ranks, for once the Moche armies encountered resistance, they split up into a melee of hand-to-hand combat. The unfortunate prisoners were disrobed of their gear and tied up nude, with the high-ranking captives being carried on litters by their defeated soldiers. In Moche III and IV, the southern valleys up to the Huarmey River were brought into the Moche sphere, their dispersed populations drawn into a few large urban-administrative centers.

In the Nepeña Valley, a major administrative and ceremonial center was established at Pañamarca from which the middle and lower valley was brought under Moche control. However, archaeologist Donald A. Proulx discovered that, in the upper valley, it was the highland Recuay culture (200 B.C. to A.D. 550) that held sway. Not well-known except for its ceramics, the Recuay culture was centered in the Callejón de Huaylas, succeeding the Chavín Religious Tradition. At a site known as Pashash, Terence Grieder found elite tombs and distinctive Recuay pottery (made from a fine white clay known as kaolin), decorated with warriors, felines, condors, and snakes—and all intermingled with Moche trade ceramics. In the upper Nepeña Valley, Proulx discovered Recuay ceramics at 42 sites and noted highland architectural characteristics at a large site named Huancarpón, leading him to conclude that the Moche and Recuay were competing for sovereignty over the valley. The Recuay also exerted pressure on the upper reaches of other neighboring valleys controlled by the Moche, and influenced the Fortaleza and Pativilca valleys south of the Moche frontier.

The colonizing march northward out of the Moche heartland is not well understood. Still, it is known that in the Piura Valley, at the northern extremes of the Moche State, Moche I and II ceramics are found in profusion (indicating an early influence or conquest).

The Moche must have moved quickly northward, subjugating the northern valleys in a series of lightning strikes both by land and by sea. In the Piura Valley, the Moche encountered the Vicús chiefdom. Looted Vicús cemeteries have yielded hundreds of Moche I and II trade ceramics similar to those in the Jequetepeque Valley. The Vicús were in a position to control trade with Ecuador and had access to important copper and gold deposits, so favored by the Moche for their superb metalwork. Also, the upper Piura Valley is within an area that receives significant annual rainfall, and its wide floodplain would have produced agricultural products attractive to the Moche. Large pyramids and mounds dot the upper Piura landscape, some dating to the Vicús Period,

Almost all known Vicús ceramics come from tombs plundered by grave robbers. However, archaeologists have begun to investigate the sites of these early Andeans, who came under Moche influence. The objects that have been studied share a strongly three-dimensional style, drawing on architectural, human, animal, and supernatural forms. The double-chambered bottle shown here typifies the large teeth and circular eyes of animal figures in Vicús ceramics.

The Sacrifice Ceremony was a ritual of major importance in the Moche religion. Prisoners captured in battle were the main object of sacrifice. The lower portion of this illustration shows two such prisoners having their throats cut. In the upper section, priests carry sacrificial blood in goblets; the most important one—the Warrior Priest, shown on the left—is presented with a goblet of blood to drink.

but they remain unexplored. The Moche royal tomb at Loma Negra, looted in 1969, demonstrates that the Moche had a strong presence in the Piura Valley, if not outright control of the Vicús populace. A possible clue to the installation of Moche power in the area may come from an El Niño that occurred in the Piura region at some point during the fourth century A.D. The upheaval caused by massive flooding may have provided the Moche with the opportunity to consolidate their control.

The Moche not only interacted with or confronted foreign powers vying for supremacy, they also maintained seaborne commerce that stretched from the Chincha Islands in the south to the Lobos Islands in the north (north of the Lambayeque Valley). This knowledge is substantiated not only by Moche artifacts recovered from offshore islands, but also by portrayals, on Moche ceramics, of seal-hunting expeditions and reed rafts loaded with cargos.

## MOCHE SOCIETY

No other Central Andean society provides such abundant information of its ritual and political activities as the Moche; this information comes to us largely through the culture's unparalleled ceramic art. Christopher B. Donnan, director of the Fowler Museum of Cultural History at U.C.L.A. and the leading Moche archaeologist, has amassed 125,000 photos of Moche artifacts whose artistic realism captures the vitality of the Moche State. Although many stirrup-spout vessels also depict ordinary animals and plants, much of the Moche art deals with ritual and political themes. Elegantly clad warriors, high-ranking personages enthroned in buildings atop temples or riding on litters—these images show the power of the ruling class. The fine-line drawings on stirrup-spout vessels portray burial, sacrifice, combat, and ritual dance themes. The

Nestled in the Lambayeque Valley, the Moche center of Sipán may have been the seat of a regional court. In recent years, the site has been the object of much examination, mainly because of its burial platform, shown at right. A rich source of information about Moche political and social structures, the tombs were unknown to archaeologists until 1987, when looting was reported at the site.

A succession of elaborate burials at Sipán from A.D. 100 to 300 were rich in finely crafted artwork, such as the ear ornaments pictured above. Unearthed as shown, the ornaments were fashioned primarily of turquoise and gold, as was a treasure trove of similar objects. From top to bottom, they represent, respectively, a warrior, a duck, and a deer.

burial scenes present nobles interred in coffins, accompanied by grave goods, vassals, and sacrificial victims.

The most elaborate scene on ceramics, and on the mural at the Moche temple of Pañamarca, is the Sacrifice Ceremony, in which a supreme leader is presented with a goblet filled with blood. In deciphering the Sacrifice Ceremony, Donnan has identified four main participants in this blood ritual. The central figure is a male ruler with rays emanating from his head and shoulders, who is being presented with a cup of blood by a person dressed as a bird. The third figure is a high-status woman with a long shirt and a head-dress of tassels, while the fourth-ranking indvidual wears an elaborate nose ornament and serrated streamers projecting from a feline headdress. Other elements of the scene include a litter and a spotted dog associated with the central figure, and attendants drawing blood from naked captives. Until recently, these scenes were thought to represent supernatural events with little relevance to actual Moche rituals.

Only 350 Moche burials have been professionally excavated, while count-less thousands of looted graves have provided hordes of Moche ceramics and metalwork to the world's museums. The graves excavated by Max Uhle at Cerro Blanco, as well as the few hundred other professionally excavated burial lots, show the wide gap between commoners, nobility, and the ruling class. Some people, of low economic stature, were buried in refuse deposits, and have no grave goods to accompany them into the afterlife; higher-status individuals, on the other hand, are accompanied by dozens of beautiful ceramic, metal, wooden, and feather artifacts, which have been well pre-served by the dry climate.

Until 1987, the richest Moche tomb was that of a Warrior-Priest, excavated by archaeologists William Duncan Strong and Clifford Evans, Jr., in 1946. On the last day of their excavations at Huaca de la Cruz in the Virú Valley, they uncovered the tomb of a 40- to 45-year-old man in a cane coffin. The man was in the company of two sacrificed llamas, a small boy, and two women who, judging by their posture, must have been tossed into the grave. Resting in and around the coffin were 28 Moche IV pots, and three wooden staffs with carved ends—one in the form of an owl, a second as a feline deity, and a third decorated with battle scenes. Gourd bottles, feather fans, a bird headdress, and a small number of metal objects completed the burial repertory. Although spectacular when compared to the other known Moche graves, the Warrior-Priest of Virú was a Moche noble, but not a Moche king.

In February of 1987, just over 40 years after the tomb of the Warrior-Priest had been uncovered, came the discovery of the magnificent and unequaled royal tombs of Sipán, in the Lambayeque Valley. Peruvian archaeologist Walter Alva, director of the Museo Nacional Brüning de Lambayeque, was alerted by the police that they had just confiscated 30 gold and copper objects from looters conducting clandestine digging at the little-known site, later dated to A.D. 100 to 300. Secured by police armed with machine guns, Alva began to explore the gaping crater and mound of the looted royal tomb, which was part of a large Moche pyramid complex where this ruler had lain at rest for 2000 years. Alva was joined by Christopher B. Donnan. As the work continued in clearing the platform mound, which was constructed of marked adobe bricks, they came upon a second tomb, this one roofed with logs. In the months that followed, the excavators gradually exposed the contents of what was to prove a sumptuous tomb.

The central individual was a man 35 to 45 years of age, buried in a wooden coffin; surrounding him were the cane coffins of two men—one with a dog—and three women, two sacrificed llamas, and a boy. The remains of two other people were found at some distance, one with both feet cut off, placed in the upper part of the chamber to guard the ruler for eternity. In niches around the coffin were hundreds of Moche pots. The central coffin held some of the most spectacular artifacts ever found in the Americas: gold headpieces, scepters, earspools, a face mask, and elegantly designed shell-bead collars. Imagine the astonishment of Alva and Donnan when they realized that the royal personage they had uncovered wore all the trappings of the central figure in the Sacrifice Ceremony.

Unearthed in Tomb 2 at Sipán, this burial seems to attest to an abundance of turquoise interred with a Moche lord. Closer examination reveals the blue-green color to be that of oxidized copper. Originally gilded, the copper was in the form of disks, triangles, and squares, as well as plates bearing human figures.

But this was not all that the royal tombs of Sipán had in store for Alva and Donnan, for the third tomb proved as rich as the second. And, to the astonishment of the incredulous archaeologists, the royal personage turned out to be the second figure in the Sacrifice Ceremony. A fourth tomb was also uncovered and it too contained the heretofore unseen splendor of an earlier ruler. At the time of this writing, excavation proceeds at Sipán; the opulence of future royal tombs, along with new information about Moche royalty, awaits the careful attention of excavators.

In 1991, at San José de Moro in the Jequetepeque Valley, Donnan and archaeologist Luis Jaime Castillo exposed another royal tomb. In the room-sized chamber lay the remains of a royal woman with head tassels of silver-copper alloy and goblets used in the Sacrifice Ceremony. This royal personage, found so soon after the other two, was none other than the female figure in the Sacrifice Ceremony painted and carved in the mural at Pañamarca! Now only the last male figure awaits discovery.

The royal tombs of Sipán, as I have stated, are by far the richest ever found in the Americas. The Moche royalty amassed tremendous wealth, which was placed in the tomb to be used in the afterlife. The deposition of spectacular regalia with each royal tomb provided the metalsmiths, lapidaries, weavers, ceramicists, and other specialists with a vast amount of work. The same artisans were also commissioned to create new ritual garb for the successors of the deceased rulers, so they could take their rightful place in the Sacrifice Ceremony and as heads of the ruling class. The quantity of foreign goods in the tombs attests to far-flung trade by land and sea. The tomb of the female figure boasts Cajamarca pottery from the highlands, Nievería pottery from the Lima area, *Spondylus* from Ecuador, and lapis lazuli from Chile.

Each valley under Moche domination had an administrative center with a royal court, a mausoleum, and a temple where the Sacrifice Ceremony, the most sacred Moche ritual, was performed. Alva and Donnan speculate that the Sipán royalty were related through kinship and marriage to the ruling elite in other valleys, much as the royalty of Europe once operated to expand control over vast territories. The genealogy of these valley rulers or governors included ties to the original royal family at Cerro Blanco in the Moche Valley.

### CRISIS IN THE MOCHE STATE

The Moche State began to show signs of stress between about A.D. 500 and 600, when it lost control of its southern valleys. The Moche Valley then became the southern boundary

The massive Huaca Fortaleza is the focal point of Pampa Grande, located in the Lambayeque Valley. Pampa Grande became the Moche capital after a shift in power resulted in the loss of some southern valley sites. The upper-valley location helped the authorities control the irrigation system that was so crucial to the Moche economy.

Relying on an economy of artistic devices, Moche ceramic workers excelled in capturing details from everyday life, as seen in this figure of a llama. A rope attached to its ear, the dutiful beast takes a pause from its burden and rests on its knees.

of the state, and the major focus of Moche power shifted to the huge site of Pampa Grande in the Lambayeque Valley, 34 miles (55 kilometers) inland and 125 miles (200 kilometers) north of Cerro Blanco, the earlier Moche capital. Pampa Grande, which has been excavated by archaeologist Izumi Shimada, covers 2.3 square miles (6 square kilometers) with pyramids, elite compounds, workshops, storage facilities, and residential sectors; indeed, it was a large urban sprawl. The main pyramid, Huaca Fortaleza (Fortress Mound), is 591 by 902 feet (180 by 275 meters) wide and 180 feet (55 meters) high, rivaling Huaca del Sol as one of the largest adobe structures in the Americas. The immense site of Pampa Grande boasted some 20,000 to 30,000 inhabitants.

In the Moche Valley, the old capital continued to be occupied, but in Moche V a new and heavily fortified urban center arose at Galindo, 12 miles (20 kilometers) from the ocean. Galindo, excavated by archaeologist Garth Bawden, is spread over 1.9 square miles (5 square kilometers), and consists of small pyramids, courts, residential sectors for commoners and elite, and storage areas.

A major settlement shift occurred between Moche IV and Moche V, and saw the relocation of lower valley Moche centers to the upper valley sites of Pampa Grande and Galindo. These new locales facilitated control over the main intake canals that provided precious irrigation water—a commodity upon which the Moche economy was heavily dependent—and strengthened defenses against incursions from the highlands.

The Late Moche was a period of environmental degradation, with extensive evidence of flooding at Cerro Blanco and at other Moche sites throughout the

coast. As mentioned in Chapter 1, the Quelccaya Ice Cap offers an annual moisture record for the last 1500 years, a record now used by archaeologists as an environmental yardstick in correlating environmental shifts with cultural changes. The ice-cap core has recorded El Niños in A.D. 511-512, as well as in 546, 576, 600, 610, 612, 650, and 681. Such intense rainfall and flooding on this normally hyperarid coast would not only have destroyed irrigation and agricultural field systems and communication networks, it would also have caused the disappearance of marine resources, and thus the widespread destruction of village and urban centers. In the 1982-83 mega-Niño, northern Peru was cut off for months, and had to be sent supplies by sea and air from Lima. But in the pre-Hispanic period, of course, there were no national or international relief agencies to aid the devastated Moche State. The Moche had survived earlier floods, but this succession of El Niños was not the only disaster to impact the irrigation-based economy of the northern coastal valleys: the Quelccaya ice sequence also reflects long periods of drought between A.D. 524 and 540, 562 and 594, and 636 and 645. The A.D. 562-94 drought was especially severe, for there was a 30 percent decrease in precipitation in the Andes. Because the source of the coastal rivers lies in the highlands, lower rainfall resulted in less water in the rivers for irrigation agriculture. It thus becomes clear why the Moche relocated their major centers to the upper valleys, where scarce water could be managed more effectively.

The alternating floods and droughts took a heavy toll on the abilities of the Moche to sustain their irrigation economy, and within the first 100 years of the Middle Horizon (A.D. 600 to 700), the Moche State collapsed, after more than 500 years of spectacular achievements in statecraft. The Moche capital at Cerro Blanco suffered one further blow during Late Moche, when sand seas buried the urban areas, leaving only the gigantic Huaca del Sol and Huaca de la Luna as testaments to the past elegance of the state.

South of the Moche State, during the Early Intermediate Period, the little-known Lima culture had its administrative center at Maranga, now surrounded by the Peruvian capital. The Temple of Pachacamac, famous in Inca times for its oracle, was also established south of Lima at this time. Still farther south, in a five-valley region, the early cultures of the Paracas region gave rise to the famous Nasca society.

## THE NASCA

The people of this society are renowned not only for their exquisite polychrome ceramics and elaborate textiles, but also for the Nazca Lines, or geoglyphs. Fascinating to scholars and non-scholars alike, the geoglyphs were until recently a source of frustration for both camps, who were unable to decipher their functions and meaning. (Note that archaeologists use the spelling Nasca to designate the culture, with Nazca used for geographical and geological discussions.)

Nasca society was centered in the five valleys from Chincha to Acari, and at its heart was the Grande River Basin. This unique coastal watershed is composed of nine highland tributaries that join to form a single river at a point 22 miles (35 kilometers) from the coast. Due to the narrowness of the river valleys, with their limited floodplains and uncertain water supply, the Nasca were unable to develop valley-wide irrigation systems like those on the north coast. (As with the Moche, they were dependent upon rainfall in the far distant highlands.) The irrigated areas were more like farming oases separated by stretches of little-used valley floors. A number of these narrow rivers disappeared underground for miles, but the ingenious Nasca dug vertical shafts to tap the subsurface water, and then connected the shafts by tunnels to surface reservoirs; from there, they irrigated their fields. Most experts feel that these subsurface aqueducts, still in use today, were constructed by the Nasca; but archaeologists Monica Barnes and David Fleming insist that this method of water-tapping was introduced from Spain, where it is more than 1000 years old.

Although Nasca pottery is elaborately painted with animal and supernatural designs, it does not provide the archaeologist with the window on Nasca culture as does that of the Moche. The essential distinction between the art of the two cultures is that, while the Moche portrayed elaborate scenes of ritual ceremonies or warfare, the Nasca emphasis was on painted scenes of single figures—animals, plants, humans, or human heads. Still, we have been able to determine eight Nasca phases, with the artistic trends of the 800 years of Nasca domination and influence showing increasing concern with warfare.

In Early Nasca, there is realism in presenting animals, plants, and a human/animal hybrid deity with splaying whiskers called the Mythical Being by archaeologists. The crisp polychrome paintings on bowls, jars, platters, and double-spout-and-bridge bottles (bottles with two spouts joined by a handle), are set against an uncluttered background in what is referred to as the Monumental Style.

With its stirrup-spout design, this vessel is undeniably of Moche origin. While the spout itself varies little among vessels of this sort, the reservoir—usually fashioned after a human or animal form—is often highly individual. Many objects appear to have been modeled after particular people, while others, such as this warrior figure, suggest general types.

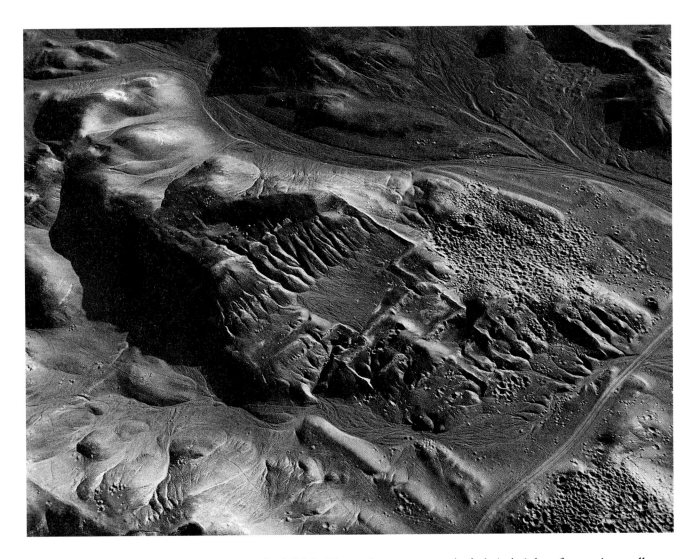

Southeast of the town of Nazca, between the Nazca and Ingenio valleys, the ancient pilgrimage center of Cahuachi is now barely recognizable, even from the air. It once boasted temples, plazas, and pyramids, but erosion and looting have robbed it of its original splendor. Unlike many important Andean archaeological sites, Cahuachi is believed to have had very few permanent residents.

In Middle Nasca the potters reached their height of ceramic excellence, dazzling the eye with 10 to 12 colors. The natural figures of Early Nasca became more abstract, and more mythic. Warriors holding human trophy heads and clubs dripping with blood reflect increasing warfare in Nasca society as local chiefdoms competed for the limited agricultural resources in the arid coastal valleys. However, this warfare theme was not manifested in the erection of fortifications, as was the case in the Moche region.

In Late Nasca, the stylized designs become interconnected figures that are expanded to fill up the empty background of Early Nasca art, a style referred to as Proliferous by ceramic specialists.

Artistic creativity in textiles followed the Paracas tradition of excellence and included an extensive use of alpaca wool imported by llama caravans from the highlands. Every known weaving technique of the Central Andes was mastered by the Nasca, whose ponchos, mantles, and painted textiles attest to the richness of a culture where textile wealth was a measure of status.

The region in and between the Nazca and Ingenio valleys is the fulcrum of Nasca culture, for here is the great pilgrimage center of Cahuachi, the urban site of Ventilla, and the world-famous sacred landscape of the Nazca Lines. Investigated by Max Uhle, Julio C. Tello, Alfred L. Kroeber, and William Duncan Strong in the first half of the 20th century, Cahuachi is unfortunately one of the most heavily looted sites in the Central Andes.

Cahuachi, located at one of the few natural springs in the Grande River Basin, covers 370 acres (150 hectares) with 40 mounds that are, in reality, natural hills that have been terraced to construct temples. The scarcity of domestic refuse has led archaeologist Helaine Silverman to conclude that Cahuachi was not a city but rather a pilgrimage center with a small resident population. Cahuachi was established in Nasca 1, and by Nasca 3 it had become a great ceremonial center; but, by Nasca 4, it had reverted to a vast cemetery. It had lost its significance as a pilgrimage center, and now became a sacred ground for the burial of the Nasca dead.

Twelve miles (20 kilometers) directly north of Cahuachi, connected by a Nazca Line, is the 494-acre (200-hectare) urban site of Ventilla, the largest Nasca site known in the Grande River drainage. Discovered in 1988 by Silverman, it is obscured by recently planted trees, but surface ceramics indicate it was occupied at the same time as Cahuachi (Nasca 1-4). The hundreds of other sites recently discovered by Silverman and her colleagues are all under 9 acres (4 hectares) in size and are interpreted as small farming villages.

If Nasca was a state, there would be at least three or more levels of settlement types, such as a capital, regional administrative centers, and local producing communities of farmers. Unlike at Sipán, there are no burials that can be considered royal tombs; unlike Moche, Nasca left no evidence of craft specialization, regional administration, or storage centers—features that identified the Moche as a social-political-religious organization at the level of a state. Silverman thus interprets Nasca as a confederacy of regional chiefdoms ruled by a small elite. Each valley consisted of several chiefdoms whose populace revered Cahuachi as a sacred center, where they worshipped at individual shrines maintained by separate social groups. The low population estimate of 10,000 to 15,000 would have been adequate to form small chiefdoms in the nine valleys of the Grande River drainage.

## NASCA IN CRISIS

By Middle Nasca (Nasca 5), water flow into the Grande River drainage was reduced by the same catastrophic drought that affected the Moche. (This is when the Nasca probably turned to tapping subsurface water to irrigate their fields.) The failure of the gods to provide lifegiving water may have led the

The subject matter of Nasca ceramics ranged widely, as did stylistic approaches. Some periods favored mythical content, while others attempted to reproduce simple forms from nature. Certain periods were known for relatively sparse backgrounds, while others are more detailed. The simple Proto-Nasca vase shown at right bears stylized double-headed creatures with snakelike bodies, yet their two heads, tongues exposed, suggest those of foxes.

Nasca—whose rituals focused upon water—to abandon Cahuachi. The urban center of Ventilla was also deserted as the inhabitants dispersed to cultivate the ever-shrinking farmland. In her extensive survey of the Nazca and Ingenio valleys, Silverman found that after A.D. 500 (Nasca 6 and 7) there was a significant decrease in the number of farming hamlets, reflecting a loss of population due to the drought. By late Nasca times, the population was drawn into a few large centers, possibly reflecting the emergence of a state-level social-political-religious organization in the Nazca region for the first time.

## THE NAZCA LINES

Although the Nazca Lines, or geoglyphs, had been briefly mentioned by Julio C. Tello, Toribio Mejía Xesspe, and Alfred L. Kroeber, it was not until 1941, when historical geographer Paul Kosok examined the lines on aerial photographs taken by the Peruvian Air Force, that the immensity of the desert markings became well known. Kosok called the lines "the largest astronomy book in the world," and he was joined in his interpretation by mathematician Maria Reiche. Both interpreted the maze of lines as representing a giant calendrical system used by the Nasca to predict the yearly agricultural cycle and to plan the ceremonial cycle. Yet subsequent investigations could not confirm the calendrical interpretation, for the lines went in many different directions, even crossing each other in a confusing array. Since that time, there have also been

Nasca ceramics are famed both for their rich symbolism and for their technical finesse. Burials are the main excavation source, yielding beautifully crafted pieces, as well as a means of correlating individual styles with particular phases of Nasca development. A feature of all epochs is colorful painted imagery. This vessel depicts a hybrid figure combining feline, human, and fish elements.

the fanciful interpretations by Erich von Däniken, in *Chariots of the Gods?* that the Nazca Lines indicated landing strips for ancient astronauts. This view received great attention, but no scientific support.

The Nazca Lines cover 77 square miles (200 square kilometers), over two percent of the vast Nazca Plains. Of the thousands of geoglyphs, fewer than 50 represent human, animal, or supernatural figures; the majority are straight lines, rectangles, triangles, and quadrangles, with trapezoids being the most prevalent. There are more than 807 miles (1300 kilometers) of lines, reaching individual lengths of up to 12 miles (20 kilometers). Some of the lines converge on knolls and many of the straight lines and trapezoids move up and down hills. The construction of lines is a very simple matter, for the desert is paved by a single layer of loose stones, which are easily cleared to expose a surface lighter in color. Archaeoastronomer Anthony Aveni, employing 12 Earthwatch volunteers, built a small line in 90 minutes; he extrapolates from this exercise that the largest trapezoids could have been made by 100 people working 10 hours a day for two days.

A fresh look at one of the world's greatest enigmas was initiated in the 1980s, when Anthony Aveni, Helaine Silverman, anthropologist Gary Urton, and others conducted rigorous studies of the lines. They soon demonstrated that the lines were not aligned to specific stars and did not represent a calendrical system for determining the seasons of the year, but

Speculation and controversy have long surrounded the Nazca Lines, a maze of geometric markings created by clearing surface stones to reveal the lighter layer beneath. Certain organic patterns, visible from hilltops, depict such creatures as a monkey or a bird, while purely geometric lines, such as those shown here, probably were laid out as ritual pathways.

instead functioned as ritual pathways. The lines date to Nasca 3 and 4, about the same time that the pilgrimage center of Cahuachi was at its height. A number of the lines are associated with Cahuachi, and many connect with other Nasca sites. The Nazca Lines have been compared with the ritual pathways leading to the Coricancha, the Inca Temple of the Sun in Cuzco. These were sacred routes to ceremonial centers or sacred locations maintained by specific social groups whose rituals revolved around the all-consuming concern with water. The giant figures of fish, monkeys, spiders, and birds cluster on the south side of the Ingenio Valley, but they are not mere doodles in the Nazca Plain, for astronomer Phyllis Pitluga has shown that the animals relate to the astro-mythology of the Nasca and correlate with figures in the Milky Way. With the abandonment of Cahuachi and

Ventilla, the building of Nazca Lines also ceased, and, except for a few isolated later examples of line construction, the brilliance of Nasca culture ended with the great drought.

**BEGINNINGS OF CIVILIZATION IN THE LAKE TITICACA BASIN**

In Chapter 5, it was argued that the evolution of the complex societies in the Lake Titicaca Basin coincided with the rise of water levels in Lake Titicaca. This rise contributed to the rich fish and aquatic resources that completed the tripartite economic system of fishing, agriculture, and herding upon which the later Tiwanaku Empire was founded. Two powerful capital cities were established on this rich resource base at each end of Lake Titicaca: Pukará, 37 miles (60 kilometers) northwest of this inland sea; and Tiwanaku, 9 miles (15 kilometers) to the south.

Pukará (400 B.C. to A.D. 100) was short-lived in comparison with Tiwanaku (400 B.C. to A.D. 1000), but in its 500 years of existence its priest-rulers used the already well-established llama-caravan trade to exert their control or influence as far northward as Cuzco, some 93 miles (150 kilometers) away, and south 560 miles (900 kilometers) into northern Chile. The site of Pukará was not only a temple center with elite residences, but also an urban sprawl covering more than 1.5 square miles (4 square kilometers). The iconography of the site's polychrome ceramics, as well as the cut-and-polished stonework of its civic and ceremonial core, included highland animals—the puma, other felines, birds, llamas—and human figures holding trophy heads. The stepped platforms at Pukará, with facings of cut stone and rectangular sunken courtyards surrounded by elite residences and storage rooms, are strikingly similar to those at Chiripa temples. These architectural elements and the Yaya-Mama religion are found in the Tiwanaku capital.

The future capital of the Tiwanaku Empire begins to take shape between A.D. 100 and 400; then, after A.D. 600, it becomes the seat of power of an empire stretching from the Titicaca Basin into southern coastal Peru and the northern coastal valleys of Chile. Excavations at Tiwanaku by Bolivian archaeologists have revealed an early settlement with Pukará-like ceramics, prompting archaeologists Alan Kolata and Carlos Ponce Sanginés to conclude that the ancestral roots of Pukará and Tiwanaku are either to be found in Chiripa or at some yet undiscovered source for the Yaya-Mama Religious Tradition.

In the late Early Intermediate Period, powerful civilizations arose in the southern Central Andes that were to change forever that region's cultural landscape. In the subsequent Middle Horizon, described in Chapter 7, the Tiwanaku Empire spread to the south and the west between A.D. 500 and 1000, and, in the Ayacucho Basin of the southern Peruvian highlands, the Middle Horizon Huari Empire expanded northward and eastward after A.D. 600, dominating or influencing much of Peru. In the Middle Horizon, the fulcrum of power shifted from the Peruvian north coast to the southern Central Andes.

The central deity of the Tiwanaku pantheon is the Gateway God, who stares out from the Gateway of the Sun within the massive walled
between the Gateway God and the Chavín Staff God have led many archaeologists to believe that the earlier Chavín religion underlies the

compound called the Kalasasaya. The similarities
Tiwanaku tradition.

# 7

# THE STAFF GOD RULES

The first empires, the Tiwanaku and the Huari, dominate or influence much of the Central Andes during the years of the Middle Horizon—A.D. 600 to 1000. Empires, as distinguished from states, control extensive territory, and incorporate conquered foreign states. The Tiwanaku capital in Bolivia and the Huari capital in southern Andean Peru emerge as the power centers of expansionist states, the Tiwanaku spreading southward and the Huari conquering to the north.

The first of these precocious empires is the Tiwanaku, which developed in the southern Lake Titicaca Basin. By A.D. 200, the Tiwanaku Empire had eclipsed the Pukará to become the most powerful empire in the southern Central Andes. Although the phases of development are not well understood, it is known that in Tiwanaku I and II (400 B.C. to A.D. 100), the capital of the empire began to rise in the southern Lake Titicaca Basin. In Tiwanaku III (A.D. 100 to 400), construction began on massive public buildings and raised agriculture fields, and by Tiwanaku IV (A.D. 400 to 800), the empire spread beyond its Lake Titicaca Basin boundaries. Tiwanaku V (A.D. 800 to 1000) finally brought to an end 600 years of mastery over 154,400 square miles (400,000 square kilometers) of the southern Central Andes.

## TIWANAKU: THE PENULTIMATE ANDEAN CITY

The roots of the Tiwanaku capital can be found in the early village underlying the 1.5-square-mile (4-square-kilometer) civic-ceremonial core of one of the great cities in the Americas. Settled by 400 B.C. on the Tiwanaku River, which empties into Lake Titicaca 9.3 miles (15 kilometers) to the north, the small farming village evolved into a regal city of multi-terraced platform pyramids, courts, and urban areas, covering a total of 2.31 square miles (6 square kilometers) between A.D. 100 and 1000. Because archaeologists have concentrated on the heavily looted monumental architecture of the city, little is known of the 30,000 to 60,000 urban dwellers or of the city's crafts or administrative functions; we also know little about the storage system that was required for the bounty of surplus foods from the agricultural fields, about the vast llama herds on the puna, and about the abundant fish caught in the lake.

The core of this imperial capital was surrounded by a moat that restricted access to the temples and to areas frequented by royalty. According to archaeologist Alan Kolata, the moat was ceremonial and not defensive; but it was also functional, serving to drain the yearly torrential rainfall through an elaborate system of subterranean drainage channels that ran throughout the pyramid platforms, the sunken courts, and the civic-ceremonial precinct to the Tiwanaku River. Within this sacred space is found the largest terraced pyramid of the city—the Akapana.

Once believed to be a modified hill, the Akapana has proven to be a massive human construction with a base 656 feet (200 meters) square and a height of 55.8 feet (17 meters). Its base is formed of beautifully cut and joined facing stone blocks. Within the cut-stone retaining walls are six T-shaped terraces with vertical stone pillars, an architectural technique that is also used in most of the other Tiwanaku monuments. The retaining walls of the six terraces enclose a dirt-filled core probably resulting from the digging of the moat. On the summit of the Akapana, reached by wide staircases, there was a sunken court with an area 164 feet (50 meters) square, serviced by the subterranean drainage system. Kolata's excavations adjacent to the sunken court revealed the

The Tiwanaku capital, near the shores of Lake Titicaca, was the center of a powerful, self-sustaining empire in the southern Central Andes. The Huari empire controlled the highland region of Peru.

122

Tiwanaku's elegant symmetry shows to greatest advantage when seen from the air, giving a clearer idea of the extent of the ancient world's highest city. At the top right of the photograph rise the eroded remains of the Akapana pyramid. The large square enclosure with sunken court is the Kalasasaya, with the smaller Putuni complex located to the lower right. Above the Kalasasaya can be seen the Semi-subterranean Temple.

residences of the elite, while, under the patio the remains of a number of seated individuals, believed to have been priests, faced a man with a ceramic vessel that displayed a puma—an animal sacred to Tiwanaku. Ritual offerings of llamas and ceramics, as well as high-status goods made of copper, silver, and obsidian, were also encountered in this elite residential area. The cut-stone building foundations supported walls of adobe brick, which have been eroded away by the yearly torrential rains over the centuries.

Associated with the Akapana are four temples: the Semi-subterranean, the Kalasasaya, the Putuni, and the Kheri Kala. The first of these, the Semi-subterranean Temple, was studded with sculptured stone heads set into cut-stone facing walls, and in the middle of the court was located a now-famous monolithic stela. Named for archaeologist Wendell C. Bennett, who conducted the first archaeological research at Tiwanaku in the 1930s, the Bennett Stela represents a human figure wearing elaborate clothes and a

Tiwanaku's largest terraced pyramid, the Akapana, was situated amid the residences of the capital's elite. The size of the Akapana led archaeologists initially to assume it was a natural hill. This view shows an excavated section of terracing. The pyramid has been heavily eroded by centuries of torrential rains, but the cut and dressed blocks used to construct the terraces bespeak the quality of its original masonry.

crown. This figure is holding a ceremonial drinking cup, called a *kero*, in one hand and a scepter in the other. The fine carving on the stela portrays llamas and plants, along with the Tiwanaku Gateway God and his winged attendants. Ethnohistorian R. Tom Zuidema has interpreted the designs on the Bennett Stela as representing a calendrical system. The stela, he argues, is the embodiment of the Tiwanaku religious concern with agriculture and herding, of which an important element was forecasting the changing seasons of the year.

Adjacent to the Semi-subterranean Temple is the Kalasasaya, a rectangular walled compound on top of a 394-by-427-foot (120-by-130-meter) platform with a central sunken court. In the central courtyard was erected another monolithic statue, similar to the Bennett Stela. Called the Ponce Stela after Bolivian archaeologist Carlos Ponce Sanginés, it probably faced the Bennett Stela in the sunken court, uniting these two religious temples in the veneration of mythical ancestors and Tiwanaku royalty.

Tiwanaku's greatest icon is the image on the Gateway of the Sun, situated in a corner of the Kalasasaya. This monolithic stone doorway is thought to have once graced the Puma Punku platform pyramid outside the encircling moat of Tiwanaku. Called the Gateway or Staff God, it is the central deity of the Tiwanaku pantheon. The Gateway God wears an elaborate headdress, dangling with low-relief carvings of human trophy heads and projecting a burst of rays at the end of which are circles and pumas. Standing, facing forward on a three-tiered temple, the Gateway God holds a pair of staffs crowned with condors, emblems of the mighty warrior. The two staffs are seen by Kolata as an *atlatl*, or spearthrower, and a sling for hurling stones. Accompanying the

The Kalasasaya was a rectangular compound enclosed by stone walls up to two stories high. This view of the imposing front wall, with its impressive central entrance still intact, exhibits the structure's masonry style, which utilized gargantuan vertical slabs along with smaller, finely cut blocks. The compound's spacious platform contained a central sunken court, visible in the foreground, and was flanked by two rows of one-room buildings.

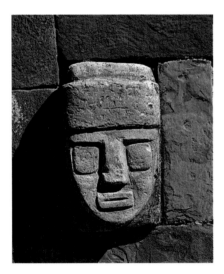

This cut-stone head is one of many adorning the walls of the Kalasasaya at Tiwanaku. Visual details such as these contributed to the awe-inspiring grandeur and sacred solidity of the compound's inner walls.

regal figure are 30 winged human-bird figures running in profile, each bearing a pair of condor staffs similar to those of the Gateway God, and 11 faces covered by sun masks. Elements of the Gateway theme are found throughout the Tiwanaku realm on sculpture, ceramics, textiles, and metalwork.

The Gateway God is an ancient deity in the Lake Titicaca Basin, for it is present at Pukará, and attendants carved in profile—similar to the 30 human-bird figures described above—are common on ceramics. The front-facing Pukará deity is also commonly depicted holding an agricultural digging stick and the lead rope of a llama, with the animal sometimes bearing packs. The Pukará deity not only symbolizes the subsistence pattern of the Pukará—based on agriculture and herding—but is also emblematic of the long-distance llama caravan trade upon which the Pukará economy was dependent.

Scholars have remarked on the similarities of the Chavín Staff God to the Gateway figure, and many believe that the Chavín deity and the components of the Chavín religion may underlie the development of the vibrant religious tradition of the Pukará and the Tiwanaku. Looking back to our discussions on the iconography at Chavín de Huántar, the latest sculpture was the front-facing Raimondi Staff God, with its elaborate headdress. Although it is not known precisely where the Raimondi Stone was erected originally, we do know that it was located in the New Temple with the Black and White Portal. The two columns of the Black and White Portal bear supernatural bird attendants, similar to those at Tiwanaku; and recently excavated columns, apparently intended to be set up at the Portal, are carved with Raimondi Stone designs. This Chavín cluster of Staff God and attendants

In an experiment to replicate ancient land-management techniques, an archaeological team reconstructed these raised agricultural fields in the Lake Titicaca Basin. Canals between the elevated fields not only contained irrigation water, but also fish, which were used for food and for fertilizer. The canal water has been found to raise the local temperature, thus protecting against frost and permitting a second annual crop.

may represent the same Staff God theme that later appears at the monolithic gateway at Tiwanaku. Just how or in what religious form the pantheon of the Staff God was introduced into the Lake Titicaca Basin is not known, but the demise of the Chavín cult occurred by 200 B.C., while the Pukará and Tiwanaku emerged early in 400 B.C., allowing 200 years for the introduction of Chavín Staff God iconography to the Lake Titicaca Basin.

The central themes of the Gateway God tableau and of its great monolithic statues are dedicated to ensuring the continued abundance of agricultural, herding, and fishing resources. It is not known what incantations the priests used to persuade the god to maintain the kingdom's economic well-being.

Rising above the plain of the city, outside the moat, is the smaller twin of the Akapana. The pyramid, known as the Puma Punku, has a base 492 feet (150 meters) square and is 16 feet (5 meters) in height. With its three terraces, usual drainage systems, and sunken summit courtyard, the Puma Punku is a late addition to the royal architecture of Tiwanaku. Erected after A.D. 600, it replaced the Akapana as the principal religious temple. The newly consecrated Puma Punku was under construction at the time that the Tiwanaku were rapidly expanding their empire. However, the city's elite central core was not abandoned, and many of the sunken temples were remodeled or built at this time, while offerings continued to be deposited at the Akapana.

The magnificent royal city of Tiwanaku was calculated to inspire awe in the commoners. Alas, the walls of the temples and the stone monolithic statues and gateways are now shorn of their gold, textiles, and painted surfaces, which for centuries had shimmered from afar in the bright sunlight.

### THE ECONOMIC KEY TO TIWANAKU CIVILIZATION

In the Lake Titicaca Basin, the Pukará and Tiwanaku engineers developed an ingenious system to bring wetlands into agricultural production. Called raised-field agriculture, this land-reclamation strategy utilized canals 16 to 30 feet (5 to 11 meters) apart and up to 656 feet (200 meters) long; the excavated soil was piled in between, creating wide planting beds. The canals supported fish and aquatic plants that were used not only as food, but also for fertilizer. Between the harvests, llama herds were brought to graze on the fields, where they deposited their natural fertilizer.

Experiments by archaeologists Clark L. Erickson and Alan Kolata have demonstrated that raised fields and their intervening water channels created a warmer localized environment. This was crucial in order to protect crops against frequent frosts, which destroy the livelihood of local farmers today on an average of once every five years. It was found that Erickson and Kolata's reconstructed water channels acted as solar collectors, raising the heat over the fields by 10° to 20° Fahrenheit (4.5° to 9° Celsius) during the day. At night, a heat envelope protected the fields from frost, which today can kill up to 90 percent of agricultural production. Erickson and Kolata found that the yields of modern fields, using dry-farming techniques (without benefit of rainfall), is 1 to 4 tons of crops, while raised fields produced up to 23 tons of food.

Raised fields require a major labor investment, which was managed by the priest-ruler elites as early as Pukará. This achievement was responsible for an agricultural revolution, and at the height of Tiwanaku more than 202,622 acres (82,000 hectares) of raised fields had been built on the northern, western, and southern edges of Lake Titicaca. In his experimental raised fields, Kolata has produced two yearly crops in a region that today only supports a single crop. Kolata estimates that in the 73.4-square-mile (190-square-kilometer) heartland of Tiwanaku, between 570,000 and 1,111,500 people could be supported by double cropping, or 285,000 to 555,570 by single cropping, if 75 percent of the raised fields were in production. This achievement is an astounding feat of engineering, for Pampa Koani, the largest of the three valleys surrounding the Tiwanaku capital, supports only 2000 farmers today! The population of the ancient Tiwanaku heartland, meanwhile, is conservatively estimated by Kolata to have been about 365,000, of whom 115,000 lived in the capital and satellite cities, with the remaining 250,000 engaged in farming, herding, and fishing.

Tiwanaku society was self-sustaining, for its agricultural, herding, and fishing resource base was more than sufficient to support the complex state administrative apparatus and the population under its control. The tremendous agricultural surplus gained from raised-field farming provided products not only for the empire, but also for the extensive commerce with its provinces.

The collapse of the Tiwanaku Empire, between A.D. 1000 and 1100, meant the end of the necessary state control for the development and maintenance of these vast reclamation and raised-field projects. Although there

Standing prominently in the central courtyard of the Kalasasaya is the monolithic statue known as the Ponce Stela, after its Bolivian discoverer. Though wind and rain erosion have left their mark on the features of the carved figure—notably on the once prominent nose—its many images are still clearly recognizable.

is some evidence that raised-field agriculture continued after Tiwanaku, it was not practiced by the local Aymara farmers when Cieza de León made his reconnaissance to Tiwanaku in 1549.

Interestingly, the archaeological research of Erickson and Kolata has led to the reestablishment of raised fields; the project has become a major program of the Peruvian and Bolivian governments to increase agricultural production in the Lake Titicaca Basin and in the Bolivian lowlands. This is a rare instance of archaeological investigation making a significant contribution (other than through archaeological tourism) to the national food-producing economies of countries under study.

## TIWANAKU SOCIETY

In the southern Lake Titicaca Basin, the Tiwanaku established the satellite sites of Oje, Khonko Wankané, Pajchiri, and Lukurmata. These and other administrative centers of fewer than 10,000 inhabitants have the characteristic terraced platforms and temples with sunken courts, thus duplicating the civic-ceremonial architecture of the capital city. Lukurmata, on the edge of the lake, is the only regional capital to have received much archaeological attention. Excavations by archaeologists Marc P. Bermann and Alan Kolata demonstrate that Lukurmata began as a small village in A.D. 1, and that by Tiwanaku III (A.D. 300 to 500), it had begun to receive the attention of rulers in the capital city. By Tiwanaku IV, Lukurmata had also become a moated city, with the distinctive temple architecture of Tiwanaku.

Just what were these bureaucratic centers administering? Certainly, some were involved in coordinating the production of lake and herding resources, but most were responsible for the management of labor forces necessary to turn vast tracts of wetlands into productive agricultural fields—the most productive ever constructed in the Central Andes. These gigantic earthmoving projects reshaped the landscape of the Tiwanaku heartland, including the construction of causeways and dikes. The causeways, or raised roadbeds, crossed the raised fields to transport agricultural surplus to the administrative centers; from there, they were further transported for use in the extensive trade exchange network of the Tiwanaku Empire. In the Pampa Koani Valley, a 7.5-mile (12-kilometer) section of the Catari River was straightened by erecting levees of earth and cut stone; flooding was thus controlled, and new areas opened for raised-field agriculture. Irrigation canals brought water to the fields, and aqueducts funneled mountain water to sustain the raised fields during periods of drought.

Little is known of the royalty of Tiwanaku—nor of the hundreds of thousands of subjects under their rule. One illuminating find occurred in the capital city, in a palace adjacent to the Putuni platform, with red-orange, blue, and green adobe walls placed on a cut-stone block foundation. In the courtyard of the palace, shaft tombs were found in each corner, only one of which was undisturbed; it held the body of an elite woman, probably once wrapped in exquisite Tiwanaku textiles that disintegrated long ago. Her wealth consisted of copper bracelets, a collar of precious lapis lazuli, turquoise, and other exotic tubular stone beads, a miniature gold mask, and a separate offering of gold pins, a copper mirror, and a unique, long-necked lead flask.

In the Kalasasaya, investigators have found portraits of individual rulers and possible royal tombs, but no royal tombs comparable to those at Sipán have yet been located. More extensive research at the looted capital and in the satellite cities may reveal the opulence of the ruling class; however, the elite burials in the Akapana do not have the wealth one associates with royalty. Tiwanaku gold artifacts are not plentiful in comparison with those of the Moche, but as we have observed with the Paracas and Nasca cultures, it was spectacular textiles that were the emblems of wealth and power. Examples of Tiwanaku weaving art are rare in the highlands, yet on the desert coast, remarkable imported textiles are preserved. Tunics, hats, bags, belts, and mantles with the complex imagery of the Gateway of the Sun were woven in many colors from llama and alpaca wool and from cotton. Overall, the personal trappings of the nobles of Tiwanaku are comprised of spectacular textiles, polychrome ceramics, and rare gold masks.

### THE SPREAD OF THE EMPIRE

After consolidating their domination over the southern valleys of the Lake Titicaca Basin, the Tiwanaku began to conquer their neighbors. Sometime between A.D. 400 and 500, the Tiwanaku rulers brought the western and northern side of Lake Titicaca into their sphere of control. In those newly conquered areas, they established the administrative centers that brought the state architecture and the religion of the Staff God to the subjugated populace. By A.D. 600, Tiwanaku control had been extended eastward to the Cochabamba Valley in Bolivia, northward into the Moquegua Valley of southern Peru, and southward into the Andes and coastal valleys of northern Chile.

Tiwanaku's spread into the Cochabamba Valley on the eastern slopes of the Andes was motivated by a desire to bring maize-producing lands into their economic systems. As mentioned earlier, maize beer was and is an important beverage in the Andes; even today, it features as payment in regional labor exchange and in rituals. It is not clear whether the Tiwanaku went so far as to colonize the eastern slope valleys of the Cochabamba, or merely gained access to the valley's crops and goods through the llama caravan trade network.

We do know that the Tiwanaku did colonize the Moquegua Valley on the coast of southern Peru, 186 miles (300 kilometers) from the Titicaca Basin. Archaeologist Paul Goldstein's excavations at Omo in the central Moquegua Valley revealed the largest Tiwanaku settlement outside of Bolivia, consisting of 94 acres (38 hectares) of residences, cemeteries, and an adobe temple with three walled courts in the architectural style of Tiwanaku.

Molded from clay and richly adorned with painted images, this cylindrical *kero*, or ritual drinking cup, represents a widely used design. The flared ends and the raised center band are elements found in keros throughout the Tiwanaku area. Commonly used for the drinking of maize beer, or *chicha*, cups such as this accompanied religious and political ritual.

Although Omo was colonized by A.D. 500 (Tiwanaku IV), it was not until after A.D. 700 (Tiwanaku V) that Omo became a prominent Tiwanaku civic-ceremonial center. The local and imported ceramics and textiles display the Gateway God and the pantheon of Tiwanaku iconography. The establishment of a satellite city in Moquegua gave the Tiwanaku outright control over the area, allowing access not only to coastal resources, but also to maize, cotton, coca, and other crops not available in the windswept Titicaca Basin. The Tiwanaku master hydraulic engineers created an elaborate irrigation system to increase agricultural production, the surpluses being sent by llama caravans to the Tiwanaku heartland.

In the northern coastal valleys and in highland oases of Chile, thousands of tombs with Tiwanaku high-status textiles and ceramics reflect the local elite's participation in the extensive network of trade by llama caravan. From Lake Poopó, 311 miles (500 kilometers) south of Tiwanaku, the caravans carried basalt (volcanic stone) for the manufacture of heavy tools, such as hoes and mauls. Along the Chilean coast and in highland areas, foodstuffs were traded, and lapis lazuli and other precious stones were secured for the Tiwanaku rulers. There is increasing evidence that areas of northern Chile were colonized by the Tiwanaku, for in the San Pedro Atacama oasis in the Chilean desert highlands, a local cemetery with Tiwanaku elite tombs has produced spectacular textiles and ceramics. It is not clear whether this strong Tiwanaku presence merely represents Tiwanaku traders or actual colonization and domination of the local populace.

The period of colonization and/or extensive trade interaction is not well dated, but by A.D. 600 to 700, the Tiwanaku had spread their economic net over much of the southern Andes. Was there any economic impetus for its branching out of its heartland? The answer appears to be yes. The Great Drought that had disastrous consequences for the Moche State and the chiefdoms of the Nasca must have raised havoc with the raised-field agricultural system around A.D. 600. Accordingly, the Quelccaya Ice Cap shows a marked decrease in agricultural activity (evidenced by minimal dust accumulation in the core after A.D. 620) as rainfall dropped in the southern Andes at the onset of the Great Drought. It is at this time that the Tiwanaku initiated colonization and intensive trade interaction with distant regions. Thus the Tiwanaku were motivated to seek new sources of foodstuffs; at stake was the survival of hundreds of thousands of subjects suffering from this natural disaster.

It has also recently been shown by Alan Kolata and hydraulic engineer Charles Ortloff that a second drought followed another peak of Tiwanaku agricultural activity in the Titicaca Basin after A.D. 1000. This drought signaled the death knell of the Tiwanaku Empire, which collapsed between A.D. 1000 and 1100.

With the collapse, stiff competition for the shrinking agricultural lands resulted in strife throughout the southern Andes, where fortified settlements appeared for the first time. It was not for another 400 years that the Tiwanaku

The ruined capital of the Huari Empire is situated on a hilly plateau in the southern Peruvian Andes, north of the modern city of Ayacucho. With its origins as a small farming village, Huari grew by stages into a complex city with distinct ceremonial and residential sectors. Much of the urban core was terraced to create habitable areas that were then subdivided into separate irregular sections.

heartland would again be controlled by a number of local kingdoms for a short period before the Inca conquered the region.

### THE HUARI EMPIRE

In 1896, when Max Uhle excavated at the great oracle center of Pachacamac, he discovered ceramics and textiles displaying the Staff God; he immediately made the connection between the Gateway God of Tiwanaku and this distant site on the coast, labeling this culture Coastal Tiahuanaco (Tiwanaku). Since the art style was not exactly like that of Tiwanaku, some scholars wondered if there was another, yet undiscovered, site from which Coastal Tihuanaco had emanated. In 1548, Cieza de León had traveled past a candidate for just such a site in the Ayacucho Basin of the southern Peruvian Andes. Discovered again in 1931 by Julio C. Tello, the site turned out to be the enormous urban center of Huari (also called Wari), 15.5 miles (25 kilometers) north of the modern city of Ayacucho. But it was not until the excavations of Wendell C. Bennett in 1950 that Huari was firmly established as the main center for the dissemination of a Tiwanaku-like ceramic and textile art style throughout the coast and highlands of Peru.

In 1964, archaeologist Dorothy Menzel's tour de force analysis of Huari ceramics from many sites allowed her to follow the development of the Huari Empire in the Ayacucho Basin, its expansion northward to Cajamarca, and its eventual collapse—all in just 200 years. Menzel divided the Middle Horizon into four epochs, with the first two separated into 1A (A.D. 600 to 650), 1B (A.D. 650 to 700), 2A (A.D. 700 to 750), and 2B (A.D. 750 to 800).

In the 1970s and 1980s, the Huari capital received the attention of archaeologists Luis G. Lumbreras and William Isbell and their colleagues, who revealed that the urban core of Huari had covered an area of 741 acres (300 hectares), and the inhabited urban area 3707 acres (1500 hectares). In the early stages of its growth from a small farming village, Huari developed into a city with ceremonial and residential sectors distinguished by their unique patio architecture; the patio spaces were bordered by three or four long, multistoried buildings grouped into large walled enclosures. Although some cut-and-polished stone was used, most of the walls—generally over 20 feet (6 meters) in height—were constructed of irregular stones.

By 1A, the small village had gained city status with its monumental architecture and large population, and by 1B an urban grid was evident, with the towering walls intersected by streets. The city had a subterranean water channel system to drain rainwater and bring water to the inhabitants. A number of

The weaving style known as tapestry was frequently employed during the Huari period, and involved the use of cotton for the warp and camelid-fiber for the weft. It was well suited to designs with complex imagery such as the blue condor on this Huari or Tiwanaku panel.

spectacular chambers of dressed (cut and polished) basalt in the Cheqo Wasi sector of the city may have been the mausoleums of Huari rulers. With the establishment of the capital, many of the surrounding Early Intermediate farming and herding towns, villages, and hamlets were abandoned as their populations were drawn into the capital city and its satellite administrative centers.

### ORIGIN AND SPREAD OF HUARI

At the Huari pottery-making center of Conchapata, near Ayacucho, investigators have found huge offerings of smashed oversized urns; similarly, three tons of oversized urns—broken into sherds—were found at Pacheco in the Nazca Valley by Tello in 1927. Significantly, the urns at both locations originally bore polychrome paintings of the Tiwanaku Gateway or Staff God and his attendants. There is no doubt that the Staff God was disseminated from the Lake Titicaca Basin, 435 miles (700 kilometers) away, into the Ayacucho Basin of southern Peru. But the absence of architecture typical of the Tiwanaku capital—monolithic stone statues, gateways, terraced pyramid platforms with rectangular sunken courts—clearly indicates that the Tiwanaku rulers did not impose their rule over the Ayacucho Basin. What is puzzling is just how the Tiwanaku Staff God was introduced to these other areas.

The God of the oversized urns was transformed by the Huari into an agricultural god, who, instead of holding weapons of war, has corn plants in its hand and on the rays of its headdress. The Pukará Staff God also had agrarian overtones, and it has been speculated that the Huari iconography may have been introduced to the region by the Pukará. Admittedly, there is scant evidence for Pukará in the area, but Pukará ceramics have recently been found in the Moquegua Valley, just 373 miles (600 kilometers) to the south of the Ayacucho Basin.

But the sudden appearance of the Tiwanaku Staff God at Conchapata and at Huari may, in fact, be due to the expansion of the Tiwanaku Empire out of its heartland during the Great Drought of circa A.D. 600. In some unknown manner, the Tiwanaku religion was introduced to Ayacucho, sparking the rise of an independent state—Huari—that quickly consolidated the surrounding valleys and began its own rapid expansion.

Archaeologist Katharina J. Schrieber's research in the nearby Carhuarazo Valley provides a clear picture of how the Huari rulers reshaped the local economy. Before the Huari invasion, the valley had six villages between 2.5 and 5 acres (1 and 2 hectares), each inhabited by farmers and herders concentrating on highland tuber crops, llamas, and alpacas for their livelihood. These villages were situated at between 10,824 and 11,808 feet (3300 and 3600 meters), but when the Huari imposed their administration on the valley, they immediately moved the population down into new villages in the quechua environmental zone, at 9840 to 11,000 feet (3000 to 3300 meters), where maize cultivation could be maximized. In addition to building administrative centers in the Huari architectural style at Jincamocco and three other locations, the new lords expended great energy in the construction of massive terraced agricultural systems. With the shift to maize agriculture from highland tuber crops, the population of the valley suddenly found itself caught up in the ever-expanding Huari political and economic system, with its great predilection for maize, both as food and in beer, for labor exchange and ritual offerings.

The rapid expansion of the Huari out of the Ayacucho Basin in epoch 2 was also partly in response to the deteriorating climatic conditions brought on by the Great Drought that occurred about A.D. 600. As they swept throughout the Peruvian highlands, the Huari emphasized the step terracing of the steep hillsides, which could be irrigated from higher altitudes. It is unclear whether they conquered distant groups by force of arms or peacefully inserted their powerful presence in the provinces, there to control the road systems—over which trade and commerce flowed throughout the empire—and also food production. The erection of administrative centers followed the rigid patio-system enclosure and the cellular architectural system of the Imperial Huari.

In the Cuzco Valley, the largest Huari provincial administrative center was Pikillacta. Archaeologist Gordon McEwan has recently concluded that this great site was not a storage center, but functioned as a ceremonial and residential center holding the provincial governors, administrators, and frontier garrisons. Pikillacta covers an area of .8 square mile (2 square kilometers), including llama corrals, and was comparable in size to the core of the later Inca Imperial capital in Cuzco. Pikillacta and other Huari centers and garrisons in the Cuzco region were strategically located not only to control communication routes, but also to defend their southern frontier from possible intrusions by the Tiwanaku Empire.

To the immediate north, there are a series of Huari administrative centers connected by 560 miles (900 kilometers) of road systems along the backbone of the Andes. And in the far north was erected the second-largest provincial Huari site: Viracochapampa. Here the Huari had moved into a region that was

Four-cornered tasseled hats were worn by both the Huari and Tiwanaku elite. This Huari hat with avian motif is woven with a warp of knotted cotton, with colored threads of camelid fiber looped and cut to form pile.

The steep cliffs of Cerro Baúl (Trunk Mountain) rise from the Moquegua Valley, an area once dominated by the Tiwanaku. The Huari moved into the valley by force, building a stronghold atop the mesa. At 1968 feet (600 meters) above its base, and with a well-defended path leading to the summit, this center ensured Huari control over the region.

already under the control of the Huamachuco State, with its 1-square-mile (2.5-square-kilometer) capital Marca-Huamachuco. Excavations by archaeologists John R. Topic and Theresa Lange Topic at Viracochapampa—a typical Huari enclosure center—suggests that the Huari did not subjugate the local populace, but that they did control the trade farther to the north in Ecuador. Although Viracochapampa was never completed, the Topics estimate that 580 people could have built this Huari site in less than two years, certainly not a great burden on the local populace. Just how the Huari interacted with the Huamachuco State is not known, though it is known that this local state remained in power upon the retreat of the Huari from the region.

The only evidence of expansion by military force comes from the Moquegua Valley, where the Huari encountered the well-established Tiwanaku colonies at Omo. Twelve miles (20 kilometers) upstream from Omo, the Huari built a multistoried center on the top of Cerro Baúl (Trunk Mountain). Cerro Baúl is an impressive mesa rising 1968 feet (600 meters) from the valley floor, a location that made it an ideal Huari fortification. Even the one steep path to this "Masada of the Andes" (referring to Masada in Israel, where Jewish Zealots held out against Roman forces) was fortified. There were also fortified Huari towns in the upper Moquegua Valley. Recent investigations by archaeologists Michael E. Moseley and Robert A. Feldman have demonstrated that when the Huari intruded into this Tiwanaku-dominated valley, the Tiwanaku pulled out, only to return later, by A.D. 700, when the Huari abandoned their heavily fortified zone around Cerro Baúl. At this time the Tiwanaku arrived in Omo in greater strength, and set up a strong ceremonial-civic center.

The city of Pikillacta was the largest and southernmost of the highland Huari centers. The site was home to provincial officials and also served as a frontier garrison. As well as controlling communication routes, Pikillacta was also useful in defending the Huari from attack by the powerful Tiwanaku Empire. With an area of .8 square mile (2 square kilometers), the city was roughly the same size as the later Inca imperial capital, Cuzco. Some of the walls of Pikillacta, traces of which can be seen in this photograph, stood up to 33 feet (10 meters) in height.

The Huari intrusions to the coast did not lead to the installation of their distinctive administrative centers, for the coastal valleys had already been fully exploited for their agricultural potential by valley-wide irrigation systems. The main impact of the Huari religion was on the coastal valleys from the Chillón Valley to the Nazca region, an area that could easily be reached from the Huari heartland via the network of highland-coastal roads. Farther to the north, in the Moche heartland, there is no extensive evidence of Huari penetration, even though the adjacent highlands did have a Huari presence. Still, this nearby force was known to the Moche, for ceramics with distinctly Huari designs are to be found scattered between the Casma and Lambayeque valleys.

The Huari Empire had collapsed by A.D. 800 at the close of epoch 2B, possibly having overstretched its ability to dominate local tribes, chiefdoms, and states. In the Carhuarazo Valley, Huari sites were abandoned as the population moved into fortified villages and towns, a sign of increasing strife.

Shortly thereafter, around A.D. 1000-1100, as we have seen, an appalling drought ended the Tiwanaku Empire. With the demise of Tiwanaku, the Staff God and its retinue disappear from the archaeological record. However, it is important to remember that for around 2000 years the deity had been a religious focus of the Chavín, Tiwanaku, and Huari civilizations. Out of the power vacuum left by the fall of the Tiwanaku and Huari empires, there arose two new forces in the Late Intermediate Period: the Chimú Empire of the Peruvian north coast and the powerful Inca of the Cuzco Basin. One of them was destined to become the greatest empire in the Americas in the Late Horizon.

The Chimú carried on the metalworking tradition of the Moche, smelting metals in small furnaces by blowing on hot coals through long tubes. the metal into fine sheets, from which animal and human ornaments, such as this gold and turquoise mask, were created in low relief.

Stone hammers were used to flatten and smooth

# EMPIRES IN COLLISION

The archaeological record of the last 12,000 years is finally joined, during the Late Intermediate Period (A.D. 1100 to 1470), by the written record of Spanish chroniclers, who not only compiled the history of the Inca Empire but went on to record the tantalizing oral traditions of their predecessors on the Peruvian north coast. For the first time, we are introduced to the kings and nobles by name, and their deeds bring us insights into two of the New World's greatest civilizations: the Chimú and the Inca.

The portrayal of the Sicán Lord, with his distinctive headdress, is a central theme in Sicán art. Both the gold *tumi* (ceremonial knife) shown at right, and the camelid-fiber tapestry fragment below, incorporate this image.

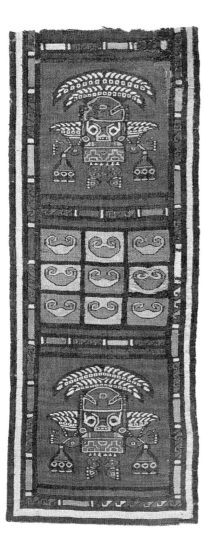

Upon the collapse of the Tiwanaku Empire, the Dark Ages enveloped the Lake Titicaca Basin, but on the north coast of Peru a number of local states emerged from the ruins of the Moche State. After the fall of the Moche, which was laid low in large part because of the Great Drought of about A.D. 600 and recurrent El Niño floods, the Sicán State arose in the Lambayeque Valley, while in the Moche Valley the Chimú rose to power, destined ultimately to dominate more than 621 miles (1000 kilometers) of the coast.

## NAYMLAP AND THE SICÁN LORD

The north coast of Peru is blessed with more than two-thirds of the country's irrigable floodplain and intervalley plains, and today supports more than 50 percent of the population on the coast. There, in one of the most productive valleys of the Lambayeque region—the Leche—the successors of the late Moche at Pampa Grande built their new capital at Batán Grande. Between A.D. 900 and 1100 the city comprised 17 truncated pyramids, plazas, palaces, and residential areas, covering 1.5 square miles (4 square kilometers). Batán Grande was to become one of the great metallurgical centers in the Central Andes, producing in its smelters tons of copper for consumption by the state and for long-distance trade with Ecuador and other parts of Peru. The Sicán lords also directed the expansion of the valley-wide irrigation systems, which included the construction of huge intervalley canals to bring water from one valley to another. Ceramics were mass-produced in molds, and the dominant motif was a personage with a square to trapezoidal face and "comma" eyes, known as the Sicán Lord (or the Tin Woodman, of *The Wizard of Oz* fame), flanked by either animal or human attendants.

Who was the Sicán Lord? Although the oral history of Sicán is fragmentary, the legend of Naymlap provides a fascinating account of the establishment of the Sicán State. Recorded by Miguel Cabello de Balboa in 1586, the story related that the Lambayeque Valley was invaded by a warrior called Naymlap, whose forces came on a fleet of balsa rafts. Naymlap was accompanied by his wife Ceterni and 40 officials, including eight chief attendants who took care of his every desire. Naymlap and his retinue established their capital at Chot, and there they set up a green stone idol to be revered by all. Upon his death, Naymlap's son Cium assumed the leadership of the kingdom, and he was succeeded by nine rulers until Fempellec took power. Fempellec attempted unsuccessfully to move the green stone idol. This sacrilege, followed by his seduction by the devil in the form of a woman, angered the gods; they brought down upon the hapless population 30 days of rain and flooding followed by a year of famine. In order to appease the gods, the priests and nobles tied Fempellec up and cast him into the sea. But this did not save the kingdom.

Although some investigators feel this is an entirely apocryphal legend, there is archaeological evidence to support the events in the Naymlap tale. Christopher B. Donnan has excavated at the pyramid and palace of Chotuna 2.5 miles (4 kilometers) from the ocean in the lower Lambayeque Valley, and has concluded that this was the site that the legendary Naymlap founded. Donnan dates the invasion to circa A.D. 750 and the end of the Naymlap Dynasty to A.D. 1100, leaving 350 years of rule by 11 kings. There is abundant evidence for massive flooding at Chotuna, Batán Grande, and other sites in the Lambayeque region dated to A.D. 1100. At that time, Chotuna was abandoned and the Naymlap dynasty came to an end as Batán Grande was deliberately burned and the capital was transferred to Túcume in the Leche Valley, where the Sicán constructed the gargantuan linear pyramid of Huaca Larga, or Long Pyramid. (*Huaca* is variously translated as "mound," "pyramid," or "shrine".) Within 250 years, the reorganized Sicán State fell to invaders from the south.

At the Sicán capital of Túcume, in the Leche Valley, stands the greatest complex of monumental adobe structures in the Americas. The capital of the Sicán State was transferred here sometime after A.D. 1100. Túcume's builders used the hill of La Raya as a natural focus for a complex of at least 26 adobe pyramids, a number of which are visible in this aerial photograph. At far right, the remnants of the massive linear pyramid known as Huaca Larga (Long Pyramid) extend into the base of the hill.

### THE CHIMÚ EMPIRE

The Sicán State was conquered by the Chimú, who expanded out of the Moche Valley, 124 miles (200 kilometers) to the south. The Chimú were centered at Chan Chan, a city founded on the coast when Galindo was abandoned at the end of the Moche State. Chan Chan rapidly developed into one of the great capitals of the Americas. The first of the grand walled palaces, or *ciudadelas* (little cities), was built by A.D. 900. By the time the Inca conquered the Chimú in the A.D. 1470s, Chan Chan had grown into an imperial capital with pyramids, nobles' estates, 10 ciudadelas, and thousands of residences of specialized craftsmen producing textiles and metals for the state. The population at its height is estimated at 26,000 artisans—both men and women—the Chimú king and nobles, and 3000 retainers supporting the elite.

Since Chan Chan has been investigated by a number of archaeologists, some of the ciudadelas bear the names of prominent figures in Peruvian archaeology, such as Rivero, Tschudi, Squier, Uhle, Bandelier, and Tello. The city encompasses an area of 7.7 square miles (20 square kilometers), with the core of 10 palaces covering 2.3 square miles (6 square kilometers). The city of Chan Chan and the organization of the Chimú State in the

Moche Valley was extensively researched by Michael E. Moseley and his colleagues between 1969 and 1974, the first large multidisciplinary research project since the Virú Valley program of the 1940s.

The early ciudadelas have quite diverse interior partitioning, but the last six were all built according to a rigid architectural plan. By circa A.D. 1100 to 1200, all palaces were rectangular, high-walled constructions, divided into three sections. Entering at the north end of the 30-foot-high (9-meter-high) walled compound, the visitor was ushered via corridors into a large courtyard decorated with friezes of maritime scenes. After stating his or her business, the visitor was directed to the first section, comprised of around 10 U-shaped *audiencias* (audience rooms). There, administrators dealt with matters of the state, such as management of the irrigation system, labor taxation, trade and commerce, and military matters. In the second section, at the center of the ciudadela, were rows of storerooms, sunken wells, and the palaces of the Chimú kings. The third section is assumed to have been used by retainers in support activities (food preparation, for example) to maintain the elaborate administrative and palace complex.

In either the central or the third sections were built the once-magnificent flattopped platform mausoleums of the Chimú kings. All the tombs were plundered by the Spanish, but the excavation of the small detached burial platform of Las Avispas revealed a T-shaped central tomb surrounded by 25 deep cells. The splendor of the noble burial platform in Las Avispas, associated with Ciudadela Laberinto (labyrinth), must have rivaled that of the Sipán rulers, but only fragmentary evidence remains of the ceremonial burial of this elite personage. To the surprise of the excavators, the cells held the bodies of women stacked like cordwood. An estimated 300 sacrificial victims of between 17 and 24 years of age had been dispatched to serve the noble in his afterlife. Little is known of the contents of the tombs themselves, since the Spanish authorities granted mining contracts on the resting places of the Chimú kings and nobles, but they must have been sumptuous beyond belief.

Outside the ciudadelas there were 30 multiroomed residences of nobles and thousands of houses and workshops arranged haphazardly in four *barrios*, or residential sections. In the ciudadelas and throughout the city, 125 walk-in wells tapped the water table upon which the city's inhabitants were so dependent.

The overriding emphasis of the craft production was metal objects and textiles, commodities of wealth to confirm the status of the elite and to exchange through the long-distance trade system of the Chimú. The city accommodated the traveling herders and their llamas in two caravansaries, which combined the services of an inn and a livery stable. The storage areas in the ciudadelas were used to house foreign wealth and distribute commodities to and from the provinces, either by llama caravans or by seagoing rafts. The total storage capacity of all the Chimú administrative centers in the provinces could be contained in the warehouses of just one of the late ciudadelas at Chan Chan; but even the

The sprawling Chimú capital city of Chan Chan features at least 10 walled palaces, or *ciudadelas*. A number of these compounds are visible in this 1929 aerial photograph. As well as the ciudadelas, Chan Chan also contained thousands of residences for the artisans who produced textiles and metalwork for the Chimú State. The city's extensive system of sunken fields utilized sub-surface water to grow food for the population, as well as totora reeds for boatbuilding.

Archaeologists working at Chan Chan have reconstructed portions of the mud friezes featuring birds or geometric motifs that originally covered the interior walls of the ciudadelas.

latter pale in comparison with the subsequent Inca storehouses: one Inca administrative center could hold the combined wealth of the Chimú State.

The agricultural economy was supported by the most extensive irrigation network ever developed in the Moche Valley. Outstripping the irrigation systems of the Moche—as well as those used today—the Chimú built on a grand scale. By running their main canals farther into the desert, they were able to farm large areas of the desert north of the capital; yet even then they were not content with their valley-wide irrigation works. The Chimú engineers and surveyors laid out the Chicama-Moche canal to bring water from the Chicama River to the agricultural fields on the north side of the Moche Valley, possibly as a response to the Great Drought of circa A.D. 1000-1100 and the need to access distant water sources. This canal was several yards wide, and skirted the foothills of the valley for 33.5 miles (54 kilometers) to connect with Vichcansao, the northermost Chimú canal. For a portion of that distance, the water passed through an aqueduct 98 feet (30 meters) high. But to the dismay of the canal engineers, this incredible construction project never carried water—for in certain sections the canal ran uphill! Either the engineers had miscalculated or the area's frequent earthquakes had slightly tilted the coast, rendering the canal useless.

### THE SPREAD OF THE CHIMÚ EMPIRE

As with the Sicán, we are faced with a legend for the founding of the Chimú Dynasty. Recorded in the *Anonymous History of Trujillo* (1604), this

legend is once again based on archaeological fact. Also, as in the Sicán legend, this tale brings a ruler by balsa raft; the ruler, Taycanamo, is said to have been sent from over the sea to take possession of the Moche Valley. His son took control of the Lower Moche Valley, and his grandson, Ñançenpinco, initiated the first wave of military expansion, subjugating the coast between the Santa River in the south and the Jequetepeque Valley in the north. Another source, written in 1638, relates that Ñançenpinco's general, Pacatnamú, was responsible for capturing the Jequetepeque Valley and was rewarded for his military exploits by being appointed its governor. Six or seven rulers followed Ñançenpinco, and the last king, Minchançaman, sent his forces north and south of the established frontiers in a second wave of expansion.

Until recently, the legendary Taycanamo Dynasty of nine or ten kings was used to intepret the layout of the city of Chan Chan, with each ciudadela sequentially constructed to house the palace and administrators of a new Chimú king. But a more recent analysis of the ciudadelas and the location of the burial platform has led archaeologist Raffael Cavallaro to a new conclusion: he sees the ciudadelas as representing a dual political organization, with a primary king and secondary lords. The western line of smaller ciudadelas had neither burial platforms nor the mausoleums but they were later incorporated into the ciudadelas; the eastern ciudadelas, on the other hand, are larger, and comprise burial platforms built within the compound. This implies that the eastern palaces were the residences of the Chimú king, who, through the great wealth of the kingdom, was assured a state burial with the entombment of sacrificial victims and untold riches. The powerful leading noble in the western ciudadela did not have the state resources to plan a mausoleum, and only later when he had accrued enough wealth was he able to build a small tomb. At any one time two of the ciudadelas would have been occupied, one by the Chimú king and the other by a ranking noble of the second most powerful lineage in the kingdom. Thus the original interpretation of the construction of a new palace for each of the 10 Chimú kings is now transformed into five paired compounds, reflecting the dual political system of the Chimú.

Even though the list of kings according to the Taycanamo legend does not correlate with the architectural plan of Chan Chan, the two-stage expansion of the empire is firmly grounded in the archaeological record. After he had consolidated the Moche Valley, General Pacatnamú was then ordered by Ñançenpinco to attack the northern valleys to Jequetepeque. The Jequetepeque Valley is 75 miles (120 kilometers) north of Chan Chan, and, according to the research of archaeologist Geoffrey Conrad, Pacatnamú—now Governor—built his palace and administrative center at Farfán, the largest site in the valley. One of the six Farfán compounds is a palace similar to those at Chan Chan, and a rare burial platform at this Chimú provincial administrative center speaks of the power and prestige of Pacatnamú.

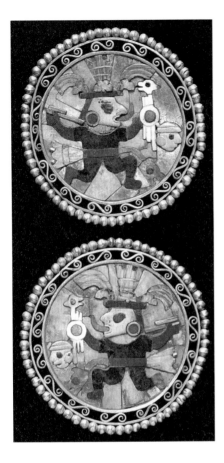

The incorporation of the Sicán State meant that the skills of the Sicán craftsmen were harnessed to the production of high-status goods for the Chimú elite. Artifacts such as the gold-and-turquoise tumbler shown on the opposite page and the gold, lapis, and turquoise earspools shown above reflect this increase in the production of luxury goods.

As in the north, the military push southward to the Chao Valley met with stiff resistance, inspiring masterly sieges on the part of the Chimú tacticians and the construction of garrisoned forts to protect territories already conquered. The first wave of expansion came on the heels of the A.D. 1000-1100 El Niño, which struck the north coast with great ferocity. As we have seen, the Sicán capital of Batán Grande was burned and abandoned at the time of the legendary Fempellec flood. This flood, recorded in the Quelccaya ice core as well as in flood deposits at sites throughout the coast, may have been the major factor in instigating the Chimú invasion of weakened neighboring societies. The irrigation canals of the Chimú in the Moche Valley had been devastated, leaving the king one alternative if he wished to maintain his kingdom: the incorporation of new agricultural lands in the valleys to the north and south. Now, after generations of constant military action, the Chimú rapidly spread farther north and south.

The second wave of expansion extended the Chimú frontiers southward to the Chillón Valley, near Lima, and led to the conquest of the Late Sicán State in the Lambayeque region by A.D. 1350. In the southern Casma Valley, Manchán gained the status of a regional capital, as did Farfán in the Jequetepeque Valley, for the empire was overstretching its abilities to control distant provinces from the imperial city at Chan Chan. Once the Late Sicán capital at Túcume had been captured, the Chimú lords soon realized the importance of the vast metallurgical abilities of the Sicán; they promptly sent 5000 captured metalsmiths to Chan Chan. The final push northward, to Tumbez, resulted in the construction of an administrative base at that site—which in less than 125 years would be the first temple center captured by Francisco Pizarro in his quest for the riches of the Inca Empire.

## THE CHIMÚ MARINERS

These waves of expansion caused explosive growth at the city of Chan Chan. The storage capacities of the later ciudadelas were greatly enlarged to receive the wealth of the newly conquered territories. The victorious armies and the incorporation of valley after valley into the kingdom brought incredible wealth to the capital, enriching not only the king, but also the high-ranking nobles who were now in a position to be buried in newly constructed burial platforms in the western line of ciudadelas.

The armies moved by means of an elaborate road system connecting the coastal valleys into a single communication network—the same system that funneled tax revenues and wealth from this far-flung empire to the imperial capital of Chan Chan. The Chimú were not only a land-based military power, but also a naval force to be reckoned with. Communication and trade by large rafts gave the Chimú military the ability to invade by sea, as is clearly evident in the Naymlap and Taycanamo narratives.

There was increased commerce not only with the central coast of Peru, where Sicán pots have been found at Pachacamac, but also with Ecuador,

Central America, and western Mexico. The precious metals of the Sicán and Chimú were exchanged for Ecuadorian *Spondylus*—which, according to legend, an official of Naymlap's, known as Fonga Sigde, had crushed into dust and cast before his king in processions. The amounts of sacred *Spondylus* exchanged were enormous, requiring careful distribution of the prized resource by the Sicán and Chimú. Archaeologist Alana Cordy-Collins has identified scenes—embossed on metal objects such as earspools, disks, and cylinders, woven into textiles, and inlaid on wooden bowls—that depict people on balsa-log rafts with tethered divers working to retrieve *Spondylus*. This in itself was no mean feat, as the mollusk is found between 60 feet (18 meters) and 165 feet (50 meters) deep. Such scenes indicate that even before the Chimú conquest of Sicán, the Sicán State was involved in extensive trade with Ecuador, by land or by sea.

The idea of a maritime commercial tradition is difficult to support without the actual evidence of watercraft; fortunately, the fine-line drawings on Late Moche pottery depict reed rafts carrying cargo. The maritime theme also festoons the interior walls of the Chan Chan ciudadelas. The location of the imperial capital on the coast, then, may well have been situated to control the coastal mercantile trade. Chan Chan's extensive sunken gardens (agricultural fields dug to reach subsurface water) would have supplied *totora* reed for rafts, and it is not far-fetched to conceive of Chimú "shipyards" stretching along the beaches in front of the capital. As for concrete evidence of balsa constructions, a small, five-log balsa raft has recently been found at Chan Chan. The balsa logs for such rafts would have had to be procured from Ecuador.

There are few harbors on the Peruvian coast, but the technique of landing and launching rafts through the surf allowed skilled boatmen to approach any beachline. None of the depicted rafts is equipped with sails, but toy balsa rafts with sails have turned up in graves of the Chiribaya culture, in southern Peru. Pizarro's pilot, Bartolomé Ruiz, encountered a balsa cargo raft with triangular sails carrying 20 people on a trading expedition near the Equator, confirming the use of sails to travel against ocean currents. On board the trade raft were silver and gold crowns, jewelry, beautiful textiles, and other precious items that according to Ruiz were intended to be exchanged for *Spondylus*.

It is well known that there was a seafaring nation on Puná Island, off the coast of Ecuador; and Chincha, on the Peruvian south coast, was a powerful maritime power in the later Inca period. At Batán Grande, the few elite shaft tombs that have been discovered held enormous quantities of copper, in addition to gold and silver necklaces, masks, and artifacts inlaid with emeralds that could only have come from faraway Colombia. In a shaft tomb at Huaca Loro (Parrot Mound) at Batán Grande, archaeologist Izumi Shimada recently excavated over a ton of metal artifacts.

The maritime traffic northward must have been extensive, for it is at this time (A.D. 800 to 1200) that metallurgy is first introduced to Mexico from Ecuador or northern Peru by trading rafts. It was also at this time that the

Balsa-log rafts drawn up on the beach near the village of Ñuro, on Peru's northern coast, are a reminder of the great seagoing rafts used by the Chimú in coastal mercantile trading. These rafts are used on inshore fishing grounds that are inaccessible to larger boats.

PREVIOUS PAGE: The Chimú State controlled a thriving maritime trading network. Aboard large balsa rafts powered by sail, traders may have voyaged as far north as Mexico. This seagoing capability also enabled the Chimú to convey military forces to trouble spots along the coast. In this illustration, boatmen straddling totora-reed floats known as *caballitas* (little horses) meet a loaded raft as it approaches Chan Chan.

Mexican hairless dog was introduced to Peru. On the Galápagos Islands, 650 miles (1050 kilometers) off the Ecuador coast, the 1953 Norwegian expedition led by Thor Heyerdahl found Chimú ceramics left by these intrepid mariners. In Costa Rica, jade llama heads and ceramic vessels in the form of llamas (which are not indigenous to that country) with packs on their backs have been found. The realistic Costa Rican llama carvings and pottery vessels, coming to light so far from the northern range of llama territory, implies that the artists had actually seen these camelids, probably on a southward trading voyage from Central America. It is also intriguing that the native South American sweet potato was somehow introduced to the Cook Islands in central Polynesia by A.D. 1000, possibly by a cargo raft blown off course.

## THE INCA

For 500 years, two regions at the opposite ends of the Central Andes were the principal foci of highly productive agricultural economies, each supporting a dense population. The north coast witnessed the rise and fall of the Moche and Chimú states, while the Lake Titicaca Basin and Ayacucho saw the expansion and contraction of the Tiwanaku and Huari empires. But at the same time that the Chimú were establishing their imperial capital at Chan Chan, momentous events were occurring in the Cuzco Basin—events that would cast an ominous shadow over the Central Andes.

After Tiwanaku fell to the Great Drought of circa A.D. 1000-1100, urban civilization disappeared. Fortified villages appeared in this troubled land as diverse ethnic groups scrambled to gain access to shrinking resources. Population decreased markedly as the state-controlled, raised-field systems were abandoned, and before long the vast territory of the Tiwanaku Empire reverted to a multitude of competing and squabbling societies. Four hundred years later, in the Lake Titicaca Basin, there arose a number of Aymara kingdoms (ancestors of the modern-day Aymara people in the Titicaca Basin). Two of these—the Lupaca and the Colla—were approaching a state level of political organization, extending their control over communities along the coast and on the eastern slopes of the southern Andes. It is in the Cuzco Basin that cataclysmic events would eventually truncate the revival of these states in the Lake Titicaca Basin and submerge the still expanding Chimú Empire.

### THE ORIGINS OF THE INCA

Up to the 1940s, when John H. Rowe provided the first archaeological evidence of the origins of the Inca, the reconstruction of Inca society was based solely upon chroniclers' eyewitness accounts from the early years of the Spanish Conquest. Since Rowe's ground-breaking work, the combination of archaeological and historical research has greatly enhanced our interpretations of the rise and spread of the greatest civilization in the Americas: the Inca.

Based on his excavations in Cuzco, Rowe established a chronology that included an Early and a Late Inca Period. During the Early Period, an Inca ceramic style called Killke starts to appear in areas under Inca influence; by the Late Inca Period, the empire has spread from central Chile to southern Colombia. Archaeologist Brian S. Bauer has recently dated the beginning of the Early Inca Period to A.D. 100. Based on the distribution of Killke ceramics and settlements in the Cuzco region, Bauer has proposed that the Inca were well on the way to statehood (and into the Late Inca Period) by A.D. 1400. Because of the scant research on the origins of the Inca, it is still too early to comment on the effect on the Cuzco Basin of the severe 60-year (A.D. 1250 to 1310) drought and the warmer Medieval Warm Epoch (A.D. 1000 to 1400), during which average temperatures were roughly 2° Fahrenheit (1° Celsius) higher than normal.

In their interviews with Inca informants, the Spanish chroniclers recorded that there were 13 kings in the Inca Dynasty. The first four are considered by Rowe to be mythical figures, and the next three are undated; but the reigns of the last six pre-Conquest Inca rulers recorded by Cabello de Balboa are accepted as real by Inca historians. (There also followed a number of Spanish-installed rulers, normally not included in the Inca king lists.)

The chroniclers' narratives are fraught with problems of interpretation, but these ancient parchments nonetheless give us an extraordinary history of the rise and spread of a remarkable New World empire.

This Lambayeque jug shows a two-man totora-reed float of a configuration still used in coastal communities of Peru. Lambayeque pottery usually had one or two spouts and a handle, and, as with this example, many were pedestal-based.

The Inca were surrounded by similar proto-states that were continuously vying for control of neighboring regions. One warlike group to the northwest of Cuzco, the Chanca, exerted such pressure on the Inca that the aged king Viracocha, deciding it was fruitless to resist their impending invasion, fled to the safety of a fortress. But two seasoned generals and Viracocha's son, Prince Yupanqui, rallied the populace and threw back the Chanca attack on Cuzco. Prince Yupanqui immediately ascended to the throne and took the name *Pachacuti* (Cataclysm, or Earthshaker), and was to become one of the greatest military strategists in the Americas. After reorganizing his army, he began his campaign to expand Inca rule throughout the Central Andes, turning his attention first to the Lupaca, Colla, and other Lake Titicaca kingdoms, and bringing their economic power into the Inca fold.

In 1463 he was joined by his son Topa Inca—often called the Alexander the Great of the Andes—and together they stretched the empire north as far as Quito, Ecuador. This swift conquest was unplanned, prompted, in fact, by the disobedience of General Capac Yupanqui. Pachacuti had ordered Yupanqui to explore to the north with imperial Inca troops and a contingent of recently subjugated Chanca soldiers; the Chanca deserted the campaign in central Peru, leaving the general in the untenable position of having to report back to Pachacuti that he had lost a portion of his army. To redeem himself, Yupanqui drove northward and attacked the Cajamarca State, allies of the Chimú on the coast below. He left a garrison in Cajamarca, returned to Cuzco, and was straightaway executed having disobeyed orders by proceeding beyond the Yanamayo River and losing the Chanca contingent. This left Pachacuti and Topa Inca the difficult choice of either supporting their garrison in Cajamarca or leaving them stranded 500 miles (804 kilometers) north of the Inca frontier. Topa Inca courageously led the army north, conquering the intervening region, and relieved the Cajamarca garrison; he then continued through the Andes to Quito, Ecuador, where he turned his troops southward to the coast and attacked the Chimú from the rear. After a series of bloody campaigns, they conquered their only rival for domination of the Central Andes. The disobedience of General Capac Yupanqui, resulting in Topa Inca's end run on the Chimú Empire, had instantly transformed the Inca into an extraordinarily powerful empire. Huayna Capac took the reins of the empire after the death of his father, Topa Inca, in 1493, and pushed the frontier even farther northward to southern Colombia and eastward into the yunga zone of northeastern Peru. Huayna Capac may well have been spurred on in his northward expansion by the onset of the Little Ice Age (circa 1500 to 1900), when the temperature dropped by 2° to 5° Fahrenheit (1° to 3° Celsius); such a change in climate would certainly have had an impact on agricultural productivity.

After Pachacuti turned the empire over to Topa Inca in 1471, he devoted his attention to Cuzco, erecting a capital befitting the mightiest kingdom in the

| RULER | REIGN |
|---|---|
| Manco Capac | mythical |
| Sinchi Roca | mythical |
| Lloque Yupanqui | mythical |
| Mayta Capac | mythical |
| Capac Yupanqui | unknown |
| Inca Roca | unknown |
| Yuhuar Huacac | unknown |
| Viracocha Inca | until 1438 |
| Pachacuti Inca Yupanqui | 1438-1471 |
| Topa Inca Yupanqui | 1471-1493 |
| Huayna Capac | 1493-1528 |
| Huascar Inca | 1528-1532 |
| Atahuallpa | 1532-1533 |

**Of the 13 Inca rulers accepted by historians, four are mythical figures. It was not until the reign of Pachacuti that the Inca emerged from obscurity and commenced the rapid expansion that forged the greatest empire of the Americas.**

The impressive citadel of La Centinela, photographed in 1931, was the focus of the wealthy Chincha Kingdom, located in the Chincha Valley along Peru's south coast. The kingdom fell peacefully to Topa Inca's armies around A.D. 1476. Under the Inca, La Centinela became an administrative seat for the Chincha Valley area. The Chincha Kingdom became a major maritime trading power under the Inca.

Americas. Over the next 50 years, Topa Inca, and, later, Huayna Capac, were to integrate hundreds of diverse tribes, chiefdoms, and states into the empire. They accomplished this through an intricate network of provincial administrative, storage, and garrison centers that extended over 25,000 miles (40,000 kilometers) of roads.

By 1470, Chan Chan lay in ruins, and the workshops of the Chimú were abandoned with tools and storage bins filled with raw materials still in place. Chan Chan was looted and King Minchançaman and Chimú metal-workers were taken to Cuzco. The riches of Chan Chan were melted down to create statues of the major Inca gods and to form a ribbon of gold to encircle the Coricancha (Enclosure of Gold, or Temple of the Sun), the most sacred temple in the empire. Topa Inca installed Minchançaman's son, Chumun-caur, as the puppet king of the Chimú, who swore allegiance to the all-powerful Topa Inca.

In just under 100 years, an insignificant state in the Cuzco Basin, reacting to an invasion and turning a general's disobedience to profit, emerged to rule an area of 385,000 square miles (616,000 square kilometers), some 3416 miles (5500 kilometers) in length, with a population of 12 million. The incorporation of this vast territory into the empire was accomplished by the extraordinary administrative and logistic system of the Inca.

Under the Inca, Cuzco was the central focus of the "Land of the Four Quarters", and its fine public architecture included glittering temples tural constructions were largely dismantled by the Spanish conquistadors, and their materials used to build the churches and fortresses of

# 9

# THE ULTIMATE EMPIRE

At its apex during the Late Horizon (A.D. 1470 to 1532), Tahuantinsuyu, the Inca "Land of the Four Quarters", encompassed the Andes from southern Colombia to central Chile. In about 100 years, the Inca had established one of the greatest empires in the world, surpassing the Roman Empire in length by 620 miles (1000 kilometers). How could a small state in a southern Peruvian Andean valley so quickly conquer this vast territory? The answer lies in the extraordinary organizational and administrative abilities of the Inca. Their genius for statecraft did not develop in a vacuum, of course, for the Inca were surely aware of the states and empires that had preceded them. As archaeologist John Hyslop has pointed out, many Inca architectural features are derived from both Huari and Tiwanaku styles.

In the Cuzco Valley, there was the brooding presence of the enormous Huari administrative center of Pikillacta, and, to the south, the crumbling Tiwanaku cities—soon to become Inca centers. Pachacuti conquered the Colla in the Lake Titicaca Basin, the Inca reconsecrated the Puma Punku temple at the Tiwanaku capital as an Inca sacred place, and Tiwanaku soon became a royal Inca pilgrimage center. Pachacuti was so enamored of the fine-cut Tiwanaku stonework that he directed his stonemasons to use dressed, or cut-and-polished, stone blocks in his own imperial buildings. Even the fabled road system of the Inca had its beginnings in the already existing communication networks dating back 2000 years to the Early Horizon.

## ORGANIZATION OF THE EMPIRE

Huayna Capac, the last great Inca emperor, ruled over the vast four quarters known as Tahuantinsuyu. The imperial capital, Cuzco, was the administrative center of the empire, and the boundaries of the four quarters—known as *suyus*—originated in Cuzco's central plaza. The largest, and southernmost, quarter was Collasuyu, encompassing much of the region formerly controlled by the Tiwanaku Empire; the small territories of Antisuyu and Cuntisuyu extended to the east and west, respectively; and Chinchaysuyu stretched northward to southern Colombia. Within Tahuantinsuyu, the Inca controlled the incredible wealth of a myriad environments, and conquered peoples from the desert coast all the way to the tropical forests of the Amazon Basin.

The rapid expansion out of the Cuzco Basin necessitated an efficient administrative system to manage the newly conquered territories. The empire was divided into more than 80 provinces, many of which correlated with the territories of conquered tribes, chiefdoms, and states, each presided over by a governor. The social organization of the Inca was strictly hierarchical, and everyone knew his or her place within the society. Subjects were organized into decimal units from 10 to 10,000 households (10, 50, 100, 500, 1000, 5000, and 10,000), with each grouping headed by a leader. The divine emperor, known as the *Sapa Inca*, or Ultimate Inca, held complete and absolute authority over the empire, its people, and its resources. Considered a descendant of the Sun God, the Sapa Inca acted as the spokesperson of the Sun Deity, who was worshipped in the Coricancha, the most revered temple in the realm. The ruling class was formed by the royal nobles, who were related by blood to the Sapa Inca, and also by the Incas by Privilege. Born outside the royal family and derived from ethnic groups in the Cuzco Valley that had been incorporated into the original Inca State, the Incas by Privilege were loyal subjects who

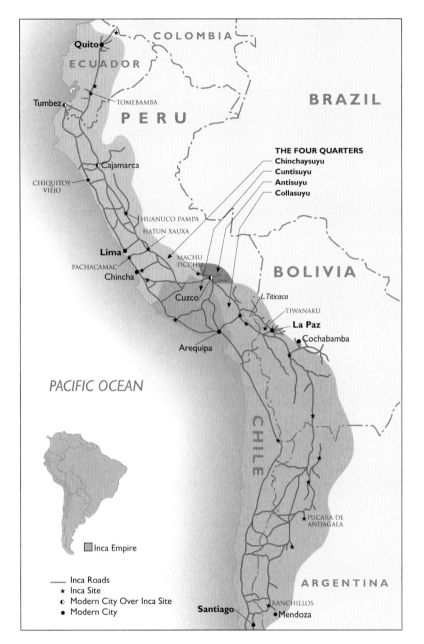

**The four quarters of the Inca Empire stretched from what is now northern Ecuador to central Chile. Control of this vast territory was facilitated by an impressive network of roads.**

THE FOUR QUARTERS
**Chinchaysuyu**
**Cuntisuyu**
**Antisuyu**
**Collasuyu**

spoke the Quechua language, and were accorded special status as administrators. The close relatives of the Sapa Inca made up the Supreme Council and each was *apu*, lord or prefect, of one of four quarters of the empire. Beneath the apus were the royal governors of the provincial capitals, and under their aegis were the numerous *curacas*, hereditary local rulers, who ruled over even smaller segments of the population.

The explosive expansion of the empire meant that Pachacuti and Topa Inca had to recruit thousands of administrators to fill bureaucratic posts throughout the realm. These lesser members of the nobility were comprised of the curaca, who provided administrators for groups ranging between 100 and 10,000 inhabitants. The curacas appointed *camayocs*, or foremen, who were responsible for between 10 and 50 taxpayers.

The millions of farmers and llama herders were taxed through a labor system that divided conquered territories into three parts: state lands, religious lands, and a portion of the "real estate" for individual use. The commoners worked the state and temple agricultural lands and herds, and the production from these vast resources was stored in state and temple warehouses. In addition to maintaining state and temple lands, the populace was required to perform labor service, called *mit'a*, by serving in the army, providing labor for the construction of public works such as state buildings, temples, fortresses, and roads, or sweat in the mines. In addition, many people maintained a plot of land of their own.

Although the Inca had no written language, the *quipu*—a series of strings with colored knots, first known from Huari times—was used to record census findings and tallies of resources or llama herds. The quipu was also used as a mnemonic device by the professional *quipucamayocs* (quipu keepers) to document Inca history. The death of the last quipu keeper, in the early colonial period, left the knotted information of the quipus indecipherable.

This colorful array of knotted strings, called a *quipu*, was once much more than an object of beauty. The quipu was valued for the information that was encoded in its knots. The Inca had no system of writing, so the quipu was used to record historical events, accounts, and census data. The knot code, known only to specialized quipu keepers, was lost after the Conquest.

The complex administrative system allowed the Sapa Inca to organize and manage his far-flung empire; but as we shall see, the governing of this mosaic of conquered peoples was fraught with problems.

### CUZCO: THE IMPERIAL CAPITAL

At 11,138 feet (3395 meters), Cuzco was one of the highest state capitals in the world. The small village at the head of the Cuzco Valley was transformed by Pachacuti into an elegant architectural model of Inca social and religious organization. The city was laid out in the shape of the sacred puma, with its head formed by Sacsahuamán, the most stupendous military, religious, and storage complex built by the Inca. Enclosed within three tiers of zigzag walls, this fortress held plazas, storehouses, a circular tower, and religious and state buildings. (Alas, these architectural treasures were removed and used for construction materials to build Spanish Cuzco.)

The imperial capital boasted an extraordinary number of royal palaces, shrines, temples, and state buildings, but it was the Coricancha that embodied the state religion and the cosmos of the Inca. Equivalent to St. Peter's Basilica in Rome, the Coricancha was adorned with sheets and bands of gold, as befitted a temple dedicated to the Sun. Blazing in the sunlight from afar, the gold sheathing was to be stripped in 1533 as part of the ransom for the last emperor, Atahuallpa, who was held prisoner by Francisco Pizarro. Inside the Coricancha, hidden from the avaricious Spaniards in a special room, was the Image of the Sun, crafted out of gold and emblazoned with jewels. (It has never been found, although a Spaniard once boasted that he had lost it in an evening of gambling in Cajamarca, giving rise to the Spanish expression "to gamble the sun before it rises".) Not only was the gold sun disk kept in the temple, but so were icons of the principal religious deities of all the conquered nations; thus did the Inca fortify the state religious pantheon, made up of gods of the sun, moon, thunder (the god of weather), sky, earth, and sea. The Coricancha held wealth beyond belief, and included a small garden about which Cieza de León said:

> There was a garden in which the earth was lumps of fine gold, and it was cunningly planted with stalks of corn that were of gold—stalk, leaves, and ears.... Aside from this, there were more than twenty sheep [actually llamas] of gold with their lambs, and the shepherds who guarded them, with their slings and staffs, all of this metal. There were many tubs of gold and silver and emeralds, and goblets, pots and every kind of vessel all of fine gold.

The Coricancha was badly burned in 1536, during the siege of then Spanish-held Cuzco by Manco Capac. (This son of Huayna Capac, who bore the same

Once the stalwart protector of the Inca capital, the fortress of Sacsahuamán, at Cuzco, was a combined military, storage, and religious complex—the greatest ever erected by the Inca. Although the fortress was largely razed by the Spaniards, the astounding close-fitting masonry, or polygonal coursing, used in the construction of its zigzag walls is still clearly visible. Originally Sacsahuamán's three tiers of walls held religious and state buildings, a tower, and plazas.

name as the first of the mythical Inca rulers, was initially a puppet Sapa Inca of the Spanish rulers; he eventually revolted against the Spanish tyranny, leading Inca armies in attempting to push out the Spanish invaders from Peru until his assassination by the Spanish around 1544.) Soon thereafter, the Dominican Fathers built the Catholic Church of Santo Domingo upon the ruins of the fabled temple. Finally, in 1950, an earthquake obliterated much of Cuzco and shook off the Spanish overlay of the Coricancha, exposing for the first time in 400 years more of the temple walls that John H. Rowe had first recorded in 1942. Four of the estimated seven temple buildings have now been restored.

One of the most hotly debated issues in Inca studies centers on the 42 imaginary sacred lines, or *ceques,* and their associated 328 shrines. The ceques are sacred pathways that converge on the Coricancha, and reflect the underlying organization of the Inca Empire. Recorded by the Jesuit scholar Bernabé Cobo in 1653, and brought to prominence by ethnohistorian R. Tom Zuidema in the 1960s, they are interpreted as a sophisticated religious and calendrical system. The ceques demarcate the four quarters, or suyus, of the empire. Three of the suyus were further subdivided by nine ceques, with the fourth, Cuntisuyu, being subdivided by 15. Until recently, it was assumed that the ceques radiated in straight lines from the Coricancha like the spokes of a wheel, but archaeologist Brian S. Bauer, using Cobo's meticulous description of the shrines situated along the lines of the Collasuyu sector, demonstrated that the ceques zigzag from shrine to shrine. It is thus the location of the shrines that dictates the course of the imaginary lines. The Coricancha must have been a religious "magnet," drawing immense power from throughout the Inca Empire.

The 328 shrines enumerated by Cobo were either human-made features such as canals, fountains, and royal houses, or natural objects, such as caves, boulders, and springs. One of the overriding concerns of the ceque system—as in previous state religious systems—was with the procurement of lifegiving water. This preoccupation is reflected in many of the shrines, as can be gathered from the partial list above. The shrines also had precise calendrical purposes, and reflected the system of sacred and sociopolitical geography surrounding the Inca capital.

The central sector of the imperial city had more than 4000 buildings, laid out in a grid pattern bordered by two canalized (straightened and walled) rivers. It is estimated that between 15,000 and 20,000 people lived in the central area with 125,000 inhabitants within 3 miles (5 kilometers) of the Coricancha. The city was divided into two halves: *hanan* (upper) and *hurin* (lower) Cuzco, each further divided into five sub-sectors pertaining to specific royal *ayllus*, or kin groups, from any one of which could come the Sapa Inca. Only the Sapa Inca and the royalty dwelt in the sacred precinct containing their palaces, temples, and public buildings. Another interesting organizational device made Cuzco a microcosm of the empire: people migrating to Cuzco from elsewhere in the empire lived in the city district corresponding geographically to their native suyu.

There was a great plaza in Cuzco called the Huacaypata that had a type of platform or dais, called an *ushnu*, used by the Sapa Inca on state occasions. The ushnu was an architectural feature of all major provincial capitals, or New Cuzcos, and from it the provincial lords received their subjugated people, reviewed troops, conducted ritual events, and dispensed justice.

The ushnu platforms united the provinces with the capital, strengthening religious and political ties, in part through the institution of child sacrifice, or *capac huchu*. An elaborate ritual, linking the sacred mountains, shrines, and temples of Tahuantinsuyu, capac huchu culminated in the sacrifice and entombment of children between six and ten years old. The children were sent from the provinces to Cuzco, where girls and boys were symbolically married. They then returned to their provinces to be sacrificed at shrines to ensure the well-being of the Sapa Inca and the empire. Through these religious rituals, Cuzco became a great pilgrimage center, uniting the diverse cultures of the empire under one religious umbrella. Evidence of a number of child sacrifices has been found on mountaintops and volcanoes—gifts of appeasement to the mountain gods. Many of the sacrificial victims are perfectly preserved (by the freezing temperatures and the dryness of the air) with their offerings. Evidence of such sacrifices has also been found on the sacred Island of the Sun in Lake Titicaca, in the coastal center of Pachacamac, and also on La Plata Island in southern Ecuador.

Other human sacrifices were made on the death of the Sapa Inca, whose body was mummified and kept in his palace to be waited upon by his royal descendants. The deceased Sapa Inca was greatly revered as an oracle, and was brought out for public ceremonies.

The most famous wall still standing in Cuzco is the finely dressed stone wall of the *acllahuasi*, the house of the chosen women (or *mamacuna)*, where more than 1000 women wove fine clothing and made *chicha* (maize beer) for offerings to the sun. When they left the walls of the acllahuasi, it was to serve the royalty in the royal quarters.

During his life, the Sapa Inca maintained royal estates and country palaces outside the city. The well-known tourist sites of Pisac, Ollantaytambo, and Machu Picchu were formerly the estates of Pachacuti. Archaeologist Susan Niles, using the detailed writings of earlier chroniclers, investigated the estate of Huayna Capac in the Yucay Valley and Huascar's palaces at Calca, in the Vilcanota-Urubamba Valley.

Today it is almost possible to walk in the footsteps of the Inca royalty; and even in their ruined state, the massive cut-stone walls, temples, and buildings continue to evoke the majesty of the Inca state. Nowhere is this revealed more than at Machu Picchu, which the Inca architects designed in harmony with the landscape on a ridge high above the Urubamba River. In 1911, Hiram Bingham began his search for this last refuge of the Incas, which had eluded explorers for hundreds of years. The Bingham party encountered a local farmer, who urged them to investigate the ruins above his hut. Climbing several thousand feet, Bingham was transfixed by the sight of buildings, temples, and hundreds of stone-faced agricultural terraces covered by a tangle of trees and undergrowth. Machu Picchu was in a remarkable state of preservation, its buildings lacking only their original thatched roofs. The site reflects the genius of

Few archaeological sites rival the majesty of Machu Picchu. Hidden by the rugged Andes, this mountain retreat eluded discovery when the Spanish conquered the Inca, and remained unknown to outsiders for nearly four centuries until its discovery in 1911 by Hiram Bingham. At the zenith of the Inca Empire, Machu Picchu was a religious site where Inca lords worshipped a pantheon of gods that included Inti, the sun itself.

Pachacuti, who built this royal residence, complete with temples and shrines, on his estate east of Ollantaytambo.

The fine masonry work in Inca state buildings has fascinated tourists and archaeologists alike. Many doubted that the "Bronze Age" Inca could possibly have quarried, moved, and dressed the cyclopean stones, some weighing over 100 tons, without the aid of extraterrestrial laser technology or powerful liquids to soften the stone for easier dressing. The answer lies, first, in the engineering genius of architects—as is the case for Neolithic Stonehenge in England and for the Egyptian pyramids—and, secondly, in large, organized teams of quarrymen, haulers, and stonemasons.

Architect Jean-Pierre Protzen's extensive research on all aspects of Inca stonemasonry has demonstrated that there were two sources of stone blocks: bedrock faces and boulders from mammoth rockfalls. The quarries all have ramps and roads along which to transport roughed-out blocks to building sites. Protzen estimates that 1800 people equipped with ropes and levers and working in tandem could drag a stone weighing 100 tons from the quarries to Pachacuti's estate at Ollantaytambo, a distance of 3 miles (5 kilometers). The Spanish chroniclers record that in the storehouses at Sacsahuamán there were huge piles of thick rope used to haul stones. Once at the building sites, the blocks were finished using quartzite hammers, and then fitted into place to form masonry walls of true elegance.

**SPREAD OF THE EMPIRE**

The Inca organized Tahuantinsuyu on a grand scale, using the strategic placement of provincial capitals, roads, and military installations to ensure tight control of their ever-expanding empire. Offensive strategy, when necessary, included coercion of the enemy into capitulation by a show of force. This strategy was of great benefit, permitting the Inca to incorporate the subjugated peoples and their economic production peacefully and without wasting time. When they met stiff resistance, they overwhelmed their enemies with armies estimated at between 10,000 and 200,000 troops. Then, after the conquest of a province, the Inca strengthened their control of local ethnic groups by extending their road system, establishing provincial capitals, and stationing garrisons.

Another factor motivating the expansion of the Inca Empire was their split inheritance system, attributed to Pachacuti. Upon the death of the Sapa Inca, his successor took over the reins of government and the state economic system, but he did not inherit his father's vast wealth. Instead, the palaces, royal

Though it now lies in ruins, the royal estate of Ollantaytambo, northwest of Cuzco, still evokes the grandeur and prestige of its builder, the Sapa Inca Pachacuti. The site is strategically located in Antisuyu—the eastern segment of the "Land of the Four Quarters"—and offered a refuge for the Inca court following the capture of Cuzco.

estates, and other possessions of the deceased emperor were considered the property of the dead king, whose mummy was now worshipped as a god by his heirs. One result of this system was that it provided considerable incentive to the new Sapa Inca to develop his own personal economic base by expanding the empire.

Many of the subjugated peoples rebelled against their oppressors, and the Sapa Inca was constantly quelling revolts. In order to minimize rebellions, the Inca developed a resettlement policy employing *mitimaes*, or colonists. Whole recalcitrant communities would be uprooted and resettled in areas within the Inca homeland, while loyal Inca colonists would be sent into troubled areas. The Inca also moved people to regions that had sparse populations in order to increase agricultural production, thus enhancing the coffers of the state.

The logistic system of the Inca provided the offensive and defensive units of the Inca army with their basic needs. Soldiers were issued supplies from storehouses situated at one-day intervals between the extensive warehouses of the provincial capitals, which were five to six days' march apart. The armies were also accompanied by llama baggage trains, human porters, and auxiliaries. In some areas, the Inca roads traversed some of the harshest terrain in the Andes, forcing the thousands of troops and their support contingents to spread out for miles along the narrow roads.

The rapid spread of the empire presented a communication problem. The solution was relay runners, who, utilizing a magnificent system of roads—which has been estimated by John Hyslop to have covered 25,000 miles (40,000 kilometers)—brought messages to Cuzco from the extremes of Tahuantinsuyu. There were two main north-south "highways," one traveling through the Andes and the other along the coast, connected by numerous east-west trunk roads. The ground routes were supplemented by the empire's famous suspension bridges placed across rushing rivers. Only three days were required for a relay of runners to reach Cuzco from Lima, and only five or six days from Quito, Ecuador! An estimated 2000 *tampu*, or way stations, were set at 12.4-mile (20-kilometer) intervals.

As the state consolidated its rule over region after region, the Inca imposed their architecture, language, political system, and religion upon the defeated groups. They also introduced their distinctive ceramic and textile art styles. The formalized Cuzco art style, based upon symmetrical patterns of bold geometric motifs, was mandated by the state to its pottery and textile specialists. The ceramics included the elegant *aryballoid* storage jars, characterized by strap handles and a lug to attach a tumpline for transport by porters. The Tiwanaku-style *kero*, or drinking cup, as well as distinctive plates and other vessels, graced the tables of the Inca and their subjects at festivals. Imperial Inca pottery is found in the Cuzco region and at state-imposed sites, but the local populace in many areas satisfied state demands by incorporating Inca shapes and designs into their own ceramic and textile traditions.

Traces of the Inca road system, including this well-preserved section near Lake Titicaca, survive throughout the Central Andes region. The roads permitted rapid communications throughout the far-flung empire, and enabled the Inca rulers to dispatch military forces needed to quell the frequent revolts by conquered peoples.

160

This colorfully painted *kero,* typical of Cuzco artwork, was used for drinking *chicha,* or maize beer. Keros were carved from wood and were painted with images that ranged from ones like this jaguar head to scenes of festivals, battles, religious ceremonies, and the Inca court. While this cup curves inward at the mouth, another common design had a flared top, like that of a beaker.

Along the Andean spine is found an imposing chain of provincial capitals of the Inca Empire, each called "New Cuzco." In the highlands north of Cuzco, the populations in the Mantaro and Huallaga valleys were small ethnic groups living in fortified hilltop settlements. When the Upper Mantaro Valley was conquered in 1460, the Inca discovered that one ethnic community, the Wanka, was really made up of a number of groups competing among themselves. As has been documented by archaeologist Terence N. D'Altroy and his colleagues, the Inca moved the 50,000 Wanka out of their fortified hilltop settlements and into the valley. They then established the provincial capital of Hatun Xauxa (which now lies under the modern town of Sausa) squarely in Wanka territory. Farther to the north, at 12,470 feet (3800 meters), is the remarkably well-preserved provincial capital of Huánuco Pampa, which has been investigated by archaeologists Craig Morris and Donald E. Thompson. Huánuco Pampa has 4000 buildings and storehouses, and boasts a magnificent cut-stone ushnu in the center of its enormous plaza. At its zenith, the city was surrounded by a number of small ethnic groups, who numbered about 55,000 people. Covering .8 square mile (2 square kilometers), Huánuco Pampa included royal dwellings and temples, a district of 50 dwellings for the mamacuna weavers and chicha brewers, and two *kallankas* (long, gabled, rectangular halls) to house troops, mit'a laborers, or guests attending state ceremonies. At the northern extreme of the empire, at what is now Cuenca, Ecuador, the Inca established their second imperial capital of Tomebamba; here, Huayna Capac spent much of his time.

Inca administrative centers on the central and south coasts were either set up in the existing civic-ceremonial structures of local states or else were constructed in a blend of imperial and local architectural styles, as at Tambo Colorado in the Pisco Valley and at Inkawasi in Cañete. At the powerful oracle center and city of Pachacamac, the Inca erected a Temple of the Sun and an elite residential complex for the Inca governor Tauri Chumpi, as well as an ushnu and an acllahuasi, the latter a fine masonry structure. Pachacamac was part of the Ichma State and had allied itself with the Inca in their suppression of the Chimú Empire. After its incorporation into the Inca Empire, the city continued to enjoy special status as a religious and pilgrimage center.

Within the former realm of the Chimú Empire on the north coast, there is little evidence of imposed administrative centers. Chiquitoy Viejo, in the Chicama Valley, for example, even includes a burial platform reminiscent of those in the Chan Chan ciudadelas; it may have been the administrative center of a Chimú puppet ruler under Inca domination. Ethnohistorian Patricia Netherly's research in the colonial archives has demonstrated that the Inca had control of the north coast, ruling through local valley lords in established administrative centers.

From the earliest pictorial chronicle of Inca civilization, this drawing by Guamán Poma de Ayala depicts Topa Inca inspecting a storehouse of maize, with the quipu keeper Apo Pomachaua at the ruler's side.

In addition to the esteem that the Inca held for Pachacamac, they also developed a favored relationship with the Lord of Chincha and his maritime kingdom. It was a great surprise when ethnohistorian María Rostworowski de Diez Canseco found a document that stated the Chincha Kingdom was a great maritime power under the Inca. The document relates that under the Chincha Lord there were 30,000 subjects, of which 12,000 were farmers, 10,000 fishermen, and 6000 merchants, ruled by 30 lords according to the usual Inca decimal system of population organization. Pedro Pizarro was told by Atahuallpa that his good friend the Lord of Chincha had 100,000 balsa rafts, certainly an exaggeration. In his research at Lo Demás, a fishing community near the Inca and pre-Inca administrative capital of Centinela in the Chincha Valley, archaeologist Daniel H. Sandweiss has revealed that the Inca conquest of the Chimú Empire shifted the center of maritime trade with Ecuador to Chincha, where under Inca control, it was greatly expanded. The Chincha merchant trade between Cuzco and Ecuadorian localities—notably, Puerto Viejo and Quito—continued the extensive maritime exchange with Ecuador established earlier by the Moche and Chimú.

## WAREHOUSING THE EMPIRE

The resources flowing into Inca storehouses were staggering, with agricultural products well represented. The Inca increased agricultural production by expanding terrace systems and bringing terrace engineering to new heights. The cascading agricultural terraces—clinging to even the most precipitous mountain slopes—brought marginal or underutilized lands into production. At the time of Spanish contact, more than 2,471,000 acres (1 million hectares) of irrigated terraces were in use. In addition to these stupendous land-reclamation works, irrigation systems were enlarged, and aqueducts, reservoirs, and stone-lined canals were constructed.

In order to store the tremendous surpluses generated by mit'a farmers, herders, and craft specialists, a decentralized system of storage was developed throughout Tahuantinsuyu. Previous storage centers paled in comparison with the Inca system of row upon row of circular and rectangular storehouses clustered around the provincial capitals and throughout the imperial heartland. In the Upper Mantaro Valley there were more than 3000 storehouses, with 1069 at Hatun Xauxa alone, 497 at Huánuco Pampa in the Huánuco region, and 325 at Pumpu in the Junín area. The few that have been excavated hold botanical evidence for maize, quinoa, potatoes, and other Andean tuber crops. Chroniclers' reports state that the storehouses also contained military supplies, clothing, sandals, firewood, and other wealth. From the warehouses, the Inca supported their administrative centers, armies, and mit'a laborers, as well as the religious festivals that were held in the great plazas of the empire. French economist Louis Baudin and others have said that the Inca Empire was a welfare state, using its stored surpluses for subjects in need, but there is little evidence for this in the chronicles.

Terrace farming continues to be practiced in much of the Andes, as shown in this view of the Colca Valley. Farmers are often prepared to cultivate terrain as steep as these mountainsides, but the practice of irrigation—a virtual necessity in areas of drought—would result in erosion here. Instead, a system of canals first introduced by the **Collagua** people draws water from springs and streams originating in the mountains.

With its classic, two-handled style, slender neck, and fern motif, the design of this Inca aryballoid jar, found near Cuzco, represents the characteristic Inca preference for painted geometric patterns over organic images. However, bees, butterflies, and stylized animals are sometimes also depicted.

The Inca Empire attained its great size in less than 100 years, under the rule of only three kings: Pachacuti, Topa Inca, and Huayna Capac. It was still in the process of expansion and consolidation when the ominous news reached Huayna Capac, at Tomebamba, in Ecuador, that a strange group of bearded men had entered Tahuantinsuyu.

### CIVIL WAR AND THE END OF THE EMPIRE

Huayna Capac died suddenly in 1528, apparently a victim of the smallpox that had spread southward from Panama in advance of the invading Spanish forces. The death of the Sapa Inca threw the empire into turmoil, with two contenders—the half-brothers Atahuallpa and Huascar—embarking on a debilitating five-year civil war for the throne. Much of the empire lay in ruins by the time Atahuallpa emerged victorious, having captured Huascar outside Cuzco in 1532.

In the summer of 1528, Francisco Pizarro and a small band of adventurers and treasure hunters had landed at Tumbez. Two men sent ashore to the Inca administrative center reported back that the temple walls were covered with gold and silver. Unable to capitalize on this first encounter with the Inca Empire, Pizarro returned to Panama and then to Spain to seek support from the Spanish throne for an invasion of Peru. In January of 1531, Pizarro left Panama with his invasion force of 200 horsemen and foot soldiers, and, by April of 1532, he had returned to Tumbez. But the city now lay in ruins due to the civil war. Leaving a garrison at San Miguel, in the Chira Valley, Pizarro, with 168 men—including both horse and foot soldiers—moved swiftly to the highland city of Cajamarca, where Atahuallpa and his army were resting at the famous baths after their hard-fought victory over Huascar.

November 16th, 1532, sounded the death knell for the Inca Empire. Pizarro, with his small force, lured Atahuallpa into a trap in the main square of Cajamarca, capturing the new Sapa Inca and slaughtering thousands of his nobles and retainers. Even the tons of gold and silver ransom piled up in an Inca room did not save Atahuallpa, for he was garroted on Pizarro's orders on July 26th, 1533. Pizarro had been the most fortunate of conquerors, for had he and his tiny army invaded at a time when the empire had not been disrupted by a civil war, the Spaniards would have faced a tougher struggle against the unified might of the Inca.

### THE AFTERMATH

In the years that followed the Conquest, the Spaniards were not only in constant military action against the remaining Inca forces, but also were fighting among themselves for the booty. Within nine years after he invaded Tahuantinsuyu, Francisco Pizarro was assassinated by rebellious Spanish soldiers. The last major Inca resistance to the foreign invaders ended with the execution of Tupac Amaru, a son of Manco Capac, in 1572; he had held out in the jungle city of Vilcabamba, the last refuge of the Inca.

The Spaniards brought death and destruction upon the former subjects of the Inca, many of whom perished in the battles and massacres of the Conquest. However, it was not this bloodshed that devastated the Inca and decimated the people of the Central Andes, but mainly the unseen enemy of European diseases. Within 100 years of the Conquest, pandemics of smallpox, measles, mumps, influenza, and typhus reduced the pre-Conquest population from an estimated 12 million inhabitants to just 670,000—a death rate of almost 95 percent! The survivors were further subjected to forced resettlement, servitude, and labor in the mines at places such as Potosí in Bolivia. The repression of the Andean peasants culminated in an uprising against Spanish authority led by José Gabriel Condorcanqui, known as Tupac Amaru II, a curaca in the Cuzco Valley. Tupac Amaru II wrested southern Peru and Bolivia from the Spaniards, but he was captured and cruelly executed in the main plaza of Cuzco in 1781.

After liberation from Spain in 1826, the new national governments of Peru and Bolivia did not treat the original inhabitants of the Andes much better than had their Spanish oppressors. Still at the bottom of the socio-economic ladder after 450 years of domination by the descendants of the Spanish invaders, they maintain a way of life today that reflects strong continuities with their Inca heritage. There are more than eight million Quechua, the descendants of the Inca, and half a million Aymara, whose ancestry harks back to the Tiwanaku Empire. Their survival as the largest native population in the Western Hemisphere can be attributed to their beloved Andes; there, in the

With a cloud-bound sky over Lake Titicaca in the background, this Bolivian Aymara woman's vibrant woven shawl recalls the textiles of the ancient people of the Andes. The half-million remaining Aymara trace their ancestry to the Tiwanaku Empire.

quechua, suni, and puna ecological zones, they maintain their adaptation to high altitudes, growing the indigenous grain and root crops that best support their agro-pastoral economic system.

### THE LEGACY

For more than 12,000 years the people of the Central Andes developed a series of civilizations whose culture and ingenuity rivaled or surpassed those of Old World societies. The record of their achievements—as hunters, herders, and fishermen, as the builders of magnificent states and empires—has only just begun to be exposed. Only in the last 100 years have the trowels of archaeologists, the archival research of ethnohistorians, and the studies of modern Andean communities by anthropologists begun to open the door on this fascinating region and its people. The campsites and monuments of these past civilizations pervade the Andean landscape, and the millions of descendants of their original builders are a poignant reminder of the Conquest that began more than 450 years ago and that has not yet ceased.

# REFERENCES

## CHAPTER ONE

Much of the resource material I used in this volume comes from the major journals on New World archaeology. These include: *American Antiquity*; *Latin American Antiquity*; *Revista de Arqueología Americana*; *Andean Past*; *Boletín de Lima*; *Bulletin de l'Institut Français d'Études Andines, Lima*; *Ñawpa Pacha* (Institute of Andean Studies, Berkeley, California); and *Revista del Museo Nacional, Lima*. Journals that I have relied upon for the reconstruction of past climate changes are: *Geoarchaeology*; *Palaeogeography, Palaeoclimatology, Palaeoecology*; *Quaternary Research;* and *Quaternary Science Reviews*. These contain numerous articles on Andean glacial and Holocene environmental change.

Readers who wish to follow the plateaus of emerging knowledge and interpretation of Central Andean cultural development should begin with Cieza de Léon (1553), edited by von Hagen, and continue with Squier (1877), Means (1931), Bennett and Bird (1949, revised 1960), and Lanning (1967). Except for Lumbreras (1974), there are few major syntheses of Central Andean archaeology until the recent publications of Bonavia (1991), Moseley (1992) and Morris and von Hagen (1993). For a comprehensive history of American archaeology see Willey and Sabloff.

BENNETT W.C. AND J.B. BIRD 1949 *Andean Cultural History*. (revised edition, 1960) The American Museum of Natural History, New York.

BONAVIA, D. 1991 *Peru: Hombre e Historia de los Orígenes al Siglo XV*, Edubanco, Lima.

BRIDGES, M. 1991 *Planet Peru: An Aerial Journey Through a Timeless Land*. The Professional Photography Division of Eastman Kodak Company; Aperture, New York.

BRUHNS, K.O. 1994 *Ancient South Americans*. Cambridge University Press, Cambridge and New York.

CLAPPERTON, C.M. 1993 Nature of Environmental Changes in South America at the Last Glacial Maximum. *Palaeogeography, Palaeoclimatology, Palaeoecology* 20: 189-208.

1993 *Quaternary Geology and Geomorphology of South America*. Elsevier, Amsterdam.

DIAZ, H.F. AND V. MARKGRAF (EDITORS) 1992 *El Niño: Historical and Paleoclimatic Aspects of the Southern Oscillation*. Cambridge University Press, Cambridge and New York.

DONNAN, C.B. 1992 *Ceramics of Ancient Peru*. Fowler Museum of Cultural History, University of California, Los Angeles.

EWBANK, T. 1855 A Description of the Indian Antiquities Brought from Chile and Peru by the United States Naval Astronomical Expedition, in *The U.S. Naval Astronomical Expedition to the Southern Hemisphere During the Years 1849-'50-'51-'52*. Volume II, pp 111-150. House of Representatives 33rd Congress, 1st Session, Executive Document No. 121, A.O.P. Nicholson, Printer, Washington.

GUAMAN POMA DE AYALA, F. 1980 (1614) *Primer Nueva Corónica y Buen Gobierno*. Critical edition by J. Murra and R. Adorno, trans. and textual analysis of Quechua by J. Urioste. 3 vols. Siglo Veintiuno, Mexico City.

LANNING, E.P. 1967 *Peru Before the Incas*. Prentice-Hall, Inc., Englewood Cliffs, New Jersey.

LUMBRERAS, L. G. 1974 *The Peoples and Cultures of Ancient Peru*, trans. by B.J. Meggers. Smithsonian Institution Press, Washington, D.C. and London.

MEANS, P.A. 1931 *Ancient Civilizations of the Andes*. Charles Scribner's Sons, New York and London.

MORRIS, C. AND A. VON HAGEN 1993 *The Inka Empire and its Andean Origins*. Abbeville Press Publishers, New York, London, Paris.

MOSELEY, M.E. 1987 Punctuated Equilibrium: Searching the Ancient Record for El Niño. *The Quarterly Review of Archaeology* 8:7-10.

1992 *The Incas and Their Ancestors: The Archaeology of Peru*. Thames and Hudson, Ltd., London.

OLIVER-SMITH, A. 1986 *The Martyred City: Death and Rebirth in the Andes*. University of New Mexico Press, Albuquerque.

PULGAR VIDAL, J. 1987 *Geografía del Perú*. Logo Press, Barcelona.

PURIN, S. (EDITOR) 1991 *Los Incas y El Antiguo Peru 1 & 2*. Sociedad Estatal Quinto Centenario, Madrid.

ROLLINS, H.B., J.B. RICHARDSON III AND D.H. SANDWEISS 1986 The Birth of El Niño: Geoarchaeological Evidence and Implications. *Geoarchaeology* 1(1):3-16.

SQUIER, E. G. 1877 *Peru: Incidents of Travel and Exploration in the Land of the Incas*. Harper & Brothers, New York.

THOMPSON, L.G., E. MOSLEY-THOMPSON, J.F. BOLZAN AND B.R. KOCI 1985 A 1500-Year Record of Tropical Precipitation in Ice Cores from the Quelccaya Ice Cap, Peru. *Science* 229:971-973.

TOWNSEND R.F. (EDITOR) 1992 *The Ancient Americas: Art from Sacred Landscapes*. The Art Institute of Chicago.

UHLE M. 1991 Pachacamac: A Reprint of the 1903 Edition by Max Uhle and Pachacamac Archaeology: Retrospect and Prospect. An Introduction by Izumi Shimada. *University Museum Monograph* 62. The University Museum of Archaeology and Anthropology, University of Pennsylvania, Philadelphia.

VON HAGEN, V. W. (EDITOR) 1959 *The Inca of Pedro de Cieza de León*. University of Oklahoma Press, Norman.

WILLEY, G.R. AND J.A. SABLOFF 1993 *A History of American Archaeology*. (3rd ed.) W.H. Freeman and Co., New York.

## CHAPTER TWO

The controversy on the date of the entrance of hunters and gatherers in South America is discussed in Meltzer and in the exchange between Lynch and Dillehay and Collins. Dillehay's et al (1992) essay presents an evaluation of the pre-11,500 sites; Junius Bird's volume discusses Fell's Cave, the southernmost early site in the Americas; and my article evaluates the Peruvian evidence for the earliest Central Andean inhabitants.

ALDENDERFER, M.S. 1989 The Archaic Period in the South-Central Andes. *Journal of World Prehistory* 3(2):117-158.

BIRD, J.B. 1988 *Travels and Archaeology in South Chile*. ed. J. Hyslop, University of Iowa Press, Iowa City.

CHAUCHAT, C. 1988 Early Hunter-Gatherers on the Peruvian Coast, in *Peruvian Prehistory: An Overview of Pre-Inca and Inca Society*. pp.41-66. ed. R. Keatinge, Cambridge University Press, Cambridge and New York.

DENEVAN, W.M., K. MATHEWSON AND G. KNAPP (EDITORS) 1987 Pre-Hispanic Agriculture Fields in the Andean Region. *British Archaeological Reports International Series* 359, Vol. 1 & 2.

DILLEHAY, T.D., G. ARDELA A. CALDERÓN, N. G. POLITIS AND M. DA CONCEICAO DE MORAES COUTINHO BELTRÃO 1992 Earliest Hunters and Gatherers of South America. *Journal of World Prehistory* 6(2):145-204.

DILLEHAY, T.D. AND M.B. COLLINS 1991 Monte Verde, Chile: A Comment on Lynch. *American Antiquity* 56:333-341.

LYNCH, T.F. 1990 Glacial-Age Man in South America? A Critical Review. *American Antiquity* 55:12-36.

1991 Lack of Evidence for Glacial-Age Settlement of South America: Reply to Dillehay and Collins and to Gruhn and Bryan. *American Antiquity* 56(2):348-355.

MELTZER, D.J. 1993 *Search for the First Americans*. St. Remy Press, Montreal; Smithsonian Books, Washington, D.C.

NATIONAL RESEARCH COUNCIL 1989 *Lost Crops of the Incas: Little-Known Plants of the Andes with Promise for Worldwide Cultivation*. National Academy Press, Washington, D.C.

PEARSALL, D.M. 1992 The Origins of Plant Cultivation in South America, in *The Origins of Agriculture: An International Perspective*. pp. 173-205, ed. C.W. Cowan and P.J. Watson, Smithsonian Institution Press, Washington D.C.

1994 Issues in the Analysis and Interpretation of Archaeological Maize in South America, in *Corn and Culture in the Prehistoric New World*. ed S. Johannessen and C.A. Hastorf. Westview Press, Boulder.

QUILTER, J. 1989 *Life and Death at Paloma: Society and Mortuary Practices in a Preceramic Peruvian Village*. University of Iowa Press, Iowa City.

RICHARDSON, J.B. III 1992 Early Hunters, Fishers, Farmers and Herders: Diverse Economic Adaptations in Peru to 4500 B.P. *Revista de Arqueología Americana* 6:71-90.

RICK, J.W. 1988 The Character and Context of Highland Preceramic Society, in *Peruvian Prehistory: An Overview of Pre-Inca and Inca Society*. pp.3-40. ed. R.W. Keatinge, Cambridge University Press, Cambridge and New York.

## CHAPTER THREE

There is increasing attention being paid to the Late Preceramic underpinnings of the rise of Central Andean civilization. See Moseley's articles which explore the economic base of the earliest temple centers. Burger's book on Chavín, cited in Chapter 5, is a marvelous synthesis of our current knowledge on this critical time period. Bird's work at Huaca Prieta will be of great interest due to the spectacular gourd and textile art from this early fishing village.

BIRD, J.B., J. HYSLOP AND M.D. SKINNER 1985 The Preceramic Excavations at the Huaca Prieta Chicama Valley, Peru. *Anthropological Papers of the American Museum of Natural History, New York*, Vol. 62, Part 1.

FELDMAN, R.A 1992 Preceramic Architectural and Subsistence Traditions. *Andean Past* 3:67-86.

GRIEDER, T., A.BUENO MENDOZA, C.E. SMITH JR. AND R.M. MALINA 1988 *La Galgada. Peru*. University of Texas Press, Austin.

IZUMI, S., AND T. SONO 1963 *Andes 2: Excavations at Kotosh, Peru, 1960*. Kadokawa Publishing Company, Tokyo.

MALPASS, M.A. AND K.E. STOTHERT 1992 Evidence for Preceramic Houses and Household Organization in Western South America. *Andean Past* 3:137-164.

MOSELEY, M.E. 1975 *The Maritime Foundations of Andean Civilization*. Cummings Publishing Company, Menlo Park, California.

1992 Maritime Foundations and Multilinear Evolution: Retrospect and Prospect. *Andean Past* 3:43-54.

QUILTER, J. 1991 Late Preceramic Peru. *Journal of World Prehistory* 5:387-438.

RICHARDSON, J.B. III 1981 Modeling the Development of Sedentary Maritime Economies on the Coast of Peru: A Preliminary Statement. *Annals of Carnegie Museum* 50:139-150.

WICKLER, W. AND U. SEIBT 1988 A Crab-Polychaete Symbiosis from Ancient Peruvian Iconography and the "Sawtoothed Snake" Problem. *Baessler-Archiv*, Neue Folge, Band 36:253-259.

## CHAPTER FOUR

Richard L. Burger's book on Chavín, cited for Chapter 5, is an authoritative discussion for this period. The volumes on temple architecture edited by Donnan, and by Millones and Onuki, the article on the Casma Valley by the Pozorskis, and the following references, will lead readers to all the relevant literature on this period, and the various interpretations of the social-political-religious organization that produced these majestic monuments.

DONNAN, C.B. (EDITOR) 1985 *Early Ceremonial Architecture in the Andes*. Dumbarton Oaks Research Library and Collection, Washington, D.C.

HAAS, J., S. POZORSKI, AND T. POZORSKI (EDITORS) 1987 *The Origins and Development of the Andean State*. Cambridge University Press, Cambridge and New York.

LATHRAP, D.W. 1970 *The Upper Amazon*. Praeger Publishers, New York and Washington.

MILLONES, L. AND Y. ONUKI (EDITORS) 1993 El Mundo Ceremonial Andino. *Senri Ethnological Studies* No. 37, National Museum of Ethnology, Osaka, Japan.

POZORSKI, S. 1983 Changing Subsistence Priorities and Early Settlement Patterns on the North Coast of Peru. *Journal of Ethnobiology* 3:15-38.

POZORSKI, S. AND T. POZORSKI 1992 Early Civilization in the Casma Valley, Peru. *Antiquity* 66:845-870.

SHADY SOLÍS, R. 1992 Sociedades del Nororiente Peruano durante el Formativo. *Pachacamac: Revista del Museo de la Naçion*, Lima 1(1):21-48.

## CHAPTER FIVE

This fascinating period brings the culmination of the ceremonial developments of the Late Preceramic and Initial periods. Again, Burger's book on Chavín is the prime source for the first of Peru's major horizons. The eminent Peruvian archaeologist, Luis G. Lumbreras, provides an excellent discussion of his research at Chavín de Huántar. Patterson's Pachacamac oracle interpretation for the spread of the Chavín cult, and Lathrap's analysis of the Tello Obelisk are important articles. Paul's book on Paracas and Kolata's on Tiwanaku (cited for Chapter 7) will lead the reader to the voluminous literature on these cultures. The Lake Titicaca research discussed in Dejoux and Iltis (eds.) will undoubtedly be as important as the Quelccaya Ice Cap in assessing the impact of climate change in the region.

BIRD, R. MCK. 1987 A Postulated Tsunami and its Effects on Cultural Development in the Peruvian Early Horizon. *American Antiquity* 52:285-303.

BURGER, R.L. 1992 *Chavín and the Origins of Andean Civilization*. Thames and Hudson, Ltd., London.

DAVENPORT, D. AND K.J. SCHREIBER 1989 The Bird of Chavín: A Parrot? *Antiquity* 63:350-356.

DEJOUX, C. AND A. ILTIS (EDITORS) 1992 Lake Titicaca: A Synthesis of Limnological Knowledge. *Monographiae Biologicae* Vol. 68, eds. H.J. Dumont and M.J.A. Werger, Kluwer Academic Publishers, Dordrecht, Boston, London.

LATHRAP, D.W. 1973 Gift of the Cayman: Some Thoughts on the Subsistence Basis of Chavín, in *Variation in Anthropology: Essays in Honor of John C. McGregor*. pp.91-105, eds. D.W. Lathrap and J. Douglas, Illinois Archaeological Survey, Urbana, Illinois.

LUMBRERAS, L.G. 1989 *Chavín de Huántar en el Nacimiento de la Civilización Andina*. Instituto Andino de Estudios Arqueológicos, Lima.

1993 Chavín de Huántar. *AVA-Materialien* 51. Kommission für Allgemeine und Vergleichende Archäologie des Deutschen Archäologischen Instituts, Bonn.

PATTERSON, T.C. 1985 Pachacamac—An Andean Oracle Under Inca Rule, in *Recent Studies in Andean Prehistory and Protohistory*. pp. 159-176, eds. D. P. Kvietok and D.H. Sandweiss, Cornell University.

PAUL, A. (EDITOR) 1991 *Paracas: Art and Architecture, Object and Context in South Coastal Peru*. University of Iowa Press, Iowa City.

WILSON, D.J. 1988 *Prehispanic Settlement Patterns in the Lower Santa Valley Peru*. Smithsonian Institution Press, Washington, D.C. and London.

## CHAPTER SIX

There are numerous works on Moche culture, but Alva and Donnan's Sipán volume is a must. The Silverman book on Cahuachi, the Nasca ceremonial center, is destined to become a classic. Aveni's edited volume on the Nazca Lines will take the mystery out of these enigmatic geoglyphs. The emergence of civilization in the Titicaca Basin is revealed in Kolata's book on Tiwanaku (cited in Chapter 7).

ALVA, W. AND C.B. DONNAN 1993 *Royal Tombs of Sipán*. Fowler Museum of Cultural History, University of California, Los Angeles.

AVENI, A. (EDITOR) 1990 The Lines of Nazca. *Memoirs of the American Philosophical Society*, Vol. 183, Philadelphia.

BARNES, M. AND D. FLEMING 1991 Filtration-Gallery Irrigation in the Spanish New World. *Latin American Antiquity* 2:48-68.

DONNAN, C.B. 1978 *Moche Art of Peru: Pre-Columbian Symbolic Communication*. Fowler Museum of Cultural History, University of California, Los Angeles.

SHIMADA, I., C.B. SCHAAF, L.G. THOMPSON AND E. MOSLEY-THOMPSON 1991 Cultural Impacts of Severe Droughts in the Prehistoric Andes: Application of a 1,500-year Ice Core Precipitation Record. *World Archaeology* 22:247-270.

SILVERMAN, H. 1990 Beyond the Pampa: the Geoglyphs in the Valleys of the Nazca. *National Geographic Research*, 6(4):435-456.

1993 *Cahuachi in the Ancient Nasca World*. University of Iowa Press, Iowa City.

**CHAPTER SEVEN**

Kolata's marvelous book presents the findings of the many investigators of Tiwanaku. Bermann's book on Lukurmata provides us with details on a local administrative center. The expansion of Tiwanaku into Peru and Chile is discussed by Goldstein and Rivera. Huari development and spread is superbly covered by Isbell and McEwan. The marvelous raised fields and the reintroduction of this ingenious agricultural field system is detailed by Erickson and Kolata.

BERMANN, M.P. 1994 *Lukurmata: Household Archaeology in Prehispanic Boliverseyia*. Princeton University Press, Princeton, New Jersey.

ERICKSON, C.L. 1988 Raised Field Agriculture in the Lake Titicaca Basin: Putting Ancient Andean Agriculture Back to Work. *Expedition* 30(3):8-16.

GOLDSTEIN, P. 1993 Tiwanaku Temples and State Expansion: A Tiwanaku Sunken-Court Temple in Moquegua, Peru. *Latin American Antiquity* 3:316-341.

ISBELL, W.H. AND G.F. MCEWAN (EDITORS) 1991 *Huari Administrative Structure: Prehistoric Monumental Architecture and State Government*. Dumbarton Oaks Research Library and Collection, Washington, D.C.

KOLATA, A. 1993 *The Tiwanaku: Portrait of an Andean Civilization*. Blackwell, Cambridge, Massachusetts and Oxford.

RIVERA M. 1991 The Prehistory of Northern Chile: A Synthesis. *Journal of World Prehistory* 5:1-47.

SCHREIBER, K.J. 1992 Huari Imperialism in Middle Horizon Peru. *Anthropological Papers*, No. 87. Museum of Anthropology, University of Michigan.

STANISH, C. 1992 *Ancient Andean Political Economy*. University of Texas Press, Austin.

THOMPSON, L.G., M.E. DAVIS, E. MOSLEY-THOMPSON AND K-B. LIU 1988 Pre-Incan Agricultural Activity Recorded in Dust Layers in Two Tropical Ice Cores. *Nature* 336:763-765.

**CHAPTER EIGHT**

There are three major edited sources on Chimu: Day and Moseley, Moseley and Cordy-Collins, and Ravines. Cavallaro presents the reinterpretation of the *ciudadelas* as paired kings' and nobles' palaces. Contact with Ecuador, Central America, and Mexico is dealt with in a number of the following articles, including the one by Fonseca and myself (which includes the llama evidence), Cordy-Collins on the hairless dog, and Hosler on metallurgy. Inca origins are reviewed in Bauer's recent work on the Cuzco Basin.

BAUER, B. 1992 *The Development of the Inca State*. University of Texas Press, Austin.

CAVALLARO, R. 1991 Large-Site Methodology. *Occasional Papers No. 5*, Department of Archaeology, University of Calgary, Alberta, Canada.

CORDY-COLLINS, A. 1994 An Unshaggy Dog Story. *Natural History* 102(2):34-41.

DAY, K.C. AND M.E. MOSELEY (EDITORS) 1982 *Chan Chan: Andean Desert City*. A School of American Research Book, University of New Mexico Press, Albuquerque.

FONSECA, O. AND J.B. RICHARDSON III 1978 South American and Mayan Cultural Contacts at the Las Huacas Site, Costa Rica. *Annals of Carnegie Museum* 47(13):299-317.

HATHER, J. AND P.V. KIRCH 1991 Prehistoric Sweet Potato (*Ipomoea batatas*) from Mangaia Island, Central Polynesia. *Antiquity* 63:350-356.

HEYERDAHL, T. AND SKJÖLSVOLD, A. 1956 Archaeological Evidence of Pre-Spanish Visits to the Galapagos Islands. *Memoirs of the Society for American Archaeology 12, American Antiquity* 22(2), Part 3.

HOSLER, D. 1988 Ancient West Mexican Metallurgy: South and Central American Origins and West Mexican Transformations. *American Anthropologist* 90:832-855.

MOSELEY, M.E. AND A. CORDY-COLLINS (EDITORS) 1990 *The Northern Dynasties: Kingship and Statecraft in Chimor*. Dumbarton Oaks Research Library and Collection, Washington, D.C.

RAVINES, R. (EDITOR) 1980 *Chanchan: Metropoli Chimú*. Instituto de Estudios Peruanos, Lima.

**CHAPTER NINE**

Of course there is a voluminous literature on the Inca Empire, but Rowe's article remains an impressive piece of scholarship on Inca culture. See Cieza de Léon, cited in Chapter 1, for an eyewitness account of the empire. Major works on Inca expansion include Malpass's edited volume, D'Altroy's superb book on the Upper Mantaro Valley, Morris and Thompson on Huánuco Pampa, Matos on Pumpu, and Sandweiss on the coastal Chincha State. Two books that are a must for anyone interested in the Inca are Hyslop's books on Inca roads and settlements. Niles identifies many of the estates of the Inca royalty. Protzen's book on Inca stonework puts to rest the speculation of how the Inca quarried and transported huge stone blocks. The controversy on the *ceque* lines is handled by Bauer and Zuidema. For the impact of the Spanish Conquest, turn to Hemming's masterful book and MacCormack for Inca religion and Spanish Catholicism. For those who wish to gain a picture of each of the Spaniards who conquered Peru, refer to Lockhart. The impact of disease in the wake of the Conquest is compiled by Cook, and Gade and Mörner cover the last 450 years of European influence in the Central Andes. Recent anthropological studies of Andean peoples include Allen, Arnold, Meyerson, Mitchell, and Rasnake.

ALLEN, C.T. 1988. *The Hold Life Has: Coca and Cultural Identity in an Andean Community.* Smithsonian Institution Press, Washington D.C.

ARNOLD, D.F. 1993 *Ecology and Ceramic Production in an Andean Community.* Cambridge University Press, Cambridge and New York.

BAUER B.S. 1992 Ritual Pathways of the Inca: An Analysis of the Collasuyu *Ceques* in Cuzco. *Latin American Antiquity* 3:183-205.

BINGHAM, A.M. 1989 *Portrait of an Explorer: Hiram Bingham, Discoverer of Machu Picchu.* Iowa State University Press, Ames.

COOK, N.D. 1981 *Demographic Collapse, Indian Peru, 1520-1620.* Cambridge University Press, Cambridge and New York.

D'ALTROY, T.N. 1992 *Provincial Power in the Inka Empire.* Smithsonian Institution Press, Washington, D.C. and London.

GADE, D.W. 1992 Landscape, System, and Identity in the Post-Conquest Andes. *Annals of the Association of American Geographers,* 82(3):460-477.

GASPARINI, G AND L. MARGOLIES 1980 *Inca Architecture.* trans. P. J. Lyon. Indiana University Press, Bloomington.

HEMMING, J. 1970 *The Conquest of the Incas.* Harcourt, Brace and Jovanovich, Inc., New York.

HYSLOP, J. 1984 *The Inka Road System.* Academic Press, New York.

1990 *Inka Settlement Planning.* University of Texas Press, Austin.

LEVINE, T.Y. (EDITOR) 1992 *Inca Storage Systems.* University of Oklahoma Press, Norman and London.

LOCKHART J. 1968 *Spanish Peru, 1532-1560: A Colonial Society.* University of Wisconsin Press, Madison.

1972 *The Men of Cajamarca: A Social and Bibliographical Study of the First Conquerors of Peru.* Institute of Latin American Studies, University of Texas Press, Austin and London.

MACCORMACK, S. 1991 *Religion in the Andes: Vision and Imagination in Colonial Peru.* Princeton University Press, Princeton, New Jersey.

MALPASS, M.A. (EDITOR) 1993 *Provincial Inca: Archaeological and Ethnohistorical Assessment of the Impact of the Inca State.* University of Iowa Press, Iowa City.

MATOS M., R. 1994 *Pumpu: Centro Administrativo Inka de la Puna Junín.* Editorial Horizonte, Lima.

MEYERSON, J. 1990 *Tambo: Life in an Andean Village.* University of Texas Press, Austin.

MITCHELL, W.P. 1991 *Peasants on the Edge: Crop, Cult, and Crisis in the Andes.* University of Texas Press, Austin.

MÖRNER M. 1985 *The Andean Past: Land, Societies and Conflicts.* Columbia University Press, New York.

MORRIS, C. AND D.E. THOMPSON 1985 *Huánuco Pampa: An Inca City and its Hinterland.* Thames and Hudson Ltd., London.

NILES, S.A, 1987 *Callachaca: Style and Status in an Inca Community.* University of Iowa Press, Iowa City.

1988 Looking for "Lost" Inca Palaces. *Expedition,* 30(3):56-64.

PATTERSON, T.C. 1991 *The Inca Empire: The Formation and Distintegration of a Pre-Capitalist State.* Berg, New York, Oxford.

PROTZEN, J-P. 1993 *Inca Architecture and Construction at Ollantaytambo.* Oxford University Press, New York, Oxford.

RASNAKE, R.N. 1988 *Domination and Cultural Resistance: Authority and Power among an Andean People.* Duke University Press, Durham and London.

ROSTWOROWSKI, DE DIEZ CANSECO, M. 1988 *Historia del Tahuantinsuyu.* Instituto de Estudios Peruanos, Lima.

ROWE, J.H. 1944 An Introduction to the Archaeology of Cuzco. *Papers of the Peabody Museum of Archaeology and Ethnology, Harvard University,* 27(2).

1946 Inca Culture at the Time of the Spanish Conquest, in *Handbook of South American Indians Volume 2: The Andean Civilizations.* pp. 183-330, ed. J.H. Steward, *Bureau of American Ethnology Bulletin* 143, Smithsonian Institution, Washington, D.C.

SANDWEISS, D.H. 1992 The Archaeology of the Chincha Fishermen: Specialization and Status in Inka Peru. *Bulletin of Carnegie Museum of Natural History* No. 29.

ZUIDEMA, R.T. 1990 *Inca Civilization in Cuzco.* University of Texas Press, Austin.

# INDEX

# PICTURE CREDITS

8,9 David Sanger
12 James B. Richardson III
14 Buddy Mays
16,17 *(both)* James B. Richardson III
18 Lonnie G. Thompson
19 Anthony Oliver-Smith
20 *(both)* Courtesy NOAA
21 James B. Richardson III
22 from Ewbank (1855)
23 from Squier (1877)
24 *(upper)* from Uhle, *Pachacamac* (1903)
24 *(lower)* Gordon R. Willey
25 *(upper)* from *American Antiquity*, Vol. 14(1)
25 *(lower)* James B. Richardson III
27 adapted from Uhle, *Pachacamac* (1903)
28,29 James B. Richardson III
32 Robert S. Peabody Museum of Archaeology,
   Phillips Academy, Andover, MA
34,35 *(both)* Thomas F. Lynch
36,37 *(both)* James B. Richardson III
39 James B. Richardson III
40 David Sanger
41 *(upper)* Buddy Mays
41 *(lower)* John W. Rick
42,43 *(both)* Deborah M. Pearsall
44,45 *(both)* Jeffrey Quilter
46,47 Thomas F. Lynch
49 Robert A. Feldman
50 from Izumi and Sono, *Excavations at Kotosh*,
   (1963)
51 Terence Grieder
53 James B. Richardson III
54 *(upper)* Jeffrey Quilter
54 *(lower)* James B. Richardson III
55 James B. Richardson III
57 Courtesy Department of Library Services,
   American Museum of Natural History,
   Neg. no. 338465, photo by John Collier
58 Courtesy Department of Library Services,
   American Museum of Natural History, Neg.
   no. 4913(3), photo by John Bigelow Taylor
60 Marie Louise Deruaz
61 Mark S. Aldenderfer

62,63 James B. Richardson III
66 Servicio Aerofotográfico Nacional, Peru
67 James B. Richardson III
68 Fernando Sánchez
69 Marilyn Bridges
71 Daniel H. Sandweiss
72 James B. Richardson III
73 Michael E. Moseley
74,75 *(both)* William H. Isbell
76 Daniel Julien
77 Courtesy Department of Library Services,
   American Museum of Natural History, Neg.
   no. 5018 (3), photo by John Bigelow Taylor
78 Munson-Williams-Proctor Institute,
   Museum of Art, Utica, NY
80,81 Daniel H. Sandweiss
84 Daniel H. Sandweiss
85 Ric Ergenbright
86 James B. Richardson III
87 The Cleveland Museum of Art, In memory
   of Mr. and Mrs. Henry Humphreys,
   Gift of their daughter, Helen, 57.494
88,89 Will Williams/Wood Ronsaville Harlin, Inc.
90 The Cleveland Museum of Art, John L.
   Severance Fund, 92.348
91 Marilyn Bridges
92 Colleen M. Beck
93 Dumbarton Oaks Research Library &
   Collections, Washington, DC
94 The Cleveland Museum of Art, John L.
   Severance Fund, 85.139
95 *(both)* Robert Frerck/Odyssey
96 The Cleveland Museum of Art,
   The Norweb Collection, 40.514
97 The Cleveland Museum of Art, In memory
   of Mr. and Mrs. Henry Humphreys,
   Gift of their daughter, Helen, 50.567
100,101 The Cleveland Museum of Art, In
   memory of Mr. and Mrs. Henry Humphreys,
   Gift of their daughter, Helen, 56.85
103,104 *(both)* James B. Richardson III
105 *(upper)* James B. Richardson III
105 *(lower)* Michael E. Moseley
106 UCLA Fowler Museum of Cultural
   History, photo by Denis J. Nervig
107 from Alva and Donnan, *Royal Tombs of
   Sipán* (1993)
108 *(upper)* Christopher B. Donnan
108 *(lower)* Donald McClelland
109 Christopher B. Donnan
110 The Art Institute of Chicago
111 *(upper)* James B. Richardson III
111 *(lower)* The Cleveland Museum of Art,
   John L. Severance Fund, 90.128
112 Robert Frerck/Odyssey
113 The Cleveland Museum of Art, Andrew R.
   Martha Jennings Fund, 89.90
114 Marilyn Bridges

116 UCLA Fowler Museum of Cultural
   History, photo by Denis J. Nervig
117 The Art Institute of Chicago
118 Marilyn Bridges
120,121 Robert Frerck/Odyssey
123 Marilyn Bridges
124 Marc P. Bermann
125 *(upper)* Marc P. Bermann
125 *(lower)* Robert Frerck/Odyssey
126 Robert Frerck/Odyssey
128 Marc P. Bermann
129 The Cleveland Museum of Art, John L.
   Severance Fund, 63.476
131 William H. Isbell
132 The Cleveland Museum of Art,
   In memory of Leonard C. Hanna Jr.,
   Gift of John Wise, 57.495
133 The Cleveland Museum of Art, J.H. Wade
   Fund, 45.378
134 Robert A. Feldman
135 Gordon McEwan
136,137 Robert Frerck/Odyssey
138 *(left)* The Cleveland Museum of Art,
   John L. Severance Fund, 91.223
138 *(right)* Robert Frerck/Odyssey
139 Daniel H. Sandweiss
141 *(upper)* Courtesy Department of Library
   Services, American Museum of Natural
   History, Neg. no. 334897
141 *(lower)* James B. Richardson III
142,143 *(both)* Robert Frerck/Odyssey
144,145 Rob Wood/ Wood Ronsaville Harlin, Inc.
146 James B. Richardson III
147 UCLA Fowler Museum of Cultural
   History, photo by Denis J. Nervig
149 Courtesy Department of Library Services,
   American Museum of Natural History,
   Neg. no. 334733
150,151 James B. Richardson III
154 Robert Frerck/Odyssey
155 Buddy Mays
156 Robert Frerck/Odyssey
158,159 *(both)* Buddy Mays
160 David Sanger
161 Mario Cervetto/Comstock
162 from Guaman Poma de Ayala, *Primer
   Nueva Corónica y Buen Gobierno* (1980)
163 *(upper)* Michael A. Malpass
163 *(lower)* Robert Frerck/Odyssey
165 David Sanger
176 Heather M. Richardson

# AUTHOR'S ACKNOWLEDGMENTS

As a teenager excavating at Fort William Henry—of *Last of the Mohicans* fame—little did I realize that one day I would write a synthesis of Central Andean archaeology. Soon afterwards, as a high school student, I joined a Smithsonian Institution expedition on the Big Bend of the Missouri River in South Dakota, researching trading posts and prehistoric earthlodge villages.

As a Master's student at Syracuse University it was my good fortune to work with William A. Ritchie, the Dean of Northeastern U.S. archaeology, on sites in New York and Martha's Vineyard Island, Massachusetts. The Martha's Vineyard experience stimulated my interest in maritime adaptations. When I entered the Ph.D. program in Anthropology at the University of Illinois, Donald W. Lathrap persuaded me to carry my maritime interests to the north coast of Peru, and he introduced me to the late Edward P. Lanning, the leading expert on coastal adaptations at that time. Illinois geographer Charles Alexander was instrumental in my using a geological approach to interpret the archaeological record.

I wish to thank the following individuals for their assistance in the writing of this volume: Monica Barnes, Garth L. Bawden, Marc P. Bermann, Richard L. Burger, Thomas D. Dillehay, David Fleming, William H. Isbell, Frances B. King, Alan L. Kolata, Thomas F. Lynch, Michael E. Moseley, Thomas C. Patterson, Harry Sanabria, Helaine Silverman, Karen E. Stothert, David J. Wilson, and Margaret Young-Sanchez.

I am profoundly grateful to Daniel H. Sandweiss who read drafts of this volume and provided many helpful suggestions. I am especially indebted to Charmaine C. Steinberg and Sylvia M. Keller who not only typed the manuscript, but provided many editorial corrections. I also wish to thank my wife Judy, daughter Heather and son James IV for their understanding and support in this endeavor. I dedicate *People of the Andes* to them and to my parents, Miriam Davenport Richardson and J. Bushnell Richardson Jr., who watched their teenage son leave on a prop plane for the Smithsonian field camp on the Big Bend of the Missouri, enabling me to fulfill my desire to become an archaeologist. I am deeply appreciative to Jeremy A. Sabloff for the opportunity to write *People of the Andes* and thank him for his encouragement throughout the writing process. I also wish to thank the staff of St. Remy Press, and particularly Philippe Arnoldi, Chantal Bilodeau, Carolyn Jackson, Chris Jackson, Alfred LeMaitre, Daniel McBain, Jenny Meltzer, and Geneviève Monette. Special thanks to Olga Dzatko, as well as to Patricia Gallagher of the Smithsonian Institution editorial staff.

*James B. Richardson III*
*Pittsburgh, Pennsylvania*